Selected Plays

Selected Plays

Christopher Fry

Oxford   New York

OXFORD UNIVERSITY PRESS

Oxford University Press, Walton Street, Oxford OX2 6DP

Oxford New York
Athens Auckland Bangkok Bombay
Calcutta Cape Town Dar es Salaam Delhi
Florence Hong Kong Istanbul Karachi
Kuala Lumpur Madras Madrid Melbourne
Mexico City Nairobi Paris Singapore
Taipei Tokyo Toronto

and associated companies in
Berlin Ibadan

Oxford is a trade mark of Oxford University Press

The Boy with a Cart first published by Oxford University Press. Second edition published 1945 by
Frederick Muller Ltd. First issued as an Oxford University Press paperback 1970
A Phoenix Too Frequent first published 1946 by Hollis & Carter. First issued as an
Oxford University Press paperback 1969
The Lady's Not For Burning first published 1949 by Oxford University Press. Second edition 1950.
First issued as an Oxford University Press paperback 1969
A Sleep of Prisoners first published 1951 by Oxford University Press. First issued as an
Oxford University Press paperback 1971
Curtmantle first published 1961 by Oxford University Press. Second edition 1965. First issued
as an Oxford University Press paperback 1971
This selection first published as an Oxford University Press paperback 1985

British Library Cataloguing in Publication Data

Data available

Library of Congress Cataloging in Publication Data

Fry, Christopher.
Selected plays.
(Oxford paperbacks)
Contents: The boy with a cart—A phoenix too
frequent—The lady's not for burning—[etc.]   I. Title.
PR6011.R9.A6   1985   822'.914   84-25047
ISBN 0-19-281873-2 (pbk.)

5 7 9 10 8 6

Printed in Great Britain by Biddles Ltd, Guildford and King's Lynn

CONTENTS

THE BOY WITH A CART

CUTHMAN, SAINT OF SUSSEX

A Play

SECOND EDITION

THE BOY WITH A CART

*First performed at Coleman's Hatch, Sussex,
1938*
*Revived at the Lyric Theatre, Hammersmith,
16 January 1950*

Cuthman	. .	RICHARD BURTON
Bess	. . . .	HAZEL TERRY
Mildred ⎫ Mrs. Fipps ⎭	. . .	DIANA GRAVES
Matt	. . . . .	LEE FOX
Tibb	. . . . .	JOHN KIDD
Cuthman's mother	. .	MARY JERROLD
Tawm	. . . .	NOËL WILLMAN
His daughter	. .	HARRIETTE JOHNS
His son-in-law	. .	ADRIAN CAIRNS
A farmer	. .	OLAF POOLEY
Alfred	. . .	DAVID OXLEY
Demiwulf	. .	ROBERT MARSDEN

Directed by John Gielgud

CHARACTERS

(In order of appearance)

CUTHMAN
BESS AND MILDRED
MATT AND TIBB   }   *Cornish neighbours*
CUTHMAN'S MOTHER
TAWM
HIS DAUGHTER
HIS SON-IN-LAW
A FARMER   }   *Villagers of Steyning*
ALFRED AND
DEMIWULF, THE SONS OF
MRS. FIPPS

*Cornish neighbours, mowers, villagers of Steyning,
and The People of South England*

Extracts from two songs by Richard Addinsell (*from the composer's manuscript*)

In our fields, fallow and burdened, in grass and furrow,
In barn and stable, with scythe, flail, or harrow,
Sheepshearing, milking or mowing, on labour that's older
Than knowledge, with God we work shoulder to shoulder;
God providing, we dividing, sowing, and pruning;
Not knowing yet and yet sometimes discerning:
Discerning a little at Spring when the bud and shoot
With pointing finger show the hand at the root,
With stretching finger point the mood in the sky:
Sky and root in joint action; and the cry
Of the unsteady lamb allying with the brief
Sunlight, with the curled and cautious leaf.

Coming out from our doorways on April evenings
When tomorrow's sky is written on the slates
We have discerned a little, we have learned
More than the gossip that comes to us over our gates.
We have seen old men cracking their memories for dry milk.
We have seen old women dandling shadows;
But coming out from our doorways, we have felt
Heaven ride with Spring into the meadows.

We have felt the joint action of root and sky, of man
And God, when day first risks the hills, and when
The darkness hangs the hatchet in the barn
And scrapes the heavy boot against the iron:
In first and last twilight, before wheels have turned
Or after they are still, we have discerned:
Guessed at divinity working above the wind,
Working under our feet; or at the end
Of a furrow, watching the lark dissolve in sun,
We have almost known, a little have known

The work that is with our work, as we have seen
The blackthorn hang where the Milky Way has been:
Flower and star spattering the sky
And the root touched by some divinity.

> Coming out from our doorways on October nights
> We have seen the sky unfreeze and a star drip
> Into the south: experienced alteration
> Beyond experience. We have felt the grip
> Of the hand on earth and sky in careful coupling
> Despite the jibbing, man destroying, denying,
> Disputing, or the late frost looting the land
> Of green. Despite flood and the lightning's rifle
> In root and sky we can discern the hand.

It is there in the story of Cuthman, the working together
Of man and God like root and sky; the son
Of a Cornish shepherd, Cuthman, the boy with a cart,
The boy we saw trudging the sheep-tracks with his mother
Mile upon mile over five counties; one
Fixed purpose biting his heels and lifting his heart.
We saw him; we saw him with a grass in his mouth, chewing
And travelling. We saw him building at last
A church among whortleberries. And you shall see
Now, in this place, the story of his going
And his building.—A thousand years in the past
There was a shepherd, and his son had three
Sorrows come together on him. Shadow
The boy. Follow him now as he runs in the meadow.

> *Enter* CUTHMAN, *running. He stops short as he sees*
> *two* NEIGHBOURS *approaching.*

CUTHMAN. Now, my legs, look what a bad place
  You've brought me into: Bess and Mildred coming:
  Two nice neighbours with long noses. Now
  I should like the sun to go down, and I could close
  As the daisy closes: put up my shutters, slap,

Here in the long grass. Whip the world away
In one collapsing gesture. And you can't
Waken a sleeping daisy with a shaking.—
Well, green is green and flesh is a different matter.
Green is under their feet, but my lot's better.
I can say to them Neighbours, believe it or not.
God is looking after my father's sheep.
But the simple truth is harder to tell than a lie.
The trouble I'll have, and the trouble they'll have to believe it!
And I wasn't looking for trouble this bright morning.

                    [*As the* NEIGHBOURS *come up to him.*

Good morning, good morning!

BESS. Good morning, Cuthman.

CUTHMAN. This is the morning to take the air, flute-clear
   And, like a lutanist, with a hand of wind
   Playing the responsive hills, till a long vibration
   Spills across the fields, and the chancelled larches
   Sing like Lenten choirboys, a green treble;
   Playing at last the skylark into rising,
   The wintered cuckoo to a bashful stutter.
   It is the first day of the year that I've king'd
   Myself on the rock, sat myself in the wind:
   It was laying my face on gold. And when I stood
   I felt the webs of winter all blow by
   And in the bone-dry runnel of the earth
   Spring restart her flood.

MILDRED.   We came to find you,
   Cuthman, expecting to find you with the sheep.

CUTHMAN. Dinner-time is passed, and my father
   Has forgotten where his son chews on a grass
   And thinks of meat.

BESS.   Cuthman-chick, your father——

CUTHMAN. I know what you will say to me: My father
　　Has my promise to be shepherd till he send
　　Another boy to take my place and tend them.
　　And, promise-bound, what do I do careering
　　Like a stone down a hill, like a holidaymaker
　　With only his own will? But they're safe,
　　Those little sheep, more than with me beside them,
　　More than with twenty Cuthmans now God minds them.

BESS. Cuthman-boy—

CUTHMAN.　　　　　　　　It is so! Not today
　　Only, but other days God took the crook
　　And watched them in the wind. One other day
　　My father let the time go by, forgetting
　　To send away the herdboy to relieve me.
　　However often I stood up on the rock
　　Shouting 'Here's Cuthman! Here's a hungry shepherd!'
　　My only relief came from the clouds that closed
　　With the sun and dodged again: the sun that tacked
　　From dinner-time into the afternoon.
　　I was as empty as a vacant barn.
　　It might have been because my stomach was empty
　　That I was suddenly filled with faith—
　　Suddenly parcelled with faith like a little wain
　　In a good hay-season and, all round, the hills
　　Lay at my feet like collies. So I took
　　My crook, and round the sheep I drew a circle
　　Saying 'God guard them here, if God will guard them';
　　Drew it, though as a fence I knew it was less
　　Good than a bubble. Then to yearling and ewe
　　And lamb I said 'Give no trouble'; laid
　　My crook against the rock and went to dinner.
　　When I came back no lamb or yearling or ewe
　　Had broken through. They gently lay together
　　Cropping the crook's limited pasture, though

The unhedged green said 'Trespass.'—This is true.
Come, and I'll show you. I have waited again
To go to dinner and father has forgotten——

BESS. Cuthman, your father is dead.

MILDRED.   We came to tell you.

CUTHMAN. You can't say that to me. I was speaking the truth.

MILDRED. We were speaking the truth.

CUTHMAN.   You came to make me sorry,
But you're breaking the sun over your knees to say
My father's dead. My father is strong and well.
Each morning my father buckles himself to,
Like a leather strap, and at night comes to the fire
His hands bare with well-water to tell
The story of Jesus. So he will talk tonight,
Clenching his hands against Gethsemane,
Opening his hands to feel the Ascension
As though after dry weeks he were feeling
The first rain. Every evening I have watched,
And his face was like a live coal under the smoking
Shadows on the ceiling.

BESS.   What can we do,
Cuthman, if you're unbelieving?

MILDRED.   Come
Down with us and see him.

CUTHMAN.   Let me alone.
No; if I come you'll take me to a place
Where truth will laugh and scatter like a magpie.
Up here, my father waits for me at home
And God sits with the sheep.

BESS.   Cuthman, you make it
Hard for us to tell you.

MILDRED.   The trouble we have
To tell him, and the trouble he has to believe.

BESS. How can we help you, Cuthman, in your trouble
If our words go by like water in a sieve?

CUTHMAN. Let me alone.

MILDRED.   It's funny the way it takes him.
I don't even know if he really understands.
I don't even know if he really thinks we're lying.

BESS. Well, I don't know. Perhaps he feels like crying
And that's why he wants us to go.

MILDRED.   It may be so.

BESS [*to* CUTHMAN]. If we can be any help——

MILDRED. If there's anything we can do——

BESS. We'd better go to his mother again, poor soul,
And get her a bite or two. She's certain not
To eat a thing unless somebody's by.

MILDRED. It's a merciful thing she had the sense to cry.

[*They go away down the hill.*

CUTHMAN. What have I done? Did I steal God away
From my father to guard my sheep? How can I keep
Pace with a pain that comes in my head so fast?
How did I make the day brittle to break?
What sin brought in the strain, the ominous knock,
The gaping seam? Was it a boast on the rock,
The garrulous game? What have I done to him?
Father, if you are standing by to help me—
Help me to cry.

[*He falls on the ground.*

THE PEOPLE OF SOUTH ENGLAND.
The day is pulled up by the root and dries,
And the sun drains to the hollow sea.
Heaven is quarried with cries.
Song dies on the tree.

The thongs of the daylight are drawn and slack.
  The dew crawls down to earth like tears.
    Root and sky break
      And will not mend with prayers.

Only the minutes fall and stack
  Like a rising drum
    Where, thin as a draught through the crack,
    Death has whistled home.

CUTHMAN [*rising to his knees*]. I have ears stopped with earth
  Not to have heard the door-catch as he went,
  The raven guling dew, the crow on the stack,
  Nor grasped the warning of the howling dog
  To bring me to my feet, to have me home;
  Heard soon enough to run and still to find him;
  For me to say 'You have been a father
  Not to lie down so soon, not to forget
  Till I forget the last hand that shall hold me.'
  Still to be able to find him, and to see
  How he put down his cup and dried his mouth
  And turned as heaven shut behind him.

THE PEOPLE OF SOUTH ENGLAND.
        How is your faith now, Cuthman?
        Your faith that the warm world hatched,
        That spread its unaccustomed colour
        Up on the rock, game and detached?

        You see how sorrow rises, Cuthman,
        How sorrow rises like the heat
        Even up to the plumed hills
        And the quickest feet.

        Pain is low against the ground
        And grows like a weed.
        Is God still in the air
        And in the seed?

Is God still in the air
Now that the sun is down?
They are afraid in the city,
Sleepless in the town.

Cold on the roads,
Desperate by the river.
Can faith for long elude
Prevailing fever?

CUTHMAN. I have stayed too long with the children, a boy
    sliding
  On the easy ice, skating the foolish silver
  Over the entangling weed and the eddying water.
  If I have only ventured the reflection
  And not the substance, and accepted only
  A brushwork sun skidding ahead of me
  And not the dealer of days and docker of time;
  Only the blue-print of a star and not
  The star; accepted only the light's boundary
  To the shadow and not the shadow, only the gloss
  And burnish of the leaf and not the leaf—
  Let me see now with truer sight, O God
  Of root and sky; let me at last be faithful
  In perception, and in action that is born
  Of perception, even as I have been faithful
  In the green recklessness of little knowledge.
  Grant this, O God, that I may grow to my father
  As he grew to Thy Son, and be his son
  Now and for always.

VOICES OF NEIGHBOURS. Cuthman! Cuthman! Cuthman!

CUTHMAN. Here's the valley breaking against the hill.

PEOPLE OF ENGLAND. Sorrow rises like the heat.

CUTHMAN. No longer dryshod can I keep my will.

PEOPLE OF ENGLAND. Nor the plumed feet.

CUTHMAN. The circle is broken and the sheep wander.
    They pull the branches of the myrtle under:
    Nibble the shadow of the cypress, trample
    The yew, and break the willow of its tears.
    This is no grief of theirs.
               [*Two* NEIGHBOURS, MATT *and* TIB, *come up to him.*

MATT.   Cuthman, your father
    Is dead.

CUTHMAN. They told me.

TIB.   Your mother is sick.

CUTHMAN.   She is grieving.

MATT. She is calling for you. We heard her voice through the
    window.

CUTHMAN. I shall come soon. But the sheep are foot-loose and
    green-
    Hungry. They will be lost in sundown, and no
    Bell-wether. Where would my mother tell me to go,
    To her or bring them home?

TIB.   You have no home,
    Cuthman.

CUTHMAN. I have no father, but my mother
    Is at home.

MATT.   Your home is sold over your head.
    There's no roof over your sorrow: nor a patch
    Of ground to know your name in; nothing, son,
    Nothing in the valley.

CUTHMAN.   My mother's at home.

TIB. Your mother is sick. What will you do, Cuthman?

CUTHMAN. I will drive my father's sheep home to my mother.
                           [*Exit* CUTHMAN.

MATT. Could we have told him the rest of it: the last
    Of the rotten business?

TIB.   I had said enough.
  I had done more damage with words than downpour
  Did the crops. Look how his wing is dragging.

MATT. Look what he still has to know. His Father dead,
  The house sold over his head, and still the blow,
  The final straw: no money in the house,
  Not a flip of silver he can toss,
  And double in his hand.

TIB.   But still we said
  Enough. And what we said he scarcely knows.
  He carries the first trouble, and the rest
  Only dog at his heels.

MATT.   Make your way down.
  None of us knows the way a neighbour feels.

                                    [*Exeunt.*

THE PEOPLE OF SOUTH ENGLAND.
  Out of this, out of the first incision
  Of mortality on mortality, there comes
  The genuflexion, and the partition of pain
  Between man and God; there grows the mutual action,
  The perspective to the vision.
  Out of this, out of the dereliction
  Of a mild morning, comes the morning's motive,
  The first conception, the fusion of root and sky;
  Grows the achievement of the falling shadow,
  Pain's patient benediction.

NEIGHBOURS [*entering*].
  One after the other we have gone to the boy,
  Offering him advice, condolences, and recommendations
  To relations in more well-to-do places.
  We have offered him two good meals a day.—
  My wife is a bad cook but she gives large helpings.—
  We have done what we could; we can't do more.

But he goes his own way. All that we say
He seems to ignore. He keeps himself apart,
Speaking only out of politeness,
Eating out his heart, and of all things on earth
He is making a cart!

One after the other we have gone to him and said,
'Cuthman, what use will a cart be to you?'
He scarcely so much as raised his head, only
Shook it, saying, 'I will tell you some other time;
I am in a hurry.'

One after the other we have gone also
To his mother, offering advice, condolences,
Recommendations to our distant relations.
His poor mother, she suffers a great deal in her legs.
And we have said to her, 'We hope you will excuse
Our asking, we hope you will not think us
Inquisitive, but what is your boy Cuthman
So busy on?'—And she replied each time:
'It is something after his own heart.'

We are none the wiser: and after all
It is none of our business, though it's only natural
We should take a certain amount of interest.

One after the other we have gone indoors
Turning it over in our minds as we went
About our chores. What will the old woman do,
Dear heart, with no roof over her head, no man,
No money, and her boy doing nothing
But make a cart?

'I will tell you some other time,' he said.
'I am in a hurry.' Well, that's his look-out.
It's not for us to worry.

> [*They go back to the village.*

Enter CUTHMAN *with a cart, and his* MOTHER.

CUTHMAN. If you turn round, Mother, you can see the village almost under your feet. You won't get another view. It's sinking like a ship. We're looking at the last of it.

MOTHER. My legs, my legs! That hill's finished them. I should have stopped at the bottom. Your grandmother used to say to me when I was a girl: 'Daughter,' she would say, 'never get above yourself. It will be your downfall.' Little did she guess what things would happen to me, and it's just as well, I was her favourite daughter.

CUTHMAN. We shall never see it again; we shall never look again at the sun on the white walls, my swaddling-clothes put out to dry. I am out of them once and for all.

MOTHER. What on earth are you doing talking about your swaddling clothes? I wish I knew what was the matter with you. You were shortened at five months. You were walking at a year. . . . Dear heart, I don't know how ever I got up as far as I have.

CUTHMAN. I have never known anything except the village and these few hills. I have two eyes, but how can I know if I have a memory for faces? I have two legs, but they've only carried me backwards and forwards like an old flight of steps. All my life I have been on a tether, but now I have slipped it and the world is green from side to side.

MOTHER. You know nothing of the world, Cuthman, and I'm thankful to say it. I am an old woman and I know too much. I have seen it. I've seen too much of it. Before I married your father I worked as a laundress at Letherwithel. That's fourteen miles away. And after we were married he brought me here, fourteen miles sitting behind him on a horse.

CUTHMAN. But now you're going to travel in style; we've got a cart for you to ride in.

MOTHER [*looking at the cart and back at* CUTHMAN]. Sometimes I think you can't be very well, Cuthman. . . . Your father and I first met one October. He had ridden over to the fair and it came on to rain.

CUTHMAN. We have more than fourteen miles to go. Last night I looked up and saw the full moon standing behind a tree. It was like a strange man walking into the room at night without knocking. It made my heart jump. . . . I don't know how many miles we'll have to go.

MOTHER. Cuthman! Look your mother in the face. What are you going to do with her?

CUTHMAN. We're going to travel.

MOTHER. I wish I knew what to do with you. The trouble is, you don't give me time to speak. You rush me up a hill so that I lose all my breath. You won't listen to reason. Where are you taking me? I insist upon knowing—don't think you can get away with those mysterious wags of your head. I shan't take another step until I know.

CUTHMAN. We're going to see the world, Mother.

MOTHER. I'm an old woman and I won't be joked to. Who gave you this man's address?

CUTHMAN. I haven't got an address, Mother.

MOTHER. I'm going to be very ill.   [*She sits on the cart.*

CUTHMAN. We shall find our way in the world, Mother, and I've made you a cart. You can rest as you go.

MOTHER. I've always stood up for you to the neighbours. They have come to me often enough and said: 'Cuthman isn't practical; he's going to find life very difficult.' And I have always said to them: 'Never you mind. Cuthman's my son, and when I was a girl his grandmother used to say to me, "Daughter, whatever else you may be, you have your wits."'—And in the end, after all the trouble I've had to bring you up, you want to use me like a barrowful of turnips.

CUTHMAN. Mother, can you remember the neighbours' faces when you came into the village riding on the back of my father's horse?

MOTHER. The neighbours' faces? I should think so indeed, like
yesterday. They were all stuck out of the windows and they were
shouting out to each other, 'What do you think of that? He's
gone out of his way to find something!' They liked the look of
me at once, they told me afterwards. We have always been very
respected in the village.

CUTHMAN. That's just it; so it wouldn't do at all to end your days
as a beggar in the place where you've always been respected; it
wouldn't do to end them in a little hovel that some one would let
us have, in a corner of one of their sheds, living on their left-
overs and perhaps a good meal at Christmas.

MOTHER. This is the finish of me, I can't survive it. There wasn't
a day in the week that I didn't have a clean apron. And now there's
no one to look after me except a fool of a son, and he wants to
trundle me all over the world like a load of fish.

CUTHMAN. What do you think I have been doing, Mother, while
I sat all day on the doorstep, working at the cart? You couldn't
get a whistle or a word out of me. But I've been thinking and
praying; and wherever we go, if we go wisely and faithfully, God
will look after us. Calamity is the forking of the roads, and when
we have gone a little way up the turn we shall find it equally green.
We have nibbled the old pasture bare, and now we must look
for longer grass.

MOTHER. I'm too old for it, too old for it. The world's no greener
than a crab in the sea, and I don't like its nip. . . . Oh, what a
disaster! What a wealth of affliction! Nothing between me and
the weather except my second-best bombasine!

CUTHMAN. You'll see; after a bit, and after a bit of worry perhaps, we shall come into our own again. You'll find yourself saying, 'This is just the place for us; just what we wanted.' And
there'll be work for me to do. I shall buckle myself to every
morning, and you shall have a white apron. These last days,
while I sat on the step, I prayed. I was praying while I worked
at the cart.

MOTHER. That's the best thing; it's always the best thing. I have been praying too. But I'm an old woman and I know the dangers. The world's a bothering place, that's what I can't make you see: the world isn't Heaven and I know it well.

CUTHMAN. But the world has more than one hill and valley and that's the comfort of it. Get easy, Mother; we're leaving.

MOTHER. I'm sick at the thought of it. Your grandmother would cry herself into her grave if she were alive to see us.

CUTHMAN. But as it is nobody is crying.

[*He turns and looks for the last time at the village.*

MOTHER [*as they go*]. It is just as well that we went away respected; that will be something to remember at any rate. I told the villagers, 'We are going away; Cuthman has found work to do.'

CUTHMAN. And hard work, too, Mother, if there are many hills. You're no feather.

[*They set off on their journey, the* MOTHER *in the cart, and a rope round* CUTHMAN'S *neck attached to the handles. As they go* CUTHMAN *begins to whistle. They are heard going away into the distance.*

THE PEOPLE OF SOUTH ENGLAND.
  Stone over stone, over the shaking track,
  They start their journey: jarring muscle and aching
  Back crunch the fading county into
  Dust. Stone over stone, over the trundling
  Mile, they stumble and trudge: where the thirsty bramble
  Begs at the sleeve, the pot-hole tugs the foot.
  Stone over stone, over the trampled sunlight,
  Over the flagging day, over the burn
  And blister of the dry boot, they flog their way
  To where the journeyless and roofless trees
  Muster against the plunging of the dark:
  Where the shut door and the ministering fire
  Have shrunk across the fields to a dog's bark,

To a charred circle in the grass.
No floorboard mouse, no tattling friend; only
The flickering bat dodging the night air,
Only the stoat clapping the fern as it runs.

Stone over stone, Cuthman has spoken out
His faith to his mother. She has been comforted
A little; begins to believe in her son.
He has made her clumsy rhymes to laugh at.
She has tried to tell him stories of his grandmother,
But it is hard to talk buffeted by a cart.

After these miles, at last when the day leans
On the wall, at last when the vagrant hour flops
In the shade, they found a protected place, a ground
Where limbs and prayers could stretch between root and
Root, between root and sky; and they slept under curfew
Or Cuthman slept. His mother was chasing fears
Until daylight. 'What is rustling in the grass?
What shakes in the tree? What is hiding in
The shadow?' And Cuthman said, 'God is there.
God is waiting with us.'

Stone over stone, in the thin morning, they plod
Again, until they come to a field where mowers
Sweep their scythes under the dry sun.

       [*The* MOWERS *at work in the field. They sing.*

MOWERS. The muscle and the meadow
    Make men sing,
   And the grass grows high
   Like lashes to a lady's eye.
   Sickle-blades go sliding by
    And so does everything,
   Grass, the year, and a merry friend
    All at last come to an end.

Enter CUTHMAN *wheeling his* MOTHER. *The* MOWERS *stop work and nudge each other.*

MOTHER. I have gone up and down stairs fifty times a day when you were a baby and your aunt lived with us. She was an invalid but you wouldn't remember her. I have dug in the garden for your father, and had all the housework to do into the bargain. You don't know the work there is to do in a house. Your father's brother came to see us (you were only two months old at the time) and he said: 'Sister, you must be made of rope. My wife has help in the house, but nevertheless when she takes a broom in her hand she bursts into tears.' And I wasn't young, you must remember. I was nearly forty years old when I married your father. But never mind that. The point is that we've come a long way, so far that it's a wonder we've still kept the sun in sight; and I've been so jogged and jerked that I think your uncle must have been right. I begin to think that I'm really made of rope.

[*At this moment the rope round* CUTHMAN'S *shoulders breaks, and his mother is rolled on to the ground. The* MOWERS *burst out laughing.*

CUTHMAN. Are you hurt, Mother? The rope broke. How are you, Mother, are you all right?

MOTHER. Oh! Oh! If your mother ever walks again you'll be luckier than you deserve. This is what it has come to. You bring me all these miles to throw me on the ground.

CUTHMAN. The rope broke, Mother. Are you hurt?

MOTHER. Of course I'm hurt. I'm more than hurt, I'm injured.

CUTHMAN. Let me help you up; see if you can walk.

MOTHER. Walk? I might as well try to fly. What are all those people laughing at?

CUTHMAN. Try to stand on your legs.

MOTHER. They're laughing at me; that's what's the matter with them. They're laughing at an old woman who has had a misfortune. I told you what kind of place the world was, Cuthman, and I shall put a stop to it. I tell you, I've a sense of humour, but I won't be laughed at. [*She gets to her feet and rounds on the* MOWERS.] I don't know who you are, but I'm glad I wasn't born in your part of the country. Where I was born we knew how to behave; we knew better than to laugh at an old woman who had come to grief. We were very respected in the village where we come from, I may tell you; but as it happens we decided to travel. [*The* MOWERS *give an even louder roar of laughter*.] All right, all right! One of these days you'll laugh for too long, you'll laugh yourselves into trouble, take my word for it.

CUTHMAN. I must make a new rope for the cart; I shall have to make it out of withies. We shall find some at the stream we just passed over, remember, Mother? Fifty yards back or so. What will you do? Would you rather stay here, or come with me?

1ST MOWER. Did you hear what the boy said? A rope of withies! What a joke!

2ND MOWER. Don't you go and make the rope too strong, baby boy. You needn't go further than the end of the earth to find a fortune!

[*They go off again into a roar of laughter.*

MOTHER. I should like to box the ears of the whole lot, but there are too many of them; it would take too long.

CUTHMAN. Let's go, Mother; let's find the withies.

MOTHER. I may be lame, but I'd walk away from this place if it was the last thing I did.

[*They go off,* CUTHMAN *wheeling the cart.*

3RD MOWER [*singing after them*].

Don't fall into the stream, Mother.
The water's very high.
We might not hear you scream, Mother
And we'd hate to see you die!

[*They laugh again, and sing it all together.*

4TH MOWER. Here, did you feel that? A drop of rain!

1ST MOWER. Never; never on your life.

4TH MOWER. I swear it was. I felt a drop of rain. Look at the
clouds coming up.

2ND MOWER. He's right. I felt a drop on my hand, and another,
and another!

3RD MOWER. Don't stand about then. For the crop's sake, get at
the hay!

> [*They feverishly set to work.*

1ST MOWER. It's no good. We can do nothing at all—the whole
sky is opening.

THE PEOPLE OF SOUTH ENGLAND.

> That is rain on dry ground. We heard it:
> We saw the little tempest in the grass,
> The panic of anticipation: heard
> The uneasy leaves flutter, the air pass
> In a wave, the fluster of the vegetation;
>
> Heard the first spatter of drops, the outriders
> Larruping on the road, hitting against
> The gate of the drought, and shattering
> On to the lances of the tottering meadow
> It is rain; it is rain on dry ground.
>
> Rain riding suddenly out of the air,
> Battering the bare walls of the sun.
> It is falling on to the tongue of the blackbird,
> Into the heart of the thrush; the dazed valley
> Sings it down. Rain, rain on dry ground!
>
> This is the urgent decision of the day,
> The urgent drubbing of earth, the urgent raid
> On the dust; downpour over the flaring poppy,
> Deluge on the face of noon, the flagellant
> Rain drenching across the air.—The day

Flows in the ditch; bubble and twisting twig
And the sodden morning swirl along together
Under the crying hedge. And where the sun
Ran on the scythes, the rain runs down
The obliterated field, the blunted crop.

[*The* MOWERS *have fled from the rain, leaving the hay to
disaster.*

THE PEOPLE OF SOUTH ENGLAND.
The rain stops.
The air is sprung with green.
The intercepted drops
Fall at their leisure; and between
The threading runnels on the slopes
The snail drags his caution into the sun.

Re-enter CUTHMAN *and his* MOTHER, *his rope of withies
fastened from the cart to his shoulder.*

CUTHMAN. All the mowers are gone.

MOTHER. If I'd been the ground under their feet I should have
swallowed the lot.

CUTHMAN. But look at the field! You might think the sky had
crashed on to it.

MOTHER. Rain! I never!

CUTHMAN. Down by the stream there wasn't even a shower; we
had a hard job keeping the sun out of our eyes. But here the
crop is ruined and everywhere is running with water. Only a
field away, and we felt nothing of it!

MOTHER. They were laughing at an old woman come to grief. I
told them how it would be. You'll go on laughing too long, I said.
And look what a plight they're in now.—Poor souls.

CUTHMAN. Mother—

MOTHER. What is it, son?

CUTHMAN. When the withies break—

MOTHER. What! When the withies break! Do you think I'll get back into that cart when I shall be expecting every bump to be my last? You don't know your mother, Cuthman. She doesn't walk up to misfortune like a horse to sugar.

CUTHMAN. I shall be ready for it this time, Mother.

MOTHER. So you will, and so shall I. My eyes will be round your neck every minute of the day.

CUTHMAN. I shall look out and keep a good hold on the handles. And when the withies break——

MOTHER. If you can tell me what happens then it will be a relief to me.

CUTHMAN. We won't go any further.

MOTHER. That's just what I was afraid of. All my bones will be broken to smithereens.

CUTHMAN. When we had gone down to the banks of the stream
And were cutting willow-shoots (listen, Mother,
This is something I must tell you: how
From today for all my days life has to be,
How life is proving) while the rain was falling
Behind us in the field though we still wore
The sun like a coat, I felt the mood
Of the meadow change, as though a tide
Had turned in the sap, or heaven from the balance
Of creation had shifted a degree.
The skirling water crept into a flow,
The sapling flickered in my hand, timber
And flesh seemed of equal and old significance.
At that place, and then, I tell you, Mother,
God rode up my spirit and drew in
Beside me. His breath met on my breath, moved
And mingled. I was taller then than death.
Under the willows I was taller than death.

MOTHER. I saw you standing quiet. I said to myself
    He has something in his heart, he has something
    That occupies him.

CUTHMAN.   We shall go as far
    As the withies take us. There, where they break,
    Where God breaks them, you shall set up
    House again and put clean paper on
    Larder shelves. And there where God breaks them
    And scoops our peace out of a strange field
    I shall build my answer in plank and brick,
    Labour out my thanks in plaster and beam
    And stone. You, Mother, and I, when God
    Brings our settled days again, will build
    A church where the withies are broken, a church to pray in
    When you have put your broom away, and untied
    Your apron.

MOTHER.   Build a church, with our own hands?

CUTHMAN. With our own hands, Mother, and with our own
    Love of God and with nothing else; for I have
    Nothing else; I have no craft or knowledge of joint
    Or strain, more than will make a cart, and even
    The cart you scarcely would call handsome. What
    Did I learn to do after I found my feet
    And found my tongue? Only to seem as intelligent
    As the neighbours' children whatever happened; to be
    Always a little less than myself in order
    To avoid being conspicuous. But now
    I am less than I would be, less
    Than I must be; my buzzing life is less
    Than my birth was or my death will be. The church
    And I shall be built together; and together
    Find our significance. Breaking and building
    In the progression of this world go hand in hand.
    And where the withies break I shall build.

MOTHER. I am always lagging a little behind your thoughts,
I am always put out of breath by them. No doubt
I shall arrive one of these days.

CUTHMAN.   In, Mother.
We shall arrive together if the cart holds good.

MOTHER. It always seems to me I take my life
In my hands, every time I get into this
Contraption.

CUTHMAN.   Listen to that! A hard week's work
And she calls it a contraption!

[*They set out again.*

THE PEOPLE OF SOUTH ENGLAND.
        For the lifetime of a sapling-rope
        Plaited in the eye of God,
        Among the unfamiliar twine
        Of England, he still must strain
        And plug the uneasy slope,
        And struggle in heavy sun, and plod
        Out his vision; still must haunt
        Along the evening battlement
        Of hills and creep in the long valleys
        In the insect's trail, the small the dogged
        Pinhead of dust, by whose desire
        A church shall struggle into the air.
        No flattering builder of follies
        Would lay foundations so deep and rugged
        A church, a church will branch at last
        Above a country pentecost,
        And the vision at last will find its people
        And the prayers at last be said.
        This is how he mutters and how
        Weariness runs off his brow.
        Already the bell climbs in the steeple,
        The belfry of his shaggy head,

And the choir over and over again
Sings in the chancel of his brain.
Across the shorn downs, to the foot,
To Steyning, the last laborious track
Is trapesed and the withies at his neck
Untwist and break.
So he tips the stone from his boot,
Laughs at the smoking stack,
At the carthorse shaking its brass,
And knows the evening will turn a friendly face.

Enter TAWM, *an old man. He keeps a look-out over his shoulder.*

TAWM. They'll be after me again, not a corner of Steyning but
they'll ferret me out; my daughter and my daughter's husband
and my daughter's daughter; my nephew and my nephew's
nephews: they'll be after me. 'There's a cold wind, Father (or
uncle or grandfather or whatever it is); take care of yourself,
wrap yourself up; it's going to rain, it's likely to snow, there's a
heavy dew.' What do they think I was born into this world for
if it wasn't to die of it?

VOICES [*off stage*]. Father! Father!

TAWM. The ferrets, the ferrets! If I climbed up on to a cloud
they'd find me out and bring me my hat.

Enter his DAUGHTER *and his* SON-IN-LAW.

DAUGHTER. Father, whatever are you thinking about? Why ever
do you want to go walking about the fields with a cold wind
blowing? I've got your supper waiting for you.

SON-IN-LAW. Here's your hat.

TAWM [*with bitterness*]. Daughter, your husband's a most obliging
man. He brings me my hat when the wind's in my hair. Thank
you, son; you're an invaluable fellow.

Enter CUTHMAN *wheeling his* MOTHER.

DAUGHTER. Who ever have we got here?   [*She giggles.*

SON-IN-LAW. They're nobody I know. I've seen everybody twenty miles around and this is none of them.

TAWM. They're strangers, likely as not. If I was challenged I shouldn't be afraid to say that these are strangers.

DAUGHTER. What does he think he's doing going around like that with the old woman? I've never seen anything like it.

> [*She giggles again.*

TAWM. You've got no understanding of geography, daughter. All the places in the world have their own ways and this young man is doing so because it's his way.

MOTHER. Cuthman, this is a very pretty place, quite a picture. The beauties of nature always make me feel honest with myself.

CUTHMAN. Mother, the withies have broken!

MOTHER. I remember when I was a girl I went up to my mother with a bunch of cornflowers in my hand—

CUTHMAN. Mother, the withies! The withies have broken!

MOTHER. Nothing has happened to me; I'm still where I was; I'm still in the cart.

CUTHMAN. I was holding it firm; but look at them, they've chafed in two. You can get out of it now, Mother; we're not going any further.

MOTHER. If ever I sit in a chair again I shan't recognize myself. What a very pretty place! Are we really stopping here, Cuthman?

CUTHMAN. Yes, Mother; we've arrived.

MOTHER. It's too much to believe all in a minute. But one thing's quite certain: it'll be a good many nights before I stop bumping about in my dreams.

> [*A crowd of* VILLAGERS *has collected. They stare at* CUTHMAN *and his* MOTHER.

CUTHMAN. Why do you think all these people are staring, Mother?

MOTHER. They're welcoming us. It's like old times. It was just like this when your father brought me home on the back of his horse.

CUTHMAN [*calling out to them*]. Could you tell me the name of this place, please?

[*The* VILLAGERS *continue to stare.*

CUTHMAN. I say! Would you mind telling us where we are?—They're dumb, Mother.

MOTHER. They like us and respect us. One of these days they'll tell us so. It was just like this when your father brought me home, and they told me afterwards they liked the look of me at once they said.

TAWM. Good evening.

CUTHMAN. Good evening.

MOTHER. Good evening.

TAWM. Can I be of any help to you at all?

CUTHMAN. Perhaps you could tell us the name of this place.

TAWM. P'r'aps I could. I've lived here seventy years, so p'r'aps I could. It's Steyning, if I remember right.

CUTHMAN. Steyning . . . The church at Steyning.

TAWM. The church? If that's what you're after you've got the wrong place; there's no church here.

A WOMAN. This is a poor place and we're poor people; we must pray on the bare ground.

CUTHMAN. I've come to build a church.

[*This causes a sensation among the* VILLAGERS.

MOTHER. It's an idea that my boy has; he has got it very much at heart. But I don't know what we can be looking like; I can't imagine at all. You must take us for tramps. Before my husband died I always hoped that one day we'd see the country together, but it really is very tiring. Some one ought to do something about the state of the roads. My husband was a farmer.

TAWM. Does the boy want work to do?

CUTHMAN. Yes, I do.

TAWM. How does he treat you, Mother? Does he pester you with shawls for your shoulders to keep the air off, with hats and over-shoes and gloves? Eh, does he? Does he protect you from draughts and shade you from the sun and hurry you out of the rain?

MOTHER. Listen, my goodness me! He asks me that, when he can see for himself how it is. My son pushes me into a cart and bumps and bangs me a million miles until I am the colour of midnight. And then he tips me out on to the hard ground as though I was refuse. And then into the cart I go again and over the hills, with the sun on me and the rain on me, and snow would have been all the same if it had come. But he is a good boy and his singing voice has improved wonderfully on the journey.

TAWM. He's a credit to you, Mother, and I shall borrow him from you when the need arises. We must find him work to do. My son is a good son, too, but he has gone off to the city. He wasn't a ferret either. Here's the farmer coming along that he was shepherd to. He'll be short-handed without my boy. [*To* CUTHMAN.] Can you manage sheep?

CUTHMAN. I looked after them for my father.

MOTHER. He's a great lover of animals, aren't you, Cuthman? And, as I say to him, animals know. Even sheep know. He can do anything he likes with them.

> [*The* FARMER *comes up to them.*

FARMER. Good evening, Tawm.

TAWM. You'll be needing another hand, I shouldn't be surprised, now that my son has gone scrimshanking off to the city.

FARMER. It's a loss, Tawm, and a pity he couldn't settle himself down like anyone else. Work's heavy enough at this time of year without being hobbled by a man short.

TAWM. Never in all my years, Mister, have I known a time when young men were scarcer.

FARMER. That's true, Tawm; there never has been such a time.

TAWM. I've been thinking, Mister; there's a young man here might do you fine. He's just such a one as my son was. He knows the difference between a man and a piece of flimsy.

FARMER [*to* CUTHMAN]. Are you a shepherd, son?

CUTHMAN. Yes, sir; I was shepherd for my father.

FARMER. Strangers, eh?

CUTHMAN. Yes, sir; strangers.

FARMER. Well, you've come at a good time. We can do with you. Is this your mother?

MOTHER. I'm his mother and there's one thing in the world I need, and that's a cushion at my back. Give me a rest and I shall begin to understand that good fortune's come our way at last.

TAWM. You can think yourself lucky, Mother, that life isn't for ever shoving a footstool under your feet.

FARMER. Come back to my house with me; we'll talk about this. There's a pot of stew on the fire that I shall be eating for three days if I can't find some one to help me out with it.

DAUGHTER [*to* TAWM]. Father, come in do. Your supper will be spoiled and you'll be in bed tomorrow with this dew soaking into your feet.

TAWM [*to* MOTHER]. You see how it is, neighbour; you see how it is.

MOTHER. It is just like old times to hear you calling me Neighbour; everything is most delightful.

CUTHMAN. I'll fetch the cart and catch you up.

[*Exeunt Omnes, except* CUTHMAN, *who goes to the cart.*

You see what comfort you have brought to us,
Old rough and ready! But your work's not over.

Those others have already forgotten the church
I've come to build, or find it hard to believe.
But when creation's tide crawled on its first
Advance across the sand of the air, and earth
Tossed its tentative hills, this place of idle
Grass where we are idling took the imprint
Of a dedication, which interminable
History could not weather away. And now
The consummation climbs on to the hill:
A church where the sun will beat on the bell, a church
To hold in its sanctuary the last light.
God be on the hill, and in my heart
And hand. God guide the hammer and the plane.
As the root is guided. Let there be a church—

> [*He grips the handles of the cart.*

Come on now, rough and ready.

> [*Exit* CUTHMAN *with the cart.*

Enter two brothers, ALFRED *and* DEMIWULF, *the sons of*
MRS. FIPPS, *who later will give her name to Fippa's Pit:*
Fippa Puteus.

ALFRED. A fat lot of good it is mooching about with a scowl on
your face. It only makes you look like a sick dog. We must make
the place too hot to hold him; there's nothing else for it.

DEMIWULF. So we will, so we certainly will! I'll make sure he
goes off with a flea in his ear!—

ALFRED. Well, let's see you. He's been here a week and you've
done precious little so far, except grind your teeth.

DEMIWULF. That's all you know. I've been speaking to people
about it.

ALFRED. And what good's that, I'd like to know? What earthly
good is it? Nobody has any ears for anyone except this ninny
hammer of a boy. There's no sociability in the village any longer,

that's what I say. Nobody ever comes to play bowls on Saturday evenings. We can't even put up a shove-ha'penny team against Bramber. Nobody can think of anything except this crazy idea of building a church.

DEMIWULF. They're a lot of gooseheads; they're a set of nincompoops, all of them, the whole lot of them! There's not a body in the village that hasn't been bitten by it, except we two and mother.

ALFRED. The farmer has given him the ground.

DEMIWULF. The builder has given him the bricks.

ALFRED. The woodman has given him the timber.

DEMIWULF. Everybody is making a fool of himself in his own way.

ALFRED. Except we two and mother.

DEMIWULF. Let's walk over to Bramber. I'm sick of the whole thing.

[*Exeunt.*

THE PEOPLE OF SOUTH ENGLAND.
    Let time rely on the regular interval
    Of days, but we do no such thing. We pull
    Down the weeks and months like a bough of cherry
    To decorate our room: strip off the year
    As lightly as we tear off the forgotten
    Calendar. But the story must be told.
    We make a country dance of Cuthman's labours
    And widely separated days become near neighbours.

    Enter CUTHMAN'S MOTHER *wearing a white apron.*

MOTHER. It's an astonishing thing how time flies. It only seems yesterday that I was being bounced all over the world, and now we've been settled in Steyning for six months as though we had lived here all our lives. Every one has been very kind. Cuthman is earning quite good money from the gentleman we met on the first evening we came. We live in a very nice little cottage. There are rather too many steps but one can't expect everything. Every day I put on a clean apron and the neighbours tell me that they liked the look of me at once. We are already very respected. And it is really wonderful the way everybody helps my son with his church. Every spare moment they have they go with him and do a little more. Besides giving the field, the gentleman we met on the first evening has also given two oxen to help with the work. I told Cuthman that I thought it was extremely generous and he ought to feel very fortunate. When I have finished my work I go down to the church and watch all the villagers singing and hammering in the cool of the day. . . . Well, I must now draw to a close. I have some milk on the fire and by this time it will probably all be boiled over.   [*Exit*.

Enter CUTHMAN, *dragging behind him an oxen-yoke. Enter to him* ALFRED *and* DEMIWULF.

CUTHMAN. Good afternoon, neighbours.

[*The* BROTHERS *pass by without speaking*.

CUTHMAN. Could you tell me—have you seen my oxen?

ALFRED [*to* DEMIWULF]. Was the boy speaking to us?

DEMIWULF. I think he was. Something about oxen.

ALFRED [*to* CUTHMAN]. Are you wanting something?

CUTHMAN. My two oxen have strayed away somewhere. They're working with us on the church and we're needing them. Have you seen them anywhere about?

ALFRED. Not a sign. We've seen two oxen belonging to your master.

CUTHMAN. My master gave them to me for the work of the church. Where did you see them?

DEMIWULF. They were on our land.

ALFRED. Trespassing.

DEMIWULF. So we shut them up.

CUTHMAN. I'm sorry they were trespassing. I'll see in future that
   they stay where they belong. If you could fetch them for me I'll
   put them to work.

ALFRED. Oh no.

DEMIWULF. Oh no. They stay where they are.

CUTHMAN. We need them.

ALFRED. Then it's a pity you let them go plunging about on other
   people's property.

DEMIWULF. Where they are they'll stay, and that's flat.

CUTHMAN. What purpose will they serve shut up in a barn? We
   need them for the building.

ALFRED. So we heard you say.

CUTHMAN. There's one thing that I'll not see any man destroy;
   there's one fire in me that no man shall put out. I am dangerous
   as I stand over the foundations of the church. I have the un-
   sleeping eyes of a watch-dog.

DEMIWULF. Go and yoke yourself. No doubt you'll find somebody
   who'll be only too pleased to drive you.

CUTHMAN. I ask you again: Let me have those oxen.

ALFRED. I'm sorry. I'm afraid there's nothing we can do about it.

CUTHMAN. Then I must move. One day I took a crook
   And drew a circle in pasture; and today
   I draw a circle here to guard the church,
   A circle of a stronger faith than I
   Could ever have mastered then. Already you slough
   Your little spite; it has deserted you,
   And all your power to stir and strength to speak
   Has fallen round your ankles, where it hangs
   With the weight of chain. And you are naked
   Without your fashion of malice, and dumb without
   Your surly tongues. But you shall help with the church

Since you refuse the oxen. You shall have
Their glory.

> [*He yokes them together. As he does so the* NEIGHBOURS
> *enter and stand a little way off.*

1ST NEIGHBOUR. Look what Cuthman is doing!

2ND NEIGHBOUR. Look! He is yoking them!

OTHERS. Can he be joking? Is this in fun?
They would never permit. They'd never allow
Liberties for the sake of a laugh.
He is angry. He is driving them
As though they were shallow-skulls,
As though they were thick-skins,
As though they were beasts of the field.

1ST NEIGHBOUR. It is neither anger nor fun.
It is the same stress that we see
Knotting his forearm and kneading his forehead
To drops of sweat when he wrestles
With timber in the framework of the church.

2ND NEIGHBOUR. What will their mother have to say about it?

MRS. FIPPS [*bursting through the crowd*].
I'll show you what their mother will have to say!
What's come over you all to stand and gape,
With outrage running to seed under your eyes?
Do you want all our days to be choked with insults
And devilment? We've stood a lot too much
Nonsense from this canting baby,
A lot too much.

[*To* CUTHMAN.] Take that off the backs of my sons and get out of
this place. Do you hear me? Get out of this place! Take it off, I
tell you! And don't let me see you or your amiable mother skulking
round these parts any longer. Do you hear what I say?

CUTHMAN. Wait a moment. Your sons have shut up the oxen that
were helping with the church. I asked them to give them back to

us, but that's something they're not prepared to do. The building
shall not be interrupted. If they'll not return the oxen they must
replace them.

MRS. FIPPS. You overbearing little brat! You'll be shut up yourself if I have anything to do with it; I'll see to it! I'll put you and
your mother on the way where you belong—in the ditch with
vagrants! My poor Alfred, my poor Demiwulf, your mother will
see that the nasty wicked boy doesn't hurt you. . . . It's your
mother talking to you. Alfred! Demiwulf! Can't you hear me?—
You've murdered them on their legs, that's what you've done.
Take that thing off their backs before I get my hands to you. Go
on! You insolent bantam! Do what I say! . . . [*A change comes
over her.*] What's happening? I'm being pushed over! I'm being
knocked down!

NEIGHBOURS. What a wind has got up! What a gale!

MRS. FIPPS. Help! Help! The wind is blowing me over!

NEIGHBOURS. Mind your heads! The chimneys will be off!
What a tornado!

MRS. FIPPS. Help! It's whirling me round!
It'll have me off my feet!

NEIGHBOURS. It will have her down!
Look at her, look at her now!

MRS. FIPPS. Help! Help!

[*The wind blows her out of sight.*

THE PEOPLE OF SOUTH ENGLAND.
The arms of the wood were not ready for this,
The turbulent boy who has pitched himself suddenly in,
The headlong ruffian hurling himself in the lap
Of the valley:
What can protect us from this ragamuffin
Who has stampeded into his manhood with
The shudder of the first anger of a rocket?
He has slammed back the ocean's stable-doors

And slapped the sturdy bases of the earth,
Wrenched and worried into the heart of heaven
And dragged a bellowing Lucifer to ground.
He has belaboured the homeflight of the day
Into a staggered bird. The word's gone round:
There will be no quarter, no pouring of oil.
The roots clutch in the soil, frantic against
The sobbing of the bough. The gates of evening
Clang in vain. Darkness will topple down
Under the guns of the enormous air.
It has lifted an old woman off her feet!
This is a matter of considerable local interest.
It is carrying her up as high as the trees,
Zigzag like a paper bag, like somebody's hat!
There hasn't been a hurricane like this
In living memory. It only shows
How ludicrous it is to strut in a storm.
Zigzag like a paper bag, like somebody's hat!
It will be a long time before we have exhausted
All the possibilities of a story
As amazing as this one is. Up! Up! Up!

NEIGHBOURS. Up! Up! Up!

> [*The* NEIGHBOURS *with shrieks and squeals rush off to
> follow the old woman's flight.*

THE PEOPLE OF SOUTH ENGLAND.
You may not think it possible, but tradition
Has it that this old woman was carried five
Miles and dropped in a pond. It's scarcely
Credible, but that is the story that got
About. And when the hurricane had dropped her
It dropped itself and the incident was closed.

CUTHMAN [*unyoking the* BROTHERS]. Well that was an upheaval.
You'd better go and look for your mother. She'll be some way
off by this time.

ALFRED. I'm not feeling very well. It's as though I was conva-
lescing after a long illness. My voice seems to be climbing back
on my tongue.

DEMIWULF. I feel like a toad crawling out from under a stone

CUTHMAN. Before you do anything else perhaps you would fetch
the oxen for me? It's time we got busy with them.

ALFRED. We'll fetch them for you at once.

DEMIWULF. At once. We're sorry if you have been put to any inconvenience.

CUTHMAN. The inconvenience was mutual. I shall be at the church.

[*Exit* CUTHMAN.

ALFRED [*as he and his brother go off*]. I wonder where mother is by
now? She always disliked long journeys, but at any rate she
hasn't got any luggage to worry about.

THE PEOPLE OF SOUTH ENGLAND.
Do you catch the time of the tune that the shepherd plays
Under the irregular bough of the oak-tree,
The tune of the tale he expects your brain to dance to,
The time of the tune as irregular as the bough?
It will not come as anything fresh to you
That instead of events keeping their proper stations
They are huddling together as though to find protection
From rain that spoils the mowers' crop
From wind sweeping old women off their feet.
We merely remind you, though we've told you before,
How things stand. We're apt to take the meticulous
Intervention of the sun, the strict
Moon and the seasons much too much for granted.

Enter CUTHMAN'S MOTHER *and* TAWM. *Enter to them some*
of the NEIGHBOURS, *downcast.*

MOTHER. I can hardly wait for my son to know. He has already
grown to love you like a father, I know that; he has often told me

so. It is nearly two years since we first met. How astonishing,
two years! Do you remember how we arrived with that dreadful
cart? I was so ashamed. You must have thought we were nothing
but riff-raff, and little did I imagine what was in store for us.
Usually my intuition is most acute; things say themselves to me.
But oddly enough nothing said to me 'One day that dear man is
going to be your husband,' nothing at all.—Here are some of the
neighbours coming from the church. It's getting on so nicely.
Good evening, neighbours. Is it nearly done?

1ST NEIGHBOUR. It'll never be done.

2ND NEIGHBOUR. It'll never be finished now.

1ST NEIGHBOUR. There'll be no church.

MOTHER. Never be finished? Tush and nonsense! What creatures
men are. You're up to the roof.

1ST NEIGHBOUR. Up to the roof we may be but we'll get no further.
The king-post has beaten us.

TAWM. You can't be beaten by a piece of timber; it isn't princely in
a man to be beaten by a piece of timber.

MOTHER. Listen to what he says and be ashamed of yourselves.
We are old, this dear man and I, and we know what is right.

1ST NEIGHBOUR. The work was almost done, and then someone
suddenly shouted 'The king-post has swung out of position!' It
had set other places wrong, that had been ready. For days we
have laboured at it, and as time went on we laboured and prayed,
but nothing will make it go into its place. We're not knowledge-
able men with these things.   It's not our work and a church isn't
like a little cottage. We've none of the proper appurtenances for
the job. There's no hope for it, even if we go on trying till we're
whiteheaded.

MOTHER. But Cuthman—he thinks of nothing but how the building grows, nothing but of the day when it will be done—where
is he? What is he doing?

2ND NEIGHBOUR. We couldn't get him away. For days he has
tugged and tusselled with us, with the blood in his face and the
veins pushing in his head. And now he has gone into a ghost.
He smoothes the stone with his hand as though it were in a fever
and sleepless. He pats it as though it were a horse that had brought
him safely through battle. And then he stands heavily in the aisle
with his misery staring to the east.

MOTHER. Poor Cuthman, poor sweet son! On our journey it was
ahead of him like riches, and every moment of his holiday time
he has run to it as though he had heaven at his shoulders. This
will damage him. I'm afraid for him and I don't mind telling you.

TAWM. Here's the boy; here he is.

Enter CUTHMAN *running. Other* NEIGHBOURS *join the group.*

MOTHER. Cuthman, what has happened to you? Son,
What is the matter?

CUTHMAN.   The king-post is in place
Again! The church will be finished.

MOTHER.   But the neighbours
Said there was no one with you. You were alone.

CUTHMAN. I was alone by the unattended pillar,
Mourning the bereaved air that lay so quiet
Between walls; hungry for hammer-blows.
And the momentous hive that once was there.
And when I prayed my voice slid to the ground
Like a crashed pediment.
There was a demolition written over
The walls, and dogs rummaged in the foundations,
And picnic parties laughed on a heap of stone.
But gradually I was aware of some one in
The doorway and turned my eyes that way and saw
Carved out of the sunlight a man who stood
Watching me, so still that there was not
Other such stillness anywhere on the earth,

So still that the air seemed to leap
At his side. He came towards me, and the sun
Flooded its banks and flowed across the shadow.
He asked me why I stood alone. His voice
Hovered on memory with open wings
And drew itself up from a chine of silence
As though it had longtime lain in a vein of gold.
I told him: It is the king-post.
He stretched his hand upon it. At his touch
It lifted to its place. There was no sound.
I cried out, and I cried at last 'Who are you?'
I heard him say 'I was a carpenter' . . .

> *[They fall upon their knees.*

There under the bare walls of our labour
Death and life were knotted in one strength
Indivisible as root and sky.

THE PEOPLE OF SOUTH ENGLAND.
The candle of our story has burnt down
And Cuthman's life is puffed like a dandelion
Into uncertain places. But the hand
Still leads the earth to drink at the sky, and still
The messenger rides into the city of leaves
Under the gradual fires of September;
The Spring shall hear, the Winter shall be wise
To warning of aconite and freezing lily,
And all shall watch the augur of a star
And learn their stillness from a stiller heaven.
And what of us who upon Cuthman's world
Have grafted progress without lock or ratchet?
What of us who have to catch up, always
To catch up with the high-powered car, or with
The unbalanced budget, to cope with competition,
To weather the sudden thunder of the uneasy
Frontier? We also loom with the earth

Over the waterways of space. Between
Our birth and death we may touch understanding
As a moth brushes a window with its wing.

Who shall question then
Why we lean our bicycle against a hedge
And go into the house of God?
Who shall question
That coming out from our doorways
We have discerned a little, we have known
More than the gossip that comes to us over our gates.

A PHOENIX TOO FREQUENT

A Comedy

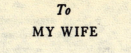

To
MY WIFE

A PHOENIX TOO FREQUENT

First produced at the Mercury Theatre, London
25 April 1946

Dynamene	. .	HERMIONE HANNEN
Doto	. .	ELEANOR SUMMERFIELD
Tegeus-Chromis	.	ALAN WHEATLEY

Directed by E. Martin Browne

Revived at the Arts Theatre, London
20 November 1946

Dynamene	.	HERMIONE HANNEN
Doto	. . .	JOAN WHITE
Tegeus-Chromis	.	PAUL SCOFIELD

Directed by Noël Willman

CHARACTERS

DYNAMENE

DOTO

TEGEUS–CHROMIS

SCENE

The tomb of Virilius, near Ephesus; night

NOTE

*The story was got from Jeremy Taylor who
had it from Petronius*

'To whom conferr'd a peacock's indecent,
A squirrel's harsh, a phoenix too frequent.'

Robert Burton quoting Martial

An underground tomb, in darkness except for the very low light of an oil-lamp. Above ground the starlight shows a line of trees on which hang the bodies of several men. It also penetrates a gate and falls on to the first of the steps which descend into the darkness of the tomb. DOTO *talks to herself in the dark.*

DOTO. Nothing but the harmless day gone into black
    Is all the dark is. And so what's my trouble?
    Demons is so much wind. Are so much wind.
    I've plenty to fill my thoughts. All that I ask
    Is don't keep turning men over in my mind,
    Venerable Aphrodite. I've had my last one
    And thank you. I thank thee. He smelt of sour grass
    And was likeable. He collected ebony quoits.
                               [An owl hoots near at hand.
    O Zeus! O some god or other, where is the oil?
    Fire's from Prometheus. I thank thee. If I
    Mean to die I'd better see what I'm doing.
        [She fills the lamp with oil. The flame burns up brightly and
        shows DYNAMENE, *beautiful and young, leaning asleep*
        beside a bier.
    Honestly, I would rather have to sleep
    With a bald bee-keeper who was wearing his boots
    Than spend more days fasting and thirsting and crying
    In a tomb. I shouldn't have said that. Pretend
    I didn't hear myself. But life and death
    Is cat and dog in this double-bed of a world.
    My master, my poor master, was a man
    Whose nose was as straight as a little buttress,

And now he has taken it into Elysium
Where it won't be noticed among all the other straightness.
                       [*The owl cries again and wakens* DYNAMENE.
Oh, them owls. Those owls. It's woken her.

DYNAMENE. Ah! I'm breathless. I caught up with the ship
But it spread its wings, creaking a cry of *Dew*,
Dew! and flew figurehead foremost into the sun.

DOTO. How crazy, madam.

DYNAMENE.   Doto, draw back the curtains.
I'll take my barley-water.

DOTO.   We're not at home
Now, madam. It's the master's tomb.

DYNAMENE.   Of course!
Oh, I'm wretched. Already I have disfigured
My vigil. My cynical eyelids have soon dropped me
In a dream.

DOTO.   But then it's possible, madam, you might
Find yourself in bed with him again
In a dream, madam. Was he on the ship?

DYNAMENE. He was the ship.

DOTO.   Oh. That makes it different.

DYNAMENE. He was the ship. He had such a deck, Doto,
Such a white, scrubbed deck. Such a stern prow,
Such a proud stern, so slim from port to starboard.
If ever you meet a man with such fine masts
Give your life to him, Doto. The figurehead
Bore his own features, so serene in the brow
And hung with a little seaweed. O Virilius,
My husband, you have left a wake in my soul.
You cut the glassy water with a diamond keel.
I must cry again.

DOTO. What, when you mean to join him?
Don't you believe he will be glad to see you, madam?
Thankful to see you, I should imagine, among
Them shapes and shades; all shapes of shapes and all
Shades of shades, from what I've heard. I know
I shall feel odd at first with Cerberus,
Sop or no sop. Still, I know how you feel, madam.
You think he may find a temptation in Hades.
I shouldn't worry. It would help him to settle down.

[DYNAMENE *weeps*.

It would only be *fun*, madam. He couldn't go far
With a shade.

DYNAMENE. He was one of the coming men.
He was certain to have become the most well-organized provost
The town has known, once they had made him provost.
He was so punctual, you could regulate
The sun by him. He made the world succumb
To his daily revolution of habit. But who,
In the world he has gone to, will appreciate that?
O poor Virilius! To be a coming man
Already gone—it must be distraction.
Why did you leave me walking about our ambitions
Like a cat in the ruins of a house? Promising husband,
Why did you insult me by dying? Virilius,
Now I keep no flower, except in the vase
Of the tomb.

DOTO. O poor madam! O poor master!
I presume so far as to cry somewhat for myself
As well. I know you won't mind, madam. It's two
Days not eating makes me think of my uncle's
Shop in the country, where he has a hardware business,
Basins, pots, ewers, and alabaster birds.

He makes you die of laughing. O madam,
Isn't it sad?

                                                 [*They both weep.*

DYNAMENE.   How could I have allowed you
To come and die of my grief? Doto, it puts
A terrible responsibility on me. Have you
No grief of your own you could die of?

DOTO.   Not really, madam.

DYNAMENE. Nothing?

DOTO.   Not really. They was all one to me.
Well, all but two was all one to me. And they,
Strange enough, was two who kept recurring.
I could never be sure if they had gone for good
Or not; and so that kept things cheerful, madam.
One always gave a wink before he deserted me,
The other slapped me as it were behind, madam;
Then they would be away for some months.

DYNAMENE.   Oh Doto,
What an unhappy life you were having to lead.

DOTO. Yes, I'm sure. But never mind, madam,
It seemed quite lively then. And now I know
It's what you say; life is more big than a bed
And full of miracles and mysteries like
One man made for one woman, etcetera, etcetera.
Lovely. I feel sung, madam, by a baritone
In mixed company with everyone pleased.
And so I had to come with you here, madam,
For the last sad chorus of me. It's all
Fresh to me. Death's a new interest in life,
If it doesn't disturb you, madam, to have me crying.

It's because of us not having breakfast again.
And the master, of course. And the beautiful world.
And you crying too, madam. Oh—Oh!

DYNAMENE. I can't forbid your crying; but you must cry
On the other side of the tomb. I'm becoming confused.
This is my personal grief and my sacrifice
Of self, solus. Right over there, darling girl.

DOTO. What here?

DYNAMENE.   Now, if you wish, you may cry, Doto.
But our tears are very different. For me
The world is all with Charon, all, all,
Even the metal and plume of the rose garden,
And the forest where the sea fumes overhead
In vegetable tides, and particularly
The entrance to the warm baths in Arcite Street
Where we first met;—all!—the sun itself
Trails an evening hand in the sultry river
Far away down by Acheron. I am lonely,
Virilius. Where is the punctual eye
And where is the cautious voice which made
Balance-sheets sound like Homer and Homer sound
Like balance-sheets? The precision of limbs, the amiable
Laugh, the exact festivity? Gone from the world.
You were the peroration of nature, Virilius.
You explained everything to me, even the extremely
Complicated gods. You wrote them down
In seventy columns. Dear curling calligraphy!
Gone from the world, once and for all. And I taught you
In your perceptive moments to appreciate me.
You said I was harmonious, Virilius,
Moulded and harmonious, little matronal

Ox-eye, your package. And then I would walk
Up and down largely, as it were making my own
Sunlight. What a mad blacksmith creation is
Who blows his furnaces until the stars fly upward
And iron Time is hot and politicians glow
And bulbs and roots sizzle into hyacinth
And orchis, and the sand puts out the lion,
Roaring yellow, and oceans bud with porpoises,
Blenny, tunny and the almost unexisting
Blindfish; throats are cut, the masterpiece
Looms out of labour; nations and rebellions
Are spat out to hang on the wind—and all is gone
In one Virilius, wearing his office tunic,
Checking the pence column as he went.
Where's animation now? What is there that stays
To dance? The eye of the one-eyed world is out.

[*She weeps.*

DOTO. I shall try to grieve a little, too.
It would take lessons, I imagine, to do it out loud
For long. If I could only remember
Any one of those fellows without wanting to laugh.
Hopeless, I am. Now those good pair of shoes
I gave away without thinking, that's a different—
Well, I've cried enough about *them*, I suppose.
Poor madam, poor master.

[TEGEUS *comes through the gate to the top of the steps.*

TEGEUS.   What's your trouble?

DOTO.   Oh!
Oh! Oh, a man. I thought for a moment it was something
With harm in it. Trust a man to be where it's dark.
What is it? Can't you sleep?

TEGEUS.   Now, listen—

DOTO.   Hush!
Remember you're in the grave. You must go away.
Madam is occupied.

TEGEUS.   What, here?

DOTO.   Becoming
Dead. We both are.

TEGEUS.   What's going on here?

DOTO.   Grief.
Are you satisfied now?

TEGEUS.   Less and less. Do you know
What the time is?

DOTO.   I'm not interested.
We've done with all that. Go away. Be a gentleman.
If we can't be free of men in a grave
Death's a dead loss.

TEGEUS.   It's two in the morning. All
I ask is what are women doing down here
At two in the morning?

DOTO.   Can't you see she's crying?
Or is she sleeping again? Either way
She's making arrangements to join her husband.

TEGEUS.   Where?

DOTO. Good god, in the Underworld, dear man. Haven't you
    learnt
About life and death?

TEGEUS.   In a manner, yes; in a manner;
The rudiments. So the lady means to die?

DOTO. For love; beautiful, curious madam.

TEGEUS.   Not curious;
I've had thoughts like it. Death is a kind of love.
Not anything I can explain.

DOTO.   You'd better come in
And sit down.

TEGEUS.   I'd be grateful.

DOTO.   Do. It will be my last
Chance to have company, in the flesh.

TEGEUS.   Do you mean
You're going too?

DOTO.   Oh, certainly I am.
Not anything I can explain.
It all started with madam saying a man
Was two men really, and I'd only noticed one,
One each, I mean. It seems he has a soul
As well as his other troubles. And I like to know
What I'm getting with a man. I'm inquisitive,
I suppose you'd call me.

TEGEUS.   It takes some courage.

DOTO.   Well, yes
And no. I'm fond of change.

TEGEUS.   Would you object
To have me eating my supper here?

DOTO.   Be careful
Of the crumbs. We don't want a lot of squeaking mice
Just when we're dying.

TEGEUS.   What a sigh she gave then.
Down the air like a slow comet.
And now she's all dark again. Mother of me.
How long has this been going on?

DOTO.   Two days.
  It should have been three by now, but at first
  Madam had difficulty with the Town Council. They said
  They couldn't have a tomb used as a private residence.
  But madam told them she wouldn't be eating here,
  Only suffering, and they thought that would be all right.

TEGEUS. Two of you. Marvellous. Who would have said
  I should ever have stumbled on anything like this?
  Do you have to cry? Yes, I suppose so. It's all
  Quite reasonable.

DOTO.   Your supper and your knees.
  That's what's making me cry. I can't bear sympathy
  And they're sympathetic.

TEGEUS.   Please eat a bit of something.
  I've no appetite left.

DOTO.   And see her go ahead of me?
  Wrap it up; put it away. You sex of wicked beards!
  It's no wonder you have to shave off your black souls
  Every day as they push through your chins.
  I'll turn my back on you. It means utter
  Contempt. Eat? Utter contempt. Oh, little new rolls!

TEGEUS. Forget it, forget it; please forget it. Remember
  I've had no experience of this kind of thing before.
  Indeed I'm as sorry as I know how to be. Ssh,
  We'll disturb her. She sighed again. O Zeus,
  It's terrible! Asleep, and still sighing.
  Mourning has made a warren in her spirit,
  All that way below. Ponos! the heart
  Is the devil of a medicine.

DOTO.   And I don't intend
  To turn round.

TEGEUS.   I understand how you must feel.
   Would it be—have you any objection
   To my having a drink? I have a little wine here.
   And, you probably see how it is: grief's in order,
   And death's in order, and women—I can usually
   Manage that too; but not all three together
   At this hour of the morning. So you'll excuse me.
   How about you? It would make me more comfortable
   If you'd take a smell of it.

DOTO.   One for the road?

TEGEUS. One for the road.

DOTO.   It's the dust in my throat. The tomb
   Is so dusty. Thanks, I will. There's no point in dying
   Of everything, simultaneous.

TEGEUS.   It's lucky
   I brought two bowls. I was expecting to keep
   A drain for my relief when he comes in the morning.

DOTO. Are you on duty?

TEGEUS.   Yes.

DOTO.   It looks like it.

TEGEUS.   Well,
   Here's your good health.

DOTO.   What good is that going to do me?
   Here's to an easy crossing and not too much waiting
   About on the bank. Do you have to tremble like that?

TEGEUS. The idea—I can't get used to it.

DOTO.   For a member
   Of the forces, you're peculiarly queasy. I wish
   Those owls were in Hades—oh no; let them stay where they are.
   Have you never had nothing to do with corpses before?

TEGEUS. I've got six of them outside.

DOTO.   Morpheus, that's plenty.
  What are they doing there?

TEGEUS.   Hanging.

DOTO.   Hanging?

TEGEUS.   On trees.
  Five plane trees and a holly. The holly-berries
  Are just reddening. Another drink?

DOTO.   Why not?

TEGEUS. It's from Samos. Here's—

DOTO.   All right. Let's just drink it.
  —How did they get in that predicament?

TEGEUS. The sandy-haired fellow said we should collaborate
  With everybody; the little man said he wouldn't
  Collaborate with anybody; the old one
  Said that the Pleiades weren't sisters but cousins
  And anyway were manufactured in Lacedaemon.
  The fourth said that we hanged men for nothing.
  The other two said nothing. Now they hang
  About at the corner of the night, they're present
  And absent, horribly obsequious to every
  Move in the air, and yet they keep me standing
  For five hours at a stretch.

DOTO.   The wine has gone
  Down to my knees.

TEGEUS.   And up to your cheeks. You're looking
  Fresher. If only—

DOTO.   Madam? She never would.
  Shall I ask her?

TEGEUS.   No; no, don't dare, don't breathe it.
  This is privilege, to come so near
  To what is undeceiving and uncorrupt
  And undivided; this is the clear fashion
  For all souls, a ribbon to bind the unruly
  Curls of living, a faith, a hope, Zeus
  Yes, a fine thing. I am human, and this
  Is human fidelity, and we can be proud
  And unphilosophical.

DOTO.   I need to dance
  But I haven't the use of my legs.

TEGEUS.   No, no, don't dance,
  Or, at least, only inwards; don't dance; cry
  Again. We'll put a moat of tears
  Round her bastion of love, and save
  The world. It's something, it's more than something,
  It's regeneration, to see how a human cheek
  Can become as pale as a pool.

DOTO.   Do you love me, handsome?

TEGEUS. To have found life, after all, unambiguous!

DOTO. Did you say Yes?

TEGEUS.   Certainly; just now I love all men.

DOTO. So do I.

TEGEUS.   And the world is a good creature again.
  I'd begun to see it as mildew, verdigris,
  Rust, woodrot, or as though the sky had uttered
  An oval twirling blasphemy with occasional vistas
  In country districts. I was within an ace
  Of volunteering for overseas service. Despair
  Abroad can always nurse pleasant thoughts of home.
  Integrity, by god!

DOTO.   I love all the world
And the movement of the apple in your throat.
So shall you kiss me? It would be better, I should think,
To go moistly to Hades.

TEGEUS.   Her's is the way,
Luminous with sorrow.

DOTO.   Then I'll take
Another little swiggy. I love all men,
Everybody, even you, and I'll pick you
Some outrageous honeysuckle for your helmet,
If only it lived here. Pardon.

DYNAMENE.   Doto. Who is it?

DOTO. Honeysuckle, madam. Because of the bees.
Go back to sleep, madam.

DYNAMENE.   What person is it?

DOTO. Yes, I see what you mean, madam. It's a kind of
Corporal talking to his soul, on a five-hour shift,
Madam, with six bodies. He's been having his supper.

TEGEUS. I'm going. It's terrible that we should have disturbed her.

DOTO. He was delighted to see you so sad, madam.
It has stopped him going abroad.

DYNAMENE.   One with six bodies?
A messenger, a guide to where we go.
It is possible he has come to show us the way
Out of these squalid suburbs of life, a shade,
A gorgon, who has come swimming up, against
The falls of my tears (for which in truth he would need
Many limbs) to guide me to Virilius.
I shall go quietly.

TEGEUS.   I do assure you—

Such clumsiness, such a vile and unforgivable
Intrusion. I shall obliterate myself
Immediately.

DOTO.   Oblit—oh, what a pity
To oblit. Pardon. Don't let him, the nice fellow.

DYNAMENE. Sir: your other five bodies: where are they?

TEGEUS.   Madam—
Outside; I have them outside. On trees.

DYNAMENE.   Quack!

TEGEUS. What do I reply?

DYNAMENE.   Quack, charlatan!
You've never known the gods. You came to mock me.
Doto, this never was a gorgon, never.
Nor a gentleman either. He's completely spurious.
Admit it, you creature. Have you even a feather
Of the supernatural in your system? Have you?

TEGEUS. Some of my relations—

DYNAMENE.   Well?

TEGEUS.   Are dead, I think;
That is to say I have connexions—

DYNAMENE.   Connexions
With pickpockets. It's a shameless imposition.
Does the army provide you with no amusements?
If I were still of the world, and not cloistered
In a colourless landscape of winter thought
Where the approaching Spring is desired oblivion,
I should write sharply to your commanding officer.
It should be done, it should be done. If my fingers
Weren't so cold I would do it now. But they are,
Horribly cold. And why should insolence matter

When my colour of life is unreal, a blush on death,
A partial mere diaphane? I don't know
Why it should matter. Oafish, non-commissioned
Young man! The boots of your conscience will pinch for ever
If life's dignity has any self-protection.
Oh, I have to sit down. The tomb's going round.

DOTO. Oh, madam, don't give over. I can't remember
When things were so lively. He looks marvellously
Marvellously uncomfortable. Go on, madam.
Can't you, madam? Oh, madam, don't you feel up to it?
There, do you see her, you acorn-chewing infantryman?
You've made her cry, you square-bashing barbarian.

TEGEUS. O history, my private history, why
Was I led here? What stigmatism has got
Into my stars? Why wasn't it my brother?
He has a tacit misunderstanding with everybody
And washes in it. Why wasn't it my mother?
She makes a collection of other people's tears
And dries them all. Let them forget I came;
And lie in the terrible black crystal of grief
Which held them, before I broke it. Outside, Tegeus.

DOTO. Hey, I don't think so, I shouldn't say so. Come
Down again, uniform. Do you think you're going
To half kill an unprotected lady and then
Back out upwards? Do you think you can leave her like this?

TEGEUS. Yes, yes, I'll leave her. O directorate of gods,
How can I? Beauty's bit is between my teeth.
She has added another torture to me. Bottom
Of Hades' bottom.

DOTO.   Madam. Madam, the corporal
Has some wine here. It will revive you, madam.
And then you can go at him again, madam.

TEGEUS. It's the opposite of everything you've said,
  I swear. I swear by Horkos and the Styx,
  I swear by the nine acres of Tityos,
  I swear the Hypnotic oath, by all the Titans—
  By Koeos, Krios, Iapetos, Kronos, and so on—
  By the three Hekatoncheires, by the insomnia
  Of Tisiphone, by Jove, by jove, and the dew
  On the feet of my boyhood, I am innocent
  Of mocking you. Am I a Salmoneus
  That, seeing such a flame of sorrow—

DYNAMENE.   You needn't
  Labour to prove your secondary education.
  Perhaps I jumped to a wrong conclusion, perhaps
  I was hasty.

DOTO.   How easy to swear if you're properly educated.
  Wasn't it pretty, madam? Pardon.

DYNAMENE.   If I misjudged you
  I apologize, I apologize. Will you please leave us?
  You were wrong to come here. In a place of mourning
  Light itself is a trespasser; nothing can have
  The right of entrance except those natural symbols
  Of mortality, the jabbing, funeral, sleek-
  With-omen raven, the death-watch beetle which mocks
  Time: particularly, I'm afraid, the spider
  Weaving his home with swift self-generated
  Threads of slaughter; and, of course, the worm.
  I wish it could be otherwise. Oh dear,
  They aren't easy to live with.

DOTO.   Not even a *little* wine, madam?

DYNAMENE. Here, Doto?

DOTO.   Well, on the steps perhaps,
  Except it's so draughty.

DYNAMENE. Doto! Here?

DOTO. No, madam;
I quite see.

DYNAMENE. I might be wise to strengthen myself
In order to fast again; it would make me abler
For grief. I will breathe a little of it, Doto.

DOTO. Thank god. Where's the bottle?

DYNAMENE. What an exquisite bowl.

TEGEUS. Now that it's peacetime we have pottery classes.

DYNAMENE. You made it yourself?

TEGEUS. Yes. Do you see the design?
The corded god, tied also by the rays
Of the sun, and the astonished ship erupting
Into vines and vine-leaves, inverted pyramids
Of grapes, the uplifted hands of the men (the raiders),
And here the headlong sea, itself almost
Venturing into leaves and tendrils, and Proteus
With his beard braiding the wind, and this
Held by other hands is a drowned sailor—

DYNAMENE. Always, always.

DOTO. Hold the bowl steady, madam.
Pardon.

DYNAMENE. Doto, have you been drinking?

DOTO. Here, madam?
I coaxed some a little way towards my mouth, madam,
But I scarcely swallowed except because I had to. The hiccup
Is from no breakfast, madam, and not meant to be funny.

DYNAMENE. You may drink this too. Oh, how the inveterate body,
Even when cut from the heart, insists on leaf,
Puts out, with a separate meaningless will,

Fronds to intercept the thankless sun.
How it does, oh, how it does. And how it confuses
The nature of the mind.

TEGEUS.   Yes, yes, the confusion;
That's something I understand better than anything.

DYNAMENE. When the thoughts would die, the instincts will set
    sail
For life. And when the thoughts are alert for life
The instincts will rage to be destroyed on the rocks.
To Virilius it was not so; his brain was an ironing-board
For all crumpled indecision: and I follow him,
The hawser of my world. You don't belong here,
You see; you don't belong here at all.

TEGEUS.   If only
I did. If only you knew the effort it costs me
To mount those steps again into an untrustworthy,
Unpredictable, unenlightened night,
And turn my back on—on a state of affairs,
I can only call it a vision, a hope, a promise,
A— By that I mean loyalty, enduring passion,
Unrecking bravery and beauty all in one.

DOTO. He means you, or you and me; or me, madam.

TEGEUS. It only remains for me to thank you, and to say
That whatever awaits me and for however long
I may be played by this poor musician, existence,
Your person and sacrifice will leave their trace
As clear upon me as the shape of the hills
Around my birthplace. Now I must leave you to your husband.

DOTO. Oh! You, madam.

DYNAMENE.   I'll tell you what I will do.
I will drink with you to the memory of my husband,

Because I have been curt, because you are kind,
And because I'm extremely thirsty. And then we will say
Good-bye and part to go to our opposite corruptions,
The world and the grave.

TEGEUS.   The climax to the vision.

DYNAMENE [*drinking*]. My husband, and all he stood for.

TEGEUS.   Stands for.

DYNAMENE.   Stands for.

TEGEUS. Your husband.

DOTO.   The master.

DYNAMENE.   How good it is,
How it sings to the throat, purling with summer.

TEGEUS. It has a twin nature, winter and warmth in one,
Moon and meadow. Do you agree?

DYNAMENE.   Perfectly;
A cold bell sounding in a golden month.

TEGEUS. Crystal in harvest.

DYNAMENE.   Perhaps a nightingale
Sobbing among the pears.

TEGEUS.   In an old autumnal midnight.

DOTO. Grapes.—Pardon. There's some more here.

TEGEUS.   Plenty.
I drink to the memory of your husband.

DYNAMENE.   My husband.

DOTO.   The master.

DYNAMENE. He was careless in his choice of wines.

TEGEUS.   And yet
Rendering to living its rightful poise is not
Unimportant.

DYNAMENE.   A mystery's in the world
Where a little liquid, with flavour, quality, and fume
Can be as no other, can hint and flute our senses
As though a music played in harvest hollows
And a movement was in the swathes of our memory.
Why should scent, why should flavour come
With such wings upon us? Parsley, for instance.

TEGEUS. Seaweed.

DYNAMENE.   Lime trees.

DOTO.   Horses.

TEGEUS.   Fruit in the fire.

DYNAMENE. Do I know your name?

TEGEUS.   Tegeus.

DYNAMENE.   That's very thin for you,
It hardly covers your bones. Something quite different,
Altogether other. I shall think of it presently.

TEGEUS. Darker vowels, perhaps.

DYNAMENE.   Yes, certainly darker vowels.
And your consonants should have a slight angle.
And a certain temperature. Do you know what I mean?
It will come to me.

TEGEUS.   Now *your* name—

DYNAMENE.   It is nothing
To any purpose. I'll be to you the She
In the tomb. You have the air of a natural-historian
As though you were accustomed to handling birds' eggs,
Or tadpoles, or putting labels on moths. You see?
The genius of dumb things, that they are nameless.
Have I found the seat of the weevil in human brains?
Our names. They make us broody; we sit and sit

To hatch them into reputation and dignity.
And then they set upon us and become despair,
Guilt and remorse. We go where they lead. We dance
Attendance on something wished upon us by the wife
Of our mother's physician. But insects meet and part
And put the woods about them, fill the dusk
And freckle the light and go and come without
A name among them, without the wish of a name
And very pleasant too. Did I interrupt you?

TEGEUS. I forget. We'll have no names then.

DYNAMENE.   I should like
You to have a name, I don't know why; a small one
To fill out the conversation.

TEGEUS.   I should like
You to have a name too, if only for something
To remember. Have you still some wine in your bowl?

DYNAMENE. Not altogether.

TEGEUS.   We haven't come to the end
By several inches. Did I splash you?

DYNAMENE.   It doesn't matter.
Well, here's to my husband's name.

TEGEUS.   Your husband's name.

DOTO. The master.

DYNAMENE.   It was kind of you to come.

TEGEUS. It was more than coming. I followed my future here,
As we all do if we're sufficiently inattentive
And don't vex ourselves with questions; or do I mean
Attentive? If so, attentive to what? Do I sound
Incoherent?

DYNAMENE.   You're wrong. There isn't a future here,
Not here, not for you.

TEGEUS.   Your name's Dynamene.

DYNAMENE. Who—Have I been utterly irreverent? Are you—
Who made you say that? Forgive me the question,
But are you dark or light? I mean which shade
Of the supernatural? Or if neither, what prompted you?

TEGEUS. Dynamene——

DYNAMENE.   No, but I'm sure you're the friend of nature,
It must be so, I think I see little Phoebuses
Rising and setting in your eyes.

DOTO.   They're not little Phoebuses,
They're hoodwinks, madam. Your name is on your brooch.
No little Phoebuses to-night.

DYNAMENE.   That's twice
You've played me a trick. Oh, I know practical jokes
Are common on Olympus, but haven't we at all
Developed since the gods were born? Are gods
And men both to remain immortal adolescents?
How tiresome it all is.

TEGEUS.   It was you, each time,
Who said I was supernatural. When did I say so?
You're making me into whatever you imagine
And then you blame me because I can't live up to it.

DYNAMENE. I shall call you Chromis. It has a breadlike sound.
I think of you as a crisp loaf.

TEGEUS.   And now
You'll insult me because I'm not sliceable.

DYNAMENE. I think drinking is harmful to our tempers.

TEGEUS. If I seem to be frowning, that is only because
    I'm looking directly into your light: I must look
    Angrily, or shut my eyes.

DYNAMENE.   Shut them.—Oh,
    You have eyelashes! A new perspective of you.
    Is that how you look when you sleep?

TEGEUS.   My jaw drops down.

DYNAMENE. Show me how.

TEGEUS.   Like this.

DYNAMENE.   It makes an irresistible
    Moron of you. Will you waken now?
    It's morning; I see a thin dust of daylight
    Blowing on to the steps.

TEGEUS.   Already? Dynamene,
    You're tricked again. This time by the moon.

DYNAMENE.   Oh well,
    Moon's daylight, then. Doto is asleep.

TEGEUS.   Doto
    Is asleep . . .

DYNAMENE. Chromis, what made you walk about
    In the night? What, I wonder, made you not stay
    Sleeping wherever you slept? Was it the friction
    Of the world on your mind? Those two are difficult
    To make agree. Chromis—now try to learn
    To answer your name. I won't say Tegeus.

TEGEUS.   And I
    Won't say Dynamene.

DYNAMENE.   Not?

TEGEUS.   It makes you real.
    Forgive me, a terrible thing has happened. Shall I

Say it and perhaps destroy myself for you?
Forgive me first, or, more than that, forgive
Nature who winds her furtive stream all through
Our reason. Do you forgive me?

DYNAMENE.   I'll forgive
Anything, if it's the only way I can know
What you have to tell me.

TEGEUS.   I felt us to be alone;
Here in a grave, separate from any life,
I and the only one of beauty, the only
Persuasive key to all my senses,
In spite of my having lain day after day
And pored upon the sepals, corolla, stamen, and bracts
Of the yellow bog-iris. Then my body ventured
A step towards interrupting your perfection of purpose
And my own renewed faith in human nature.
Would you have believed that possible?

DYNAMENE.   I have never
Been greatly moved by the yellow bog-iris. Alas,
It's as I said. This place is for none but the spider,
Raven and worms, not for a living man.

TEGEUS. It has been a place of blessing to me. It will always
Play in me, a fountain of confidence
When the world is arid. But I know it is true
I have to leave it, and though it withers my soul
I must let you make your journey.

DYNAMENE.   No.

TEGEUS.   Not true?

DYNAMENE. We can talk of something quite different.

TEGEUS.   Yes, we can!
Oh yes, we will! Is it your opinion

That no one believes who hasn't learned to doubt?
Or, another thing, if we persuade ourselves
To one particular Persuasion, become Sophist,
Stoic, Platonist, anything whatever,
Would you say that there must be areas of soul
Lying unproductive therefore, or dishonoured
Or blind?

DYNAMENE.   No, I don't know.

TEGEUS.   No. It's impossible
To tell. Dynamene, if only I had
Two cakes of pearl-barley and hydromel
I could see you to Hades, leave you with your husband
And come back to the world.

DYNAMENE.   Ambition, I suppose,
Is an appetite particular to man.
What is your definition?

TEGEUS.   The desire to find
A reason for living.

DYNAMENE.   But then, suppose it leads,
As often, one way or another, it does, to death.

TEGEUS. Then that may be life's reason. Oh, but how
Could I bear to return, Dynamene? The earth's
Daylight would be my grave if I had left you
In that unearthly night.

DYNAMENE.   O Chromis——

TEGEUS.   Tell me,
What is your opinion of Progress? Does it, for example,
Exist? Is there ever progression without retrogression?
Therefore is it not true that mankind
Can more justly be said increasingly to Gress?

As the material improves, the craftsmanship deteriorates
And honour and virtue remain the same. I love you,
Dynamene.

DYNAMENE. Would you consider we go round and round?

TEGEUS. We concertina, I think; taking each time
A larger breath, so that the farther we go out
The farther we have to go in.

DYNAMENE.   There'll come a time
When it will be unbearable to continue.

TEGEUS. Unbearable.

DYNAMENE.   Perhaps we had better have something
To eat. The wine has made your eyes so quick
I am breathless beside them. It *is*
Your eyes, I think; or your intelligence
Holding my intelligence up above you
Between its hands. Or the cut of your uniform.

TEGEUS. Here's a new roll with honey. In the gods' names
Let's sober ourselves.

DYNAMENE.   As soon as possible.

TEGEUS.   Have you
Any notion of algebra?

DYNAMENE.   We'll discuss you, Chromis.
We will discuss you, till you're nothing but words.

TEGEUS. I? There is nothing, of course, I would rather discuss,
Except—if it would be no intrusion—you, Dynamene.

DYNAMENE. No, you couldn't want to. But your birthplace,
Chromis,
With the hills that placed themselves in you for ever
As you say, where was it?

TEGEUS.   My father's farm at Pyxa.

DYNAMENE. There? Could it be there?

TEGEUS.   I was born in the hills
Between showers, a quarter of an hour before milking time.
Do you know Pyxa? It stretches to the crossing of two
Troublesome roads, and buries its back in beechwood,
From which come the white owls of our nights
And the mulling and cradling of doves in the day.
I attribute my character to those shadows
And heavy roots; and my interest in music
To the sudden melodious escape of the young river
Where it breaks from nosing through the cresses and kingcups.
That's honestly so.

DYNAMENE.   You used to climb about
Among the windfallen tower of Phrasidemus
Looking for bees' nests.

TEGEUS.   What? When have I
Said so?

DYNAMENE.   Why, all the children did.

TEGEUS. Yes: but, in the name of light, how do you *know* that?

DYNAMENE. I played there once, on holiday.

TEGEUS.   O Klotho,
Lachesis and Atropos!

DYNAMENE.   It's the strangest chance:
I may have seen, for a moment, your boyhood.

TEGEUS.   I may
Have seen something like an early flower
Something like a girl. If I only could remember how I must
Have seen you. Were you after the short white violets?
Maybe I blundered past you, taking your look,
And scarcely acknowledged how a star

Ran through me, to live in the brooks of my blood for ever.
Or I saw you playing at hiding in the cave
Where the ferns are and the water drips.

DYNAMENE. I was quite plain and fat and I was usually
Hitting someone. I wish I could remember you.
I'm envious of the days and children who saw you
Then. It is curiously a little painful
Not to share your past.

TEGEUS.   How did it come
Our stars could mingle for an afternoon
So long ago, and then forget us or tease us
Or helplessly look on the dark high seas
Of our separation, while time drank
The golden hours? What hesitant fate is that?

DYNAMENE. Time? Time? Why—how old are we?

TEGEUS.   Young,
Thank both our mothers, but still we're older than to-night
And so older than we should be. Wasn't I born
In love with what, only now, I have grown to meet?
I'll tell you something else. I was born entirely
For this reason. I was born to fill a gap
In the world's experience, which had never known
Chromis loving Dynamene.

DYNAMENE.   You are so
Excited, poor Chromis. What is it? Here you sit
With a woman who has wept away all claims
To appearance, unbecoming in her oldest clothes,
With not a trace of liveliness, a drab
Of melancholy, entirely shadow without
A smear of sun. Forgive me if I tell you
That you fall easily into superlatives.

TEGEUS. Very well. I'll say nothing, then. I'll fume
  With feeling.

DYNAMENE.   Now you go to the extreme. Certainly
  You must speak. You may have more to say. Besides
  You might let your silence run away with you
  And not say something that you should. And how
  Should I answer you then? Chromis, you boy,
  I can't look away from you. You use
  The lamplight and the moon so skilfully,
  So arrestingly, in and around your furrows.
  A humorous ploughman goes whistling to a team
  Of sad sorrow, to and fro in your brow
  And over your arable cheek. Laugh for me. Have you
  Cried for women, ever?

TEGEUS.   In looking about for you.
  But I have recognized them for what they were.

DYNAMENE. What were they?

TEGEUS.   Never you: never, although
  They could walk with bright distinction into all men's
  Longest memories, never you, by a hint
  Or a faint quality, or at least not more
  Than reflectively, stars lost and uncertain
  In the sea, compared with the shining salt, the shiners,
  The galaxies, the clusters, the bright grain whirling
  Over the black threshing-floor of space.
  Will you make some effort to believe that?

DYNAMENE.   No, no effort.
  It lifts me and carries me. It may be wild
  But it comes to me with a charm, like trust indeed,
  And eats out of my heart, dear Chromis,
  Absurd, disconcerting Chromis. You make me

Feel I wish I could look my best for you.
I wish, at least, that I could believe myself
To be showing some beauty for you, to put in the scales
Between us. But they dip to you, they sink
With masculine victory.

TEGEUS.   Eros, no! No!
If this is less than your best, then never, in my presence,
Be more than your less: never! If you should bring
More to your mouth or to your eyes, a moisture
Or a flake of light, anything, anything fatally
More, perfection would fetch her unsparing rod
Out of pickle to flay me, and what would have been love
Will be the end of me. O Dynamene,
Let me unload something of my lips' longing
On to yours receiving. Oh, when I cross
Like this the hurt of the little space between us
I come a journey from the wrenching ice
To walk in the sun. That is the feeling.

DYNAMENE.   Chromis,
Where am I going? No, don't answer. It's death
I desire, not you.

TEGEUS.   Where is the difference? Call me
Death instead of Chromis. I'll answer to anything.
It's desire all the same, of death in me, or me
In death, but Chromis either way. Is it so?
Do you not love me, Dynamene?

DYNAMENE.   How could it happen?
I'm going to my husband. I'm too far on the way
To admit myself to life again. Love's in Hades.

TEGEUS. Also here. And here are we, not there
In Hades. Is your husband expecting you?

DYNAMENE. Surely, surely?

TEGEUS. Not necessarily. I,
If I had been your husband, would never dream
Of expecting you. I should remember your body
Descending stairs in the floating light, but not
Descending in Hades. I should say 'I have left
My wealth warm on the earth, and, hell, earth needs it.'
'Was all I taught her of love,' I should say, 'so poor
That she will leave her flesh and become shadow?'
'Wasn't our love for each other' (I should continue)
'Infused with life, and life infused with our love?
Very well; repeat me in love, repeat me in life,
And let me sing in your blood for ever.'

DYNAMENE. Stop, stop, I shall be dragged apart!
Why should the fates do everything to keep me
From dying honourably? They must have got
Tired of honour in Elysium. Chromis, it's terrible
To be susceptible to two conflicting norths.
I have the constitution of a whirlpool.
Am I actually twirling, or is it just sensation?

TEGEUS. You're still; still as the darkness.

DYNAMENE. What appears
Is so unlike what is. And what is madness
To those who only observe, is often wisdom
To those to whom it happens.

TEGEUS. Are we compelled
To go into all this?

DYNAMENE. Why, how could I return
To my friends? Am I to be an entertainment?

TEGEUS. That's for to-morrow. To-night I need to kiss you,
Dynamene. Let's see what the whirlpool does

Between my arms; let it whirl on my breast. O love,
Come in.

DYNAMENE. I am there before I reach you; my body
Only follows to join my longing which
Is holding you already.—Now I am
All one again.

TEGEUS.   I feel as the gods feel:
This is their sensation of life, not a man's:
Their suspension of immortality, to enrich
Themselves with time. O life, O death, O body,
O spirit, O Dynamene.

DYNAMENE.   O all
In myself; it so covets all in you,
My care, my Chromis. Then I shall be
Creation.

TEGEUS.   You have the skies already;
Out of them you are buffeting me with your gales
Of beauty. Can we be made of dust, as they tell us?
What! dust with dust releasing such a light
And such an apparition of the world
Within one body? A thread of your hair has stung me.
Why do you push me away?

DYNAMENE.   There's so much metal
About you. Do I have to be imprisoned
In an armoury?

TEGEUS.   Give your hand to the buckles and then
To me.

DYNAMENE. Don't help; I'll do them all myself.

TEGEUS. O time and patience! I want you back again.

DYNAMENE. We have a lifetime. O Chromis, think, think
Of that. And even unfastening a buckle

Is loving. And not easy. Very well,
You can help me. Chromis, what zone of miracle
Did you step into to direct you in the dark
To where I waited, not knowing I waited?

TEGEUS.   I saw
The lamplight. That was only the appearance
Of some great gesture in the bed of fortune.
I saw the lamplight.

DYNAMENE.   But here? So far from life?
What brought you near enough to see lamplight?

TEGEUS.   Zeus,
That reminds me.

DYNAMENE.   What is it, Chromis?

TEGEUS.   I'm on duty.

DYNAMENE. Is it warm enough to do without your greaves?

TEGEUS. Darling loom of magic, I must go back
To take a look at those boys. The whole business
Of guard had gone out of my mind.

DYNAMENE.   What boys, my heart?

TEGEUS. My six bodies.

DYNAMENE.   Chromis, not that joke
Again.

TEGEUS. No joke, sweet. To-day our city
Held a sextuple hanging. I'm minding the bodies
Until five o'clock. Already I've been away
For half an hour.

DYNAMENE.   What can they do, poor bodies,
In half an hour, or half a century?
You don't really mean to go?

TEGEUS.   Only to make
My conscience easy. Then, Dynamene,
No cloud can rise on love, no hovering thought
Fidget, and the night will be only to *us*.

DYNAMENE. But if every half-hour——

TEGEUS.   Hush, smile of my soul,
My sprig, my sovereign: this is to hold your eyes,
I sign my lips on them both: this is to keep
Your forehead—do you feel the claim of my kiss
Falling into your thought? And now your throat
Is a white branch and my lips two singing birds—
They are coming to rest. Throat, remember me
Until I come back in five minutes. Over all
Here is my parole: I give it to your mouth
To give me again before it's dry. I promise:
Before it's dry, or not long after.

DYNAMENE.   Run,
Run all the way. You needn't be afraid of stumbling.
There's plenty of moon. The fields are blue. Oh, wait,
Wait! My darling. No, not now: it will keep
Until I see you; I'll have it here at my lips.
Hurry.

TEGEUS. So long, my haven.

DYNAMENE.   Hurry, hurry!

                                          [*Exit* TEGEUS.

DOTO. Yes, madam, hurry; of course. Are we there
Already? How nice. Death doesn't take
Any doing at all. We were gulped into Hades
As easy as an oyster.

DYNAMENE.   Doto!

DOTO. Hurry, hurry,
Yes, madam.—But they've taken out all my bones.
I haven't a bone left. I'm a Shadow: wonderfully shady
In the legs. We shall have to sit out eternity, madam,
If they've done the same to you.

DYNAMENE. You'd better wake up.
If you can't go to sleep again, you'd better wake up.
Oh dear.—We're still alive, Doto, do you hear me?

DOTO. You must speak for yourself, madam. I'm quite dead.
I'll tell you how I know. I feel
Invisible. I'm a wraith, madam; I'm only
Waiting to be wafted.

DYNAMENE. If only you *would* be.
Do you see where you are? Look. Do you see?

DOTO. Yes. You're right, madam. We're still alive.
Isn't it enough to make you swear?
Here we are, dying to be dead,
And where does it get us?

DYNAMENE. Perhaps you should try to die
In some other place. Yes! Perhaps the air here
Suits you too well. You were sleeping very heavily.

DOTO. And all the time you alone and dying.
I shouldn't have. Has the corporal been long gone,
Madam?

DYNAMENE. He came and went, came and went,
You know the way.

DOTO. Very well I do. And went
He should have, come he should never. Oh dear, he must
Have disturbed you, madam.

DYNAMENE. He could be said
To've disturbed me. Listen; I have something to say to you.

DOTO. I expect so, madam. Maybe I *could* have kept him out
But men are in before I wish they wasn't.
I think quickly enough, but I get behindhand
With what I ought to be saying. It's a kind of stammer
In my way of life, madam.

DYNAMENE.   I have been unkind,
I have sinfully wronged you, Doto.

DOTO.   Never, madam.

DYNAMENE. Oh yes. I was letting you die with me, Doto, without
Any fair reason. I was drowning you
In grief that wasn't yours. That was wrong, Doto.

DOTO. But I haven't got anything against dying, madam.
I may *like* the situation, as far as I like
Any situation, madam. Now if you'd said mangling,
A lot of mangling, I might have thought twice about staying.
We all have our dislikes, madam.

DYNAMENE.   I'm asking you
To leave me, Doto, at once, as quickly as possible,
Now, before—now, Doto, and let me forget
My bad mind which confidently expected you.
To companion me to Hades. Now good-bye,
Good-bye.

DOTO.   No, it's not good-bye at all.
I shouldn't know another night of sleep, wondering
How you got on, or what I was missing, come to that.
I should be anxious about you, too. When you belong
To an upper class, the netherworld might come strange.
Now I was born nether, madam, though not
As nether as some. No, it's not good-bye, madam.

DYNAMENE. Oh Doto, go; you must, you must! And if I seem
Without gratitude, forgive me. It isn't so,

It is far, far from so. But I can only
Regain my peace of mind if I know you're gone.

DOTO. Besides, look at the time, madam. Where should I go
At three in the morning? Even if I was to think
Of going; and think of it I never shall.

DYNAMENE. Think of the unmatchable world, Doto.

DOTO.   I do
Think of it, madam. And when I think of it, what
Have I thought? Well, it depends, madam.

DYNAMENE.   I insist,
Obey me! At once! Doto!

DOTO.   Here I sit.

DYNAMENE. What shall I do with you?

DOTO.   Ignore me, madam.
I know my place. I shall die quite unobtrusive.
Oh look, the corporal's forgotten to take his equipment.

DYNAMENE. Could he be so careless?

DOTO.   I shouldn't hardly have thought so.
Poor fellow. They'll go and deduct it off his credits.
I suppose, madam, I suppose he couldn't be thinking
Of coming back?

DYNAMENE.   He'll think of these. He will notice
He isn't wearing them. He'll come; he is sure to come.

DOTO. Oh.

DYNAMENE. I know he will.

DOTO.   Oh, oh.
Is that all for to-night, madam? May I go now, madam?

DYNAMENE. Doto! Will you?

DOTO.   Just you try to stop me, madam.
  Sometimes going is a kind of instinct with me.
  I'll leave death to some other occasion.

DYNAMENE.   Do,
  Doto. Any other time. Now you must hurry.
  I won't delay you from life another moment.
  Oh, Doto, good-bye.

DOTO.   Good-bye. Life is unusual,
  Isn't it, madam? Remember me to Cerberus.

> [*Re-enter* TEGEUS. DOTO *passes him on the steps.*

DOTO [*as she goes*]. You left something behind. Ye gods, what a
  moon!

DYNAMENE. Chromis, it's true; my lips are hardly dry.
  Time runs again; the void is space again;
  Space has life again; Dynamene has Chromis.

TEGEUS. It's over.

DYNAMENE.   Chromis, you're sick. As white as wool.
  Come, you covered the distance too quickly.
  Rest in my arms; get your breath again.

TEGEUS. I've breathed one night too many. Why did I see you,
  Why in the name of life did I see you?

DYNAMENE.   Why?
  Weren't we gifted with each other? O heart,
  What do you mean?

TEGEUS.   I mean that joy is nothing
  But the parent of doom. Why should I have found
  Your constancy such balm to the world and yet
  Find, by the same vision, its destruction
  A necessity? We're set upon by love
  To make us incompetent to steer ourselves,

To make us docile to fate. I should have known:
Indulgences, not fulfilment, is what the world
Permits us.

DYNAMENE. Chromis, is this intelligible?
Help me to follow you. What did you meet in the fields
To bring about all this talk? Do you still love me?

TEGEUS. What good will it do us? I've lost a body.

DYNAMENE.   A body?
One of the six? Well, it isn't with them you propose
To love me; and you couldn't keep it for ever.
Are we going to allow a body that isn't there
To come between us?

TEGEUS.   But I'm responsible for it.
I have to account for it in the morning. Surely
You see, Dynamene, the horror we're faced with?
The relatives have had time to cut him down
And take him away for burial. It means
A court martial. No doubt about the sentence.
I shall take the place of the missing man.
To be hanged, Dynamene! Hanged, Dynamene!

DYNAMENE. No; it's monstrous! Your life is yours, Chromis.

TEGEUS. Anything but. That's why I have to take it.
At the best we live our lives on loan,
At the worst in chains. And I was never born
To have life. Then for what? To be had by it,
And so are we all. But I'll make it what it is,
By making it nothing.

DYNAMENE.   Chromis, you're frightening me.
What are you meaning to do?

TEGEUS.   I have to die,
Dance of my heart, I have to die, to die,

To part us, to go to my sword and let it part us.
I'll have my free will even if I'm compelled to it.
I'll kill myself.

DYNAMENE.   Oh, no! No, Chromis!
It's all unreasonable—no such horror
Can come of a pure accident. Have you hanged?
How can they hang you for simply not being somewhere?
How can they hang you for losing a dead man?
They must have wanted to lose him, or they wouldn't
Have hanged him. No, you're scaring yourself for nothing
And making me frantic.

TEGEUS.   It's section six, paragraph
Three in the Regulations. That's my doom.
I've read it for myself. And, by my doom,
Since I have to die, let me die here, in love,
Promoted by your kiss to tower, in dying,
High above my birth. For god's sake let me die
On a wave of life, Dynamene, with an action
I can take some pride in. How could I settle to death
Knowing that you last saw me stripped and strangled
On a holly tree? Demoted first and then hanged!

DYNAMENE. Am I supposed to love the corporal
Or you? It's you I love, from head to foot
And out to the ends of your spirit. What shall I do
If you die? How could I follow you? I should find you
Discussing me with my husband, comparing your feelings,
Exchanging reactions. Where should I put myself?
Or am I to live on alone, or find in life
Another source of love, in memory
Of Virilius and of you?

TEGEUS.   Dynamene,
Not that! Since everything in the lives of men

Is brief to indifference, let our love at least
Echo and perpetuate itself uniquely
As long as time allows you. Though you go
To the limit of age, it won't be far to contain me.

DYNAMENE. It will seem like eternity ground into days and days.

TEGEUS. Can I be certain of you, for ever?

DYNAMENE.   But, Chromis,
Surely you said——

TEGEUS.   Surely we have sensed
Our passion to be greater than mortal? Must I
Die believing it is dying with me?

DYNAMENE.   Chromis,
You must never die, never! It would be
An offence against truth.

TEGEUS.   I cannot live to be hanged.
It would be an offence against life. Give me my sword,
Dynamene. O Hades, when you look pale
You take the heart out of me. I could die
Without a sword by seeing you suffer. Quickly!
Give me my heart back again with your lips
And I'll live the rest of my ambitions
In a last kiss.

DYNAMENE.   Oh, no, no, no!
Give my blessing to your desertion of me?
Never, Chromis, never. Kiss you and then
Let you go? Love you, for death to have you?
Am I to be made the fool of courts martial?
Who are they who think they can discipline souls
Right off the earth? What discipline is that?
Chromis, love is the only discipline

And we're the disciples of love. I hold you to that:
Hold you, hold you.

TEGEUS.   We have no chance. It's determined
In section six, paragraph three, of the Regulations.
That has more power than love. It can snuff the great
Candles of creation. It makes me able
To do the impossible, to leave you, to go from the light
That keeps you.

DYNAMENE.   No!

TEGEUS.   O dark, it does. Good-bye,
My memory of earth, my dear most dear
Beyond every expectation. I was wrong
To want you to keep our vows existent
In the vacuum that's coming. It would make you
A heaviness to the world, when you should be,
As you are, a form of light. Dynamene, turn
Your head away. I'm going to let my sword
Solve all the riddles.

DYNAMENE.   Chromis, I have it! I know!
Virilius will help you.

TEGEUS.   Virilius?

DYNAMENE. My husband. He can be the other body.

TEGEUS. Your husband can?

DYNAMENE.   He has no further use
For what he left of himself to lie with us here.
Is there any reason why he shouldn't hang
On your holly tree? Better, far better, he,
Than you who are still alive, and surely better
Than *idling* into corruption?

TEGEUS.   Hang your husband?
Dynamene, it's terrible, horrible.

DYNAMENE. How little you can understand. I loved
His life not his death. And now we can give his death
The power of life. Not horrible: wonderful!
Isn't it so? That I should be able to feel
He moves again in the world, accomplishing
Our welfare? It's more than my grief could do.

TEGEUS. What can I say?

DYNAMENE.   That you love me; as I love him
And you. Let's celebrate your safety then.
Where's the bottle? There's some wine unfinished in this bowl.
I'll share it with you. Now forget the fear
We were in; look at me, Chromis. Come away
From the pit you nearly dropped us in. My darling,
I give you Virilius.

TEGEUS.   Virilius.
And all that follows.

DOTO [*on the steps, with the bottle*]. The master. Both the masters.

CURTAIN

THE LADY'S NOT FOR BURNING

A Comedy

SECOND EDITION

with revisions made for the Candida Plays production, 1971
directed by the author, and the
Chichester Festival Theatre production, 1972
directed by Robin Phillips

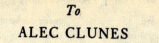

To
ALEC CLUNES

THE LADY'S NOT FOR BURNING

Arts Theatre, London: 10 *March* 1948

Richard	.	.	DEREK BLOMFIELD
Thomas Mendip		.	ALEC CLUNES
Alizon Eliot	.	.	DAPHNE SLATER
Nicholas Devize		.	MICHAEL GOUGH
Margaret Devize		.	HENZIE RAEBURN
Humphrey Devize		.	GORDON WHITING
Hebble Tyson	.	.	ANDREW LEIGH
Jennet Jourdemayne		.	SHEILA MANAHAN
The Chaplain	.	.	FRANK NAPIER
Edward Tappercoom		.	PETER BULL
Matthew Skipps	.		MORRIS SWEDEN

Directed by Jack Hawkins

Globe Theatre, London: 11 *May* 1949

Richard	.	.	RICHARD BURTON
Thomas Mendip		.	JOHN GIELGUD
Alizon Eliot	.	.	CLAIRE BLOOM
Nicholas Devize	.	.	DAVID EVANS
Margaret Devize		.	NORA NICHOLSON
Humphrey Devize		.	RICHARD LEECH
Hebble Tyson	.	.	HARCOURT WILLIAMS
Jennet Jourdemayne		.	PAMELA BROWN
The Chaplain	.	.	ELIOT MAKEHAM
Edward Tappercoom		.	PETER BULL
Matthew Skipps	.		ESME PERCY

Directed by John Gielgud *and* Esme Percy

Scenery and costumes by Oliver Messel

CHARACTERS

(in order of their appearance)

RICHARD, *an orphaned clerk*

THOMAS MENDIP, *a discharged soldier*

ALIZON ELIOT

NICHOLAS DEVIZE

MARGARET DEVIZE, *mother of Nicholas*

HUMPHREY DEVIZE, *brother of Nicholas*

HEBBLE TYSON, *the Mayor*

JENNET JOURDEMAYNE

THE CHAPLAIN

EDWARD TAPPERCOOM, *a Justice*

MATTHEW SKIPPS

SCENE

*A room in the house of Hebble Tyson, Mayor
of the small market-town of Cool Clary*

TIME
1400 either more or less or exactly

'In the past I wanted to be hung. It was worth while being hung to be a hero, seeing that life was not really worth living.'

A convict who confessed falsely to a murder, February 1947

ACT ONE

The Scene (the house of HEBBLE TYSON, *the Mayor of the little market*
 town of Cool Clary) and the appearance of the characters are as
 much fifteenth century as anything.

RICHARD, *a young copying-clerk, stands working at a desk.* THOMAS
 MENDIP, *less young, in his late twenties perhaps, and less re-*
 spectable, looks in through a great window from the garden.

THOMAS. Soul!

RICHARD.   —and the plasterer, that's fifteen groats——

THOMAS. Hey, soul!

RICHARD.   —for stopping the draught in the privy——

THOMAS.   Body!
  You calculating piece of clay!

RICHARD.   Damnation.

THOMAS.   Don't mention it. I've never seen a world
  So festering with damnation. I have left
  Rings of beer on every alehouse table
  From the salt sea-coast across half a dozen counties,
  But each time I thought I was on the way
  To a faintly festive hiccup
  The sight of the damned world sobered me up again.
  Where is the Mayor? I've business with His Worship.

RICHARD. Where have you come from?

THOMAS.   Straight from your
     local.
  Damnation's pretty active there this afternoon,
  Licking her lips over gossip of murder and witchcraft;
  There's mischief brewing for someone. Where's the Mayor?

RICHARD.   I'm the mayor's clerk.

THOMAS.   How are you?

RICHARD. Can I have your name?

THOMAS.   It's yours.

RICHARD.   Now, look——

THOMAS.   It's no earthly
  Use to me. I travel light; as light,
  That is, as a man can travel who will
  Still carry his body around because
  Of its sentimental value. Flesh
  Weighs like a thousand years, and every morning
  Wakes heavier for an intake of uproariously
  Comical dreams which smell of henbane.
  Guts, humours, ventricles, nerves, fibres
  And fat—the arterial labyrinth, body's hell.
  Still, it was the first thing my mother gave me,
  God rest her soul. What were you saying?

RICHARD.   Name
  And business.

THOMAS.   Thomas Mendip. My well-born father,
  If birth can ever be said to be well, maintains
  A castle as draughty as a tree. At every sunset,
  It falls into the river and fish swim through its walls.
  They swim into the bosom of my grandmother
  Who sits late, watching for the constellation of Orion
  Because my dead grandfather, she believes,
  Is situated somewhere in the Belt.
  That is part of the glory of my childhood.

RICHARD. I like you as much as I've liked anybody.
  Perhaps you're a little drunk. But here, I'm afraid,
  They may not take to you.

THOMAS. That's what I hope.

RICHARD. Who told you to come here?
You couldn't have chosen a less fortunate afternoon.
They're expecting company—well, a girl. Excuse me,
I must get back to the books.

THOMAS. I'll wait.

RICHARD. He'll not
See anybody; I'm sure of it.

THOMAS. Dear boy,
I only want to be hanged. What possible
Objection can he have to that?

RICHARD. Why, no, I—
To be—*want* to be hanged? How very drunk you are
After all. Who ever would want to be hanged?

THOMAS. You don't
Make any allowance for individuality.
How do you know that out there, in the day or night
According to latitude, the entire world
Isn't wanting to be hanged? Now you, for instance,
Still damp from your cocoon, you're desperate
To fly into any noose of the sun that should dangle
Down from the sky. Life, forbye, is the way
We fatten for the Michaelmas of our own particular
Gallows. What a wonderful thing is metaphor.

RICHARD. Was that a knock?

THOMAS. The girl. She knocks. I saw her
Walking through the garden beside a substantial nun.
Whsst! Revelation!

    Enter ALIZON ELIOT, *aged seventeen, talking to herself.*

ALIZON. Two steps down, she said. One, two,
The floor. Now I begin to be altogether
Different—I suppose.

RICHARD.   O God, God,
God, God, God. I can see such trouble!
Is life sending a flame to nest in my flax?
For pity's sake!

THOMAS.   Sweet pretty noose, nice noose.

RICHARD. Will you step in?

ALIZON.   They told me no one was here.

RICHARD. It would be me they meant.

ALIZON.   Oh, would it be?
Coming in from the light, I am all out at the eyes.
Such white doves were paddling in the sunshine
And the trees were as bright as a shower of broken glass.
Out there, in the sparkling air, the sun and the rain
Clash together like the cymbals clashing
When David did his dance. I've an April blindness.
You're hidden in a cloud of crimson catherine-wheels.

RICHARD. It doesn't really matter. Sit in the shadow.

THOMAS. There are plenty to choose from.

ALIZON.   Oh, there are three of us!
Forgive me.

RICHARD.   He's waiting—he wants—he says——

THOMAS.   I breathe,
I spit, I am. But take no further notice.
I'll just nod in at the window like a rose;
I'm a black and frosted rosebud whom the good God
Has preserved since last October. Take no notice.

ALIZON. Men, to me, are a world to themselves.

RICHARD. Do you think so?

ALIZON. I am going to be married to one of them, almost at once.
I have met him already.

RICHARD. Humphrey.

ALIZON. Are you his brother?

RICHARD. No. All I can claim as my flesh and blood
Is what I stand up in. I wasn't born,
I was come-across. In the dusk of one Septuagesima
A priest found an infant, about ten inches long,
Crammed into the poor-box. The money had all
Been taken. Nothing was there except myself,
I was the baby, as it turned out. The priest,
Thinking I might have eaten the money, held me
Upside down and shook me, which encouraged me
To live, I suppose, and I lived.

ALIZON. No father or mother?

RICHARD. Not noticeably.

ALIZON. You mustn't let it make you
Conceited. Pride is one of the deadly sins.

THOMAS. And it's better to go for the lively ones.

ALIZON. Which ones
Do you mean?

THOMAS. Pay no heed. I was nodding in.

ALIZON. I am quite usual, with five elder sisters. My birth
Was a great surprise to my parents, I think. There had been
A misunderstanding and I appeared overnight
As mushrooms do. My father thought
He would never be able to find enough husbands

For six of us, and so he made up his mind
To simplify matters and let me marry God.
He gave me to a convent.

RICHARD. What showing did he think he would make as God's
Father-in-law?

ALIZON.   He let his beard grow longer.
But he found that husbands fell into my sisters' laps.
So then he stopped thinking of God as eligible—
No prospects, he thought. And so he looked round and found me
Humphrey Devize. Do you think he will do?

RICHARD.   Maybe.
He isn't God, of course.

ALIZON.   No, he isn't.
He's very nearly black.

RICHARD.   Swart.

ALIZON.   Is that it?
When he dies it may be hard to picture him
Agreeable to the utter white of heaven.
Now you, you are——

RICHARD.   Purgatory-colour.

ALIZON. It's on the way to grace. Who are you?

RICHARD.   Richard,
The mayor's copying-clerk.

ALIZON.   The mayor is Humphrey's
Uncle. Humphrey's mother is the mayor's sister.
And then, again, there's Nicholas, Humphrey's brother.
Is he sensible?

RICHARD.   He knows his way about.

THOMAS. O enviable Nick.

RICHARD.   He's nodding in.

ALIZON. I'll tell you a strange thing. Humphrey Devize
 Came to the convent to see me, bringing a present
 For his almost immediate wife, he said, which is me,
 Of barley-sugar and a cross of seed-pearls. Next day
 Nicholas came, with a little cold pie, to say
 He had a message from Humphrey. And then he sat
 And stared and said nothing until he got up to go.
 I asked him for the message, but by then
 It had gone out of his head. Quite gone, you see.
 It was curious.—Now you're not speaking either.

RICHARD. Yes, of course; of course it was curious.

ALIZON. Men are strange. It's almost unexpected
 To find they speak English. Do you think so too?

RICHARD. Things happen to them.

ALIZON.   What things?

RICHARD.   Machinations of nature;
 As April does to the earth.

ALIZON.   I wish it were true!
 Show me daffodils happening to a man!

RICHARD. Very easily.

THOMAS.   And thistles as well, and ladies'
 Bedstraw and deadly nightshade and the need
 For rhubarb.

ALIZON.   Is it a riddle?

RICHARD.   Very likely.
 Certainly a considerable complication.

    Enter NICHOLAS DEVIZE, *muddy, dishevelled.*

NICHOLAS. Where are you, Alizon? Alizon, what do you think?
 I've won you from him! I've destroyed my brother!

It's me you're going to marry. What do you think
Of that?

RICHARD. You have mud in your mouth.

NICHOLAS.   You canter off.

ALIZON. No, Nicholas. That's untrue. I have to be
The wife of Humphrey.

NICHOLAS.   Heaven says no. Heaven
And all the nodding angels say
Alizon for Nicholas, Nicholas for Alizon.
You must come to know me; not so much now, because now
I'm excited, but I have at least three virtues.
How many have you got?

RICHARD.   Are you mad? Why don't you
Go and clean yourself up?

NICHOLAS.   What shall I do
With this nattering wheygoose, Alizon?
Shall I knock him down?

ALIZON.   His name is Richard, he says;
And I think he might knock you down.

THOMAS.   Nicholas,
He might. There you have a might, for once,
That's right. Forgive me; an unwarranted interruption.

NICHOLAS. Come in, come in.—Alizon, dear, this Richard
Is all very well. But I was conceived the night
The church was struck by lightning
And born in the great gale. I apologize
For boasting, but once you know my qualities
I can drop back into a quite brilliant

Humility. God have mercy upon me,
You have such little hands. I knew I should love you.

RICHARD. Just tell me: am I to knock him down? You have only
To say so.

ALIZON.   No, oh no. We only have
To be patient and unweave him. He is mixed,
Aren't you, Nicholas?

NICHOLAS.   Compounded of explosives
Like the world's inside. I'm the receipt God followed
In the creation. It took the roof off his oven.
How long will it be before you love me, Alizon?
Let's go.

> [*He picks her up in his arms.*

Enter MARGARET DEVIZE.

MARGARET. Where are you taking Alizon, Nicholas?

NICHOLAS. Out into the air, mother.

MARGARET.   Unnecessary.
She's in the air already. This room is full of it.
Put her down, Nicholas. You look
As though you had come straight out of a wheelbarrow;
And not even straight out.

NICHOLAS.   I have to tell you
I've just been reborn.

MARGARET.   Nicholas, you always think
You can do things better than your mother. You can be sure
You were born quite adequately on the first occasion.
There is someone here I don't know. Who is it, Alizon?
Did he come with you?

ALIZON.   Oh, no. A rosebud, he says,
He budded in October.

MARGARET. He's not speaking the truth.—Tch! more rain!
This is properly April.—And you're eager to see
Your handsome Humphrey. Nicholas will fetch him.
They're inseparable, really twin natures, utterly
Brothers, like the two ends of the same thought.—
Nicholas, dear, call Humphrey.

NICHOLAS.   I can't. I've killed him

MARGARET. Fetch Humphrey, Nicholas dear.

NICHOLAS.   I've killed him, dearest
Mother.

MARGARET. Well, never mind. Call Humphrey, dear.

THOMAS. Is that the other end of this happy thought,
There, prone in the flower-bed?

RICHARD.   Yes, it's Humphrey
Lying in the rain.

MARGARET.   One day I shall burst my bud
Of calm, and blossom into hysteria.
Tell him to get up. What on earth is he doing
Lying in the rain?

THOMAS.   All flesh is grass.

ALIZON. Have you really killed Humphrey?

MARGARET.   Nicholas,
Your smile is no pleasure to me.

NICHOLAS.   We fought for possession
Of Alizon Eliot. What could be more natural?
What he loves, I love. And if existence will
Disturb a man with beauty, how can he help
Trying to impose on her the boundary

Of his two bare arms?—Pandemonium, what a fight!
What a fight! Humphrey went hurtling
Like Lucifer into the daffodils.
When Babylon fell there wasn't a better thump.

MARGARET. Are you standing there letting your brother be rained
    on?
Haven't you any love for him?

NICHOLAS.   Yes, mother,
But wet as well as dry.

MARGARET.   Can Richard carry him
Single-handed?

NICHOLAS.   Why can't he use both hands?
And how did I know it was going to rain?

                              [*Exit* NICHOLAS *with* RICHARD.

MARGARET. I would rather have to plait the tails of unbroken
Ponies than try to understand Nicholas.
Oh! it's bell-ringing practice. Their ding-dong rocks me
Till my head feels like the belfry, and makes blisters
All along my nerves. Dear God, a cuckoo
As well!

THOMAS. By God, a cuckoo! Grief and God,
A canting cuckoo, that laugh with no smile!
A world unable to die sits on and on
In spring sunlight, hatching egg after egg,
Hoping against hope that out of one of them
Will come the reason for it all; and always
Out pops the arid chuckle and centuries
Of cuckoo-spit.

MARGARET.   I don't really think we need
To let that worry us now. I don't know why you're waiting,

Or who brought you, or whether I could even
Begin to like you, but I know it would be agreeable
If you left us. There's enough going on already.

THOMAS. There is certainly enough going on.
  Madam, watch Hell come
As a gleam into the eye of the wholesome cat
When philip-sparrow flips his wing.
I see a gleam of Hell in *you*, madam.
You understand those bells perfectly.
I understand them, too.
What is it that, out there in the mellow street,
The soft rain is raining on?
Is it only on the little sour grass, madam?

MARGARET. Out in the street? What could it be?

THOMAS.   It could be,
  And it is, a witch-hunt.

MARGARET.   Oh!—dear; another?

THOMAS. Your innocence is on at such a rakish angle
  It gives you quite an air of iniquity.
  Hadn't you better answer that bell? With a mere
  Clouding of your unoccupied eyes, madam,
  Or a twitch of the neck: what better use can we put
  Our faces to than to have them express kindness
  While we're thinking of something else? Oh, be disturbed,
  Be disturbed, madam, to the extent of a tut
  And I will thank God for civilization.
  This is my last throw, my last poor gamble
  On the human heart.

MARGARET.   If I knew who you were
  I should ask you to sit down. But while you're on

Your feet, would you be kind enough to see
How Humphrey is doing?

THOMAS.   If we listened, we could hear
How the hunters, having washed the dinner things,
Are now toiling up and down the blind alleys
Which they think are their immortal souls,
To scour themselves in the blood of a grandmother.
They, of course, will feel all the better for it.
But she? Grandma? Is it possible
She may be wishing she had died yesterday,
The wicked sobbing old body of a woman?

MARGARET. At the moment, as you know,
I'm trying hard to be patient with my sons.
You really mustn't expect me to be Christian
In two directions at once.

THOMAS.   What, after all,
Is a halo? It's only one more thing to keep clean.
Richard and Nicholas
Have been trying to persuade the body to stand up.

ALIZON. Why, yes, he isn't dead. He's lying on his back
Picking the daffodils. And now they are trying
To lift him.

MARGARET.   Let me look over your shoulder.
They mustn't see me taking an interest.
Oh, the poor boy looks like a shock
Of bedraggled oats.—But you will see, Alizon,
What a nice boy he can be when he wears a clean shirt.
I more than once lost my heart to clean linen
When I was a young creature, even to linen
That hung on the hedges without a man inside it.
Do I seem composed, sufficiently placid and unmotherly?

ALIZON. Altogether, except that your ear-ring
  Trembles a little.

MARGARET.   It's always our touches of vanity
  That manage to betray us.

THOMAS.   When shall I see the mayor?
  I've had enough of the horror beating in the belfry.
  Where is the mayor?

Re-enter RICHARD *and* NICHOLAS *carrying* HUMPHREY *who has a
  bunch of daffodils in his hand.*

NICHOLAS.   Here's Humphrey. Where would you like him?

MARGARET. Humphrey, why do you have to be carried?

HUMPHREY.   My dear
  Mother, I didn't knock myself down. Why
  Should I pick myself up?—Daffodils
  For my future wife.

NICHOLAS.   You swindling half-cock alderman!
  Do I have to kill you a second time?
  I've proved my right to have her.

HUMPHREY. Nothing of the sort. Officially
  Alizon is mine. What is official
  Is incontestable.—Without disrespect either
  To you, mother, or to my officially
  Dear one, I shall lie down.—Who is playing the viol?

MARGARET. The Chaplain is tuning his G string by the bells.
  It must be time for prayers. It must be time
  For something. You're both transfigured with dirt.

THOMAS. Where in thunder is the mayor? Are you deaf to the
    baying

Of those human bloodhounds out in the street?
I want to be hanged.

NICHOLAS [*to* HUMPHREY]. You dismal coprolite!
It's in my stars I should have her. Wait
Till it's dark, and go out if you dare
Bareheaded under the flash of my star Mercury.
Ignore the universe if you can. Go on,
Ignore it!—Alizon, who's going to marry you?

MARGARET. He deserves no answer.

RICHARD.   Can you tell us, Alizon?

ALIZON. I am not very used to things happening rapidly.
The nuns, you see, were very quiet, especially
In the afternoon. They say I shall marry Humphrey.

MARGARET. Certainly so. Now, Nicholas, go and get clean.

NICHOLAS. She never shall!

THOMAS.   Will someone fetch the mayor?
Will no one make the least effort to let me
Out of the world?

NICHOLAS.   Let Humphrey go and officially
Bury himself. She's not for him.
What does love understand about hereinafter-
Called-the-bride-contracted?
An April anarchy, she is, with a dragon's breath,
An angel on a tiger,
The jaws and maw of a kind of heaven, though hell
Sleeps there with one open eye; an onslaught
Unpredictable made by a benefactor
Armed to the teeth——

THOMAS.   Who benefits, before God,

By this collision of the sexes,
This paroxysm of the flesh? Let me get out!
I'll find the mayor myself
And let you go on with your psalm of love.

[*He makes for the door.*

HUMPHREY. Who the hell's that?

RICHARD.   The man about the gallows.

Enter HEBBLE TYSON *the mayor, afflicted with office.*

MARGARET. Now here's your uncle. Do, for the sake of calm,
    Go and sweeten yourselves.

THOMAS.   Is this the man
    I long for?

TYSON.   Pest, who has stolen my handkerchief?

MARGARET. Use this one, Hebble.—Go and get under the pump.

[*Exit* HUMPHREY *and* NICHOLAS.

TYSON [*blowing his nose*]. Noses, noses.

THOMAS.   Mr. Mayor, it's a joy to see you.
    You're about to become my gateway to eternal
    Rest.

TYSON.   Dear sir, I haven't yet been notified
    Of your existence. As far as I'm concerned
    You don't exist. Therefore you are not entitled
    To any rest at all, eternal or temporary,
    And I would be obliged if you'd sit down.

MARGARET. Here is Alizon Eliot, Humphrey's bride
    To be.

THOMAS. I have come to be hanged, do you hear?

TYSON. Have you filled in the necessary forms?—

So this is the young lady? Very nice, very charming.—
And a very pretty dress.
Splendid material, a florin a yard
If a groat. I'm only sorry you had to come
On a troubled evening such as this promises
To be. The bells, you know. Richard, my boy,
What is it this importunate fellow wants?

RICHARD. He says he wants to be hanged, sir.

TYSON.   Out of the question
   It's a most immodest suggestion; which I know
   Of no precedent for. Cannot be entertained.
   I suspect an element of mockery
   Directed at the ordinary decencies
   Of life.—Tiresome catarrh.—A sense of humour
   Incompatible with good citizenship
   And I wish you a good evening. Are we all
   Assembled together for evening prayers?

THOMAS.   Oh no!
   You can't postpone me. Since opening-time I've been
   Propped up at the bar of heaven and earth, between
   The wall-eye of the moon and the brandy-cask of the sun,
   Growling thick songs about jolly good fellows
   In a mumping pub where the ceiling drips humanity,
   Until I've drunk myself sick, and now, by Christ,
   I mean to sleep it off in a stupor of dust
   Till the morning after the day of judgement.
   So put me on the waiting-list for your gallows
   With a note recommending preferential treatment.

TYSON. Go away; you're an unappetizing young man
   With a tongue too big for your brains. I'm not at all sure
   It would be amiss to suppose you to be a vagrant,

In which case an unfortunate experience
At the cart's tail——

THOMAS.   Unacceptable.
Hanging or nothing.

TYSON.   Get this man away from here!
Good gracious, do you imagine the gallows to be
A charitable institution? Very mad,
Wishes to draw attention to himself;
The brain a delicate mechanism; Almighty
God more precise than a clockmaker;
Grant us all a steady pendulum.

ALL. Amen.

THOMAS. Listen! The wild music of the spheres:
Tick-tock.

RICHARD.   Come on; you've got to go.

THOMAS. Does Justice with her sweet, impartial sword
Never come to this place? Do you mean
There's no recognition given to murder here?

MARGARET. Murder?

TYSON.   Now what is it?

THOMAS.   I'm not a fool.
I didn't suppose you would do me a favour for nothing.
No crime, no hanging; I quite understand the rules.
But I've made that all right. I managed to do-in
A rag-and-bone merchant at the bottom of Leapfrog Lane.

TYSON [*staring*]. Utterly unhinged.

MARGARET.   Hebble, they're all
In the same April fit of exasperating nonsense.

Nicholas, too. He said he had killed Humphrey
But of course he hadn't. If he had I should have told you.

THOMAS. It was such a monotonous cry, that 'Raga-boa!'
Like the damned cuckoo. It was more than time
He should see something of another world.
But, poor old man, he wasn't anxious to go.
He picked on his rags and his bones as love
Picks upon hearts, he with an eye to profit
And love with an eye to pain.

RICHARD.   *Sanctus fumus!*

TYSON. Get a complete denial of everything
He has said. I don't want to be bothered with you.
You don't belong to this parish. I'm perfectly satisfied
He hasn't killed a man.

THOMAS.   I've killed two men
If you want me to be exact.
The other I thought scarcely worth mentioning:
A quite unprepossessing pig-man with a birthmark.
He couldn't have had any affection for himself.
So I pulped him first and knocked him into the river
Where the water gives those girlish giggles around
The ford, and held him under with my foot
Until he was safely in Abram's bosom, birthmark
And all. You see, it still isn't properly dry.

TYSON. What a confounded thing! Who do people
Think they are, coming here without
Identity, and putting us to considerable
Trouble and expense to have them punished?
You don't deserve to be listened to.

THOMAS.   It's habit.
I've been unidentifiably

Floundering in Flanders for the past seven years,
Prising open ribs to let men go
On the indefinite leave which needs no pass.
And now all roads are uncommonly flat, and all hair
Stands on end.

Enter NICHOLAS.

NICHOLAS.   I'm sorry to interrupt
But there's a witch to see you, uncle.

TYSON.   To see me?
A witch to see me? I will not be the toy
Of irresponsible events. Is that clear
To you all?

NICHOLAS.   Yes. But she's here.

TYSON.   A witch to see me!
Do I have to tell you what to do with her?

NICHOLAS. Don't tell me. My eyes do that only too well.
She is the one, of witches she's the one
Who most of all disturbs Hell's heart. Jimminy!
How she must make Torment sigh
To have her to add to its torment! How the flames
Must burn to lay their tongues about her.
If evil has a soul it's here outside,
The flower of sin, Satan's latest
Button-hole. Shall I ask her in?

THOMAS.   She's young,
O God, she's young.

TYSON.   I stare at you, Nicholas,
With no word of condemnation. I stare,
Astonished at your behaviour.

MARGARET. Ask her in?
  In here? Nicholas——

NICHOLAS. She's the glorious
  Undercoat of this painted world——

  [JENNET JOURDEMAYNE *stands in the doorway.*

  ——You see:
  It comes through, however much of our whiteness
  We paint over it.

TYSON. What is the meaning of this?
  What is the meaning of this?

THOMAS. That's the most relevant
  Question in the world.

JENNET. Will someone say
  Come in? And understand that I don't every day
  Break in on the quiet circle of a family
  At prayers? Not quite so unceremoniously,
  Or so shamefully near a flood of tears,
  Or looking as unruly as I surely do. Will you
  Forgive me?

TYSON. You'll find I can't be disarmed
  With pretty talk, young woman. You have no business
  At all in this house.

JENNET. Do you know how many walls
  There are between the garden of the Magpie,
  Past Lazer's field, Slink Alley and Poorsoul Pond
  To the gate of your paddock?

TYSON. I'm not to be seduced.
  I'm not attending.

JENNET. Eight. I've come over them all.

MARGARET. How could she have done?

THOMAS.   Her broomstick's in the hall.

MARGARET. Come over to this side of the room, Nicholas.

NICHOLAS. Don't worry, mother, I have my fingers crossed.

TYSON. Never before in the whole term of my office
Have I met such extraordinary ignorance
Of what is permitted——

JENNET.   Indeed, I was ignorant.
They were hooting and howling for me, as though echoes
Could kill me. So I started to run. Thank God
I only passed one small girl in a ditch
Telling the beads of her daisy-chain.
And a rumpled idiot-boy who smiled at me.
They say I have turned a man into a dog.

TYSON.   This will all be gone into
At the proper time——

JENNET.   But it isn't a dog at all.
It's a bitch; a rather appealing brindle bitch
With many fleas. Are you a gentleman
Full of ripe, friendly wisdom?

TYSON.   This
Will all be gone into at the proper——

JENNET.   If so
I will sit at your feet. I will sit anyway;
I am tired. Eight walls are enough.

MARGARET.   What do we do?
I can almost feel the rustling-in of some
Kind of enchantment already.

TYSON.   She will have
To be put in charge.

ALIZON.   Oh, must she, must she?

THOMAS. He can see she's a girl of property,
And the property goes to the town if she's a witch;
She couldn't have been more timely.

NICHOLAS.   Curious, crooked
Beauty of the earth. Fascinating.

TYSON [*to* JENNET]. Get up at once, you undisciplined girl. Have
    you never
Heard of law and order?

NICHOLAS.   Won't you use
This chair?

JENNET.   Thank you. Oh, this is the reasonable
World again! I promise not to leave behind me
Any flymarks of black magic, or any familiars
Such as mice or beetles which might preach
Demonology in your skirting-board.
It's unbelievable, the quite fantastic
Tales they tell!

TYSON.   This will be discussed
At the proper time——

THOMAS.   When we have finished talking
About my murders.

MARGARET. Are they both asking to be punished? Has death
Become the fashionable way to live?
Nothing would surprise me in their generation.

JENNET. Asking to be punished? Why, no, I have come
Here to have the protection of your laughter.
They accuse me of such a brainstorm of absurdities
That all my fear dissolves in the humour of it.
If I could perform what they say I *can* perform

I should have got safely away from here
As fast as you bat your eyelid.

TYSON.   Oh, indeed;
Could you indeed?

JENNET.   They say I have only
To crack a twig, and over the springtime weathercocks
Cloudburst, hail and gale, whatever you will,
Come leaping fury-foremost.

TYSON.   The report
May be exaggerated, of course, but where there's smoke. . .

JENNET. They also say that I bring back the past;
For instance, Helen comes,
Brushing the maggots from her eyes,
And, clearing her throat of several thousand years,
She says 'I loved . . .'; but cannot any longer
Remember names. Sad Helen. Or Alexander, wearing
His imperial cobwebs and breastplate of shining worms
Wakens and looks for his glasses, to find the empire
Which he knows he put beside his bed.

TYSON. Whatever you say will be taken down in evidence
Against you; am I making myself clear?

JENNET. They tell one tale, that once, when the moon
Was gibbous and in a high dazed state
Of nimbus love, I shook a jonquil's dew
On to a pearl and let a cricket chirp
Three times, thinking of pale Peter:
And there Titania was, vexed by a cloud
Of pollen, using the sting of a bee to clean
Her nails and singing, as drearily as a gnat,
'Why try to keep clean?'

THOMAS.   'The earth is all of earth'—

> So sang the queen:
> So the queen sung,
>   Crumbling her crownet into clods of dung.

JENNET. You heard her, too, Captain? Bravo. Is that
   A world you've got there, hidden under your hat?

THOMAS. Bedlam, ma'am, and the battlefield
   Uncle Adam died on. He was shot
   To bits with the core of an apple
   Which some fool of a serpent in the artillery
   Had shoved into God's cannon.

TYSON.   That's enough!
   Terrible frivolity, terrible blasphemy,
   Awful unorthodoxy. I can't understand
   Anything that is being said. Fetch a constable.
   The woman's tongue clearly knows the flavour
   Of *spiritu maligno*. The man must be
   Drummed out of the town.

THOMAS.   Oh, *must* he be?

RICHARD. Are you certain, sir? The constable? The lady
   Was laughing. She laughed at the very idea
   Of being a witch, sir.

TYSON.   Yes, just it, just it.
   Giving us a rigmarole of her dreams:
   Probably dreams: but intentionally
   Recollected, intentionally consented to,
   Intentionally delighted in. And so
   As dangerous as the act. Fetch the constable.

NICHOLAS. Sad, how things always are. We get one gulp
   Of dubious air from our hellmost origins
   And we have to bung up the draught with a constable.
   It's a terribly decontaminating life.

TYSON. I'll not have any frivolity.
   The town goes in terror.
   I have told you, Richard, twice, what to do.
   Are you going about it?

RICHARD.   No, sir. Not yet.

TYSON. Did you speak to me? Now be careful how you answer.

JENNET. Can you be serious? I am Jennet Jourdemayne
   And I believe in the human mind. Why play with me
   And make me afraid of you, as you did for a moment,
   I confess it. You can't believe—oh, surely, not
   When the centuries of the world are piled so high—
   You'll not believe what, in their innocence,
   Those old credulous children in the street
   Imagine of me?

THOMAS.   Innocence! Dear girl,
   Before the world was, innocence
   Was beaten by a lion all round the town.
   And liked it.

JENNET.   What, does everyone still knuckle
   And suckle at the big breast of irrational fears?
   Do they really think I charm a sweat from Tagus,
   Or lure an Amazonian gnat to fasten
   On William Brown and shake him till he rattles?
   Can they think and then think like this?

TYSON.   Will be
   Gone into at the proper time. Disturbing
   The peace. In every way. Have to arrest you.

JENNET. No!

THOMAS.   You bubble-mouthing, fog-blathering,

    Chin-chuntering, chap-flapping, liturgical,
    Turgidical, base old man! What about my murders?
    And what goes round in *your* head,
    What funny little murders and fornications
    Chatting up and down in three-four time
    Afraid to come out? What bliss to sin by proxy
    And do penance by way of someone else!
    But we'll not talk about you. It will make the outlook
    So dark. Neither about this exquisitely
    Mad young woman. Nor about this congenital
    Generator, your nephew here;
    Nor about anyone but me. I'm due
    To be hanged. Good Lord, aren't two murders enough
    To win me the medals of damnation? Must I put
    Half a dozen children on a spit
    And toast them at the flame that comes out of my mouth?
    You let the fairies fox you while the devil
    Does you. Concentrate on me.

TYSON.   I'll not
    Have it—I'll—I'll——

THOMAS.   Power of Job!
    Must I wait for a stammer? Your life, sir, is propelled
    By a dream of the fear of having nightmares; your love
    Is the fear of being alone; your world's history
    The fear of a possible leap by a possible antagonist
    Out of a possible shadow, or a not-improbable
    Skeleton out of your dead-certain cupboard.
    But here am I, the true phenomenon
    Of acknowledged guilt, steaming with the blood
    Of the pig-man and the rag-and-bone man, Crime
    Transparent. What the hell are we waiting for?

TYSON. Will you attend to me? Will you be silent?

JENNET. Are you doing this to save me?

THOMAS.   You flatter my powers,
My sweet; you're too much a woman. But if you wish
You can go down to the dinner of damnation
On my arm.

JENNET.   I dine elsewhere.

TYSON.   Am I invisible?
Am I inaudible? Do I merely festoon
The room with my presence? Richard, wretched boy,
If you don't wish to incur considerable punishment
Do yourself the kindness to fetch the constable.
I don't care for these unexpurgated persons.
I shall lose my patience.

MARGARET.   I shall lose my faith
In the good-breeding of providence. Wouldn't this happen
Now: to-day: within an hour or two
Of everyone coming to congratulate
Humphrey and Alizon. Arrangements were made
A month ago, long before this gentleman's
Murders were even thought of.

TYSON.   They don't exist,
I say——

Enter HUMPHREY.

HUMPHREY. Uncle, there's a sizeable rumpus,
Without exaggeration a how-do-you-do
Taking place in the street. I thought you should know.

TYSON. Rumpus?

HUMPHREY.   Perhaps rumpus isn't the word.
A minor kind of bloody revolution.
It's this damned rascal, this half-pay half-wit.

I should say he's certifiable. It seems
He's been spreading all around the town some tale
About drowning a pig-man and murdering old Skipps
The rag-and-bone man.

THOMAS.   Ah, old Skipps, old Skipps,
  What a surplus of bones you'll have where you've gone to now!

JENNET. Old Skipps? But he's the man——

TYSON.   Will you both be silent?
  I won't have every Tom, Dick, and Harry
  Laying information against himself before
  He's got written authority from me.

HUMPHREY.   Quite right.
  As it is, the town is hell's delight. They've looked
  For the drowned pig-man and they've looked for Skipps
  And they've looked in the places where he says he left them
  And they can't find either.

NICHOLAS.   Can't find either?

HUMPHREY. Can't find either.

MARGARET.   Of course they can't. When he first
  Mentioned murders I knew he had got hold
  Of a quite wrong end of the stick.

HUMPHREY.   They say he's the Devil.

MARGARET. I can imagine who started *that* story.

HUMPHREY. But are we so sure he isn't? Outside in the street
  They're convinced he's the Devil. And none of us ever having
  Seen the Devil, how can we know? They say
  He killed the old men and spirited them into the Limbo.
  We can't search there. I don't even know where it is.

THOMAS. Sir, it's between me and the deep blue sea.
  The wind of conscience blows straight from its plains.

HUMPHREY. Shut up.—If you're the Devil I beg your pardon.—
  They also have the idea
  He's got a girl in his toils, a witch called——

JENNET.   Jennet.
  I am she.

HUMPHREY. God.

TYSON.   Well, Humphrey, well?
  Is that the end of your information?

NICHOLAS.   Humphrey,
  Have you spoken to your little future wife
  Lately?

THOMAS. Tinder, easy tinder.

HUMPHREY.   In fact—
  In fact——

NICHOLAS.   In fact it's all a bloody revolution.

TYSON. I'm being played with, I'm sure of it; something tells me
  There is irresponsibility somewhere. Richard,
  You'll not get out of this lightly. Where's the constable?
  Why isn't he standing before me?

RICHARD.   I can see
  No need for the constable, sir.

TYSON.   No need? No need?

Enter the CHAPLAIN *with his viol.*

CHAPLAIN. I am late for prayers, I know; I know you think me
  A broken reed, and my instrument too, my better half,
  You lacked it, I'm afraid. But life has such
  Diversity, I sometimes remarkably lose

Eternity in the passing moment. Just now
In the street there's a certain boisterous interest
In a spiritual matter. They say——

TYSON.   I know what they say.

CHAPLAIN. Ah yes; you know. Sin, as well as God,
Moves in a most mysterious way. It is hard to imagine
Why the poor girl should turn Skipps into a dog.

NICHOLAS. Skipps? Skipps into a dog?

HUMPHREY.   But Skipps——

THOMAS. Skipps trundles in another place, calling
His raga-boa in gutters without end,
Transfigured by the spatial light
Of Garbage Indestructible. And I
Ought to know since I sent him there. A dog?
Come, come; don't let's be fanciful.

TYSON. They say one thing and another thing and both at once;
I don't know. It will all have to be gone into
At the proper time——

HUMPHREY.   But this is a contradiction——

CHAPLAIN. Ah, isn't that life all over? And is this
The young assassin? If he is the doer of the damage
Can it be she also? My flock are employing
Fisticuffs over this very question.

HUMPHREY. But if he could be the Devil——

THOMAS.   Good boy! Shall I set
Your minds at rest and give you proof? Come here.

                      [*He whispers in* HUMPHREY's *ear.*

HUMPHREY. That's not funny.

THOMAS.   Not funny for the goats.

HUMPHREY. I've heard it before. He says the Day of Judgement
  Is fixed for to-night.

MARGARET.   Oh no. I have always been sure
  That when it comes it will come in the autumn.
  Heaven, I am quite sure, wouldn't disappoint
  The bulbs.

THOMAS.   Consider: vastiness lusted, mother;
  A huge heaving desire, overwhelming solitude,
  And the mountain belly of Time laboured
  And brought forth man, the mouse. The spheres churned on,
  Hoping to charm our ears
  With sufficient organ-music, sadly sent out
  On the wrong wave of sound; but still they roll
  Fabulous and fine, a roundabout
  Of doomed and golden notes. And on beyond,
  Profound with thunder of oceanic power,
  Lie the morose dynamics of our dumb friend
  Jehovah.
  Why should these omnipotent bombinations
  Go on with the deadly human anecdote, which
  From the first was never more than remotely funny?
  No; the time has come for tombs to tip
  Their refuse; for the involving ivy, the briar,
  The convolutions of convolvulus,
  To disentangle and make way
  For the last great ascendancy of dust,
  Sucked into judgement by a cosmic yawn
  Of boredom. The Last Trump
  Is timed for twenty-two forty hours precisely.

TYSON. This will all be gone into at the proper——

THOMAS.   Time
   Will soon be most improper. Why not hang me
   Before it's too late?

MARGARET.   I shall go and change my dress;
   Then I shall both be ready for our guests
   And whatever else may come upon the world.

HUMPHREY. I'm sure he's mad.

CHAPLAIN.   And his information, of course,
   Is in opposition to what we are plainly told
   In the Scriptures: that the hour will come——

NICHOLAS.   Do you think
   He means it? I've an idea he's up to something
   None of us knows about, not one of us.

ALIZON [*who has found her way to* RICHARD]. Quiet Richard, son of
   nobody.

RICHARD [*whispering*]. It isn't always like this, I promise it isn't.

JENNET. May I, Jennet Jourdemayne, the daughter
   Of a man who believed the universe was governed
   By certain laws, be allowed to speak?
   Here is such a storm of superstition
   And humbug and curious passions, where will you start
   To look for the truth? Am I in fact
   An enchantress bemused into collaboration
   With the enemy of man? Is this the enemy,
   This eccentric young gentleman never seen by me
   Before? I say I am not. He says perhaps
   He is. You say I am. You say he is not.
   And now the eccentric young gentleman threatens us all
   With imminent cataclysm. If, as a living creature,
   I wish in all good faith to continue living,
   Where do you suggest I should lodge my application?

TYSON. That is perfectly clear. You are both under arrest.

THOMAS. Into Pandora's box with all the ills.
But not if that little hell–cat Hope's
Already in possession. I've hoped enough.
I gave the best years of my life to that girl,
But I'm walking out with Damnation now, and she's
A flame who's got finality.

JENNET. Do you want no hope for me either? No compassion
To lift suspicion off me?

THOMAS.   Lift? Compassion
Has a rupture, lady. To hell with lifting.

JENNET. Listen, please listen to me!

THOMAS.   Let the world
Go, lady; it isn't worth the candle.

TYSON. Take her, Richard; down to the cellars.

THOMAS.   You see?
He has the key to every perplexity.
Kiss your illusions for me before they go.

JENNET. But what will happen?

THOMAS. That's something even old nosedrip doesn't know.
                              [RICHARD *leads* JENNET *away*

TYSON. Take him away!

THOMAS.   Mr. Mayor, hang me for pity's sake,
For God's sake hang me, before I love that woman!

CURTAIN ON ACT ONE

ACT TWO

The same room, about an hour later. The CHAPLAIN *in a chair, sleeping.* TYSON *surrounded with papers.* EDWARD TAPPERCOOM, *the town's Justice, mountainously rolling up and down the room.*

TAPPERCOOM. Well, it's poss-ss-ible, it's poss-ss-ible.
I *may* have been putting the Devil to the torture.
But can you smell scorching?—not a singe
For my sins—that's from yesterday: I leaned
Across a candle. For all practical purposes
I feel as unblasted as on the day I was born.
And God knows I'm a target. Cupid scarcely
Needs to aim, and no devil could miss me.

TYSON. But his action may be delayed. We really must
Feel our way. We don't want to put ourselves wrong
With anything as positive as evil.

TAPPERCOOM. We have put him to the merest thumbscrew,
Tyson,
Courteously and impartially, the purest
Cajolery to coax him to deny
These cock-and-bull murders for which there isn't a scrap
Of evidence.

TYSON.   Ah; ah. How does he take it?
Has he denied them?

TAPPERCOOM.   On the contrary.
He says he has also committed petty larceny,
Abaction, peculation and incendiarism.
As for the woman Jourdemayne——

TYSON. Ah, yes,
Jourdemayne; what are we to make of her?
Wealthy, they tell me. But on the other hand
Quite affectingly handsome. Sad, you know.
We see where the eye can't come, eh, Tappercoom?
And all's not glorious within; no use
Saying it is.—I had a handkerchief.
Ah yes; buried amongst all this evidence.

TAPPERCOOM. Now, no poetics, Tyson. Blow your nose
And avoid lechery. Keep your eye on the evidence
Against her; there's plenty of it there. Religion
Has made an honest woman of the supernatural
And we won't have it kicking over the traces again,
Will we, Chaplain?—In the Land of Nod.
Admirable man.

TYSON. Humanity,
That's all, Tappercoom; it's perfectly proper.
No one is going to let it interfere
With anything serious. I use it with great
Discretion, I assure you.—Has she confessed?

TAPPERCOOM. Not at all. Though we administer persuasion
With great patience, she admits nothing. And the man
Won't stop admitting. It really makes one lose
All faith in human nature.

Enter MARGARET, *without her placidity.*

MARGARET. Who has the tongs?
The tongs, Hebble, the tongs, dear! Sweet
Elijah, we shall all go up in flames!

TYSON. Flames? Did you hear that, Tappercoom? Flames!
My sister said flames!

MARGARET. A log the size of a cheese
Has fallen off the fire! Well, where are they?
What men of action! Tongs, I said!—Chaplain,
They're under your feet. Very simple you'd look
As a pile of ashes.

[*Exit.*

TYSON. Oh. I beg your pardon,
Tappercoom. A blazing log.

CHAPLAIN. Would there be something
I could do? I was asleep, you know.

TYSON. All this evidence from the witchfinder. . . .

TAPPERCOOM. The advent of a woman cannot be
Too gradual. I am not a nervous man
But I like to be predisposed to an order of events.

CHAPLAIN. It was very interesting: I was dreaming I stood
On Jacob's ladder, waiting for the Gates to open.
And the ladder was made entirely of diminished sevenths.
I was surprised but not put out. Nothing
Is altogether what we suppose it to be.

TAPPERCOOM. As for the Day of Judgement, we can be sure
It's not due yet. What are we told the world
Will be like? 'Boasters, blasphemers, without natural
Affection, traitors, trucebreakers,' and the rest of it.
Come, we've still a lot of backsliding ahead of us.

TYSON. Are you uneasy, Tappercoom?

TAPPERCOOM. No, Tyson.
The whole thing's a lot of amphigourious
Stultiloquential fiddle-faddle.

Re-enter MARGARET, *head-first.*

MARGARET. Hebble!

TAPPERCOOM. For God's sake!

TYSON. What is it now? What is it?

MARGARET. The street's gone mad. They've seen a shooting star!

TYSON. They? Who? What of it?

MARGARET. I'm sure I'm sorry,
But the number of people gone mad in the street
Is particularly excessive. They were shaking
Our gate, and knocking off each other's hats
And six fights simultaneously, and some
Were singing psalm a hundred and forty—I think
It's a hundred and forty—and the rest of them shouting
'The Devil's in there!' (pointing at this house)
'Safety from Satan!' and 'Where's the woman? Where's
The witch? Send her out!'; and using words
That are only fit for the Bible. And I'm sure
There was blood in the gutter from somebody's head
Or else it was the sunset in a puddle,
But Jobby Pinnock was prising up cobblestones,
Roaring like the north wind, and you know
What he is in church when he starts on the responses.
And that old Habbakuk Brown using our wall
As it was never meant to be used. And then
They saw the star fall over our roof somewhere
And followed its course with a downrush of whistling
And Ohs and Ahs and groans and screams; and Jobby
Pinnock dropped a stone on his own foot
And roared 'Almighty God, it's a sign!' and some
Went down on their knees and others fell over them
And they've started to fight again, and the hundred and fortieth
Psalm has begun again louder and faster than ever.
Hebble dear, isn't it time they went home?

TYSON. All right, yes, all right, all right. Now why
  Can't people mind their own business? This shooting star
  Has got nothing to do with us, I am quite happy
  In my mind about that. It probably went past
  Perfectly preoccupied with some astral anxiety or other
  Without giving us a second thought. Eh, Tappercoom?
  One of those quaint astrological holus-boluses,
  Quite all right.

TAPPERCOOM.   Quite. An excess of phlegm
  In the solar system. It was on its way
  To a heavenly spittoon. How is that,
  How is that? On its way——

TYSON.   I consider it unwise
  To tempt providence with humour, Tappercoom.

MARGARET. And on the one evening when we expect company!
  What company is going to venture to get here
  Through all that heathen hullabaloo in the road?
  Except the glorious company of the Apostles,
  And we haven't enough glasses for all that number.

TAPPERCOOM. Doomsday or not, we must keep our integrity.
  We cannot set up dangerous precedents
  Of speed. We shall sincerely hope, of course,
  That Doomsday will refrain from precipitous action;
  But the way we have gone must be the way we arrive.

CHAPLAIN. I wish I were a thinking man, very much.
  Of course I feel a good deal, but that's no help to you.

TYSON. I'm not bewildered, I assure you I'm not
  Bewildered. As a matter of fact a plan
  Is almost certainly forming itself in my head
  At this very moment. It may even be adequate.

CHAPLAIN. Where did I put my better half? I laid it
  Aside. I could take it down to the gate and perhaps
  Disperse them with a skirmish or two of the bow.
  Orpheus, you know, was very successful in that way,
  But of course I haven't his talent, not nearly his talent.

TYSON. If you would allow me to follow my train of thought——

TAPPERCOOM. It's my belief the woman Jourdemayne
  Got hold of the male prisoner by unlawful
  Supernatural soliciting
  And bewitched him into a confession of murder
  To draw attention away from herself. But the more
  We coax him to withdraw his confession, the more
  Crimes he confesses to.

CHAPLAIN.   I know I am not
  A practical person; legal matters and so forth
  Are Greek to me, except, of course,
  That I understand Greek. And what may seem nonsensical
  To men of affairs like yourselves might not seem so
  To me, since everything astonishes me,
  Myself most of all. When I think of myself
  I can scarcely believe my senses. But there it is,
  All my friends tell me I actually exist
  And by an act of faith I have come to believe them.
  But this fellow who is being such a trouble to us,
  He, on the contrary, is so convinced
  He *is* that he wishes he was NOT. Now why
  Should that be?

TAPPERCOOM.   I believe you mean to tell us,
  Chaplain.

MARGARET. I might as well sit down, for all
  The good that standing up does.

CHAPLAIN.   I imagine
He finds the world not entirely salubrious.
If he cannot be stayed with flagons, or comforted
With apples—I quote, of course—or the light, the ocean,
The ever-changing . . . I mean and stars, extraordinary
How many, or some instrument or other—I am afraid
I appear rhapsodical—but perhaps the addition
Of your thumbscrew will not succeed either. The point
I'm attempting to make is this one: he might be wooed
From his aptitude for death by being happier;
And what I was going to suggest, quite irresponsibly,
Is that he might be invited to partake
Of our festivities this evening. No,
I see it astonishes you.

MARGARET.   Do you mean ask him——

TYSON. I have heard very little of what you have said, Chaplain,
Being concerned, as I am, with a certain Thought,
But am I to believe that you recommend our inviting
This undesirable character to rub shoulders
With my sister?

CHAPLAIN.   Ah; rubbing shoulders. I hadn't exactly
Anticipated that. It was really in relation to the soul
That the possibility crossed my mind——

TAPPERCOOM. As a criminal the boy is a liability.
I doubt very much if he could supply a farthing
Towards the cost of his execution. So
You suggest, Chaplain, we let him bibulate
From glass to glass this evening, help him to
A denial of his guilt and get him off our hands
Before daybreak gets the town on its feet again?

MARGARET. I wish I could like the look of the immediate
Future, but I don't.

TYSON. I'm glad to tell you
An idea has formed in my mind, a possible solution.

Enter RICHARD.

RICHARD. Sir, if you please——

TYSON. Well, Richard?

RICHARD. I should like to admit
That I've drunk some of the wine put out for the guests.

TYSON. Well, that's a pretty thing, I must say.

RICHARD. I was feeling
Low; abominably; about the prisoners,
And the row in the street that's getting out of hand—
And certain inner things. And I saw the wine
And I thought Well, here goes, and I drank
Three glassesful.

TYSON. I trust you feel better for it.

RICHARD. I feel much worse. Those two, sir, the prisoners,
What are you doing with them? I don't know why
I keep calling you Sir. I'm not feeling respectful.
If only inflicted pain could be as contagious
As a plague, you might use it more sparingly.

TAPPERCOOM. Who's this cub of a boy?

MARGARET. Richard, be sensible.
He's a dear boy but a green boy, and I'm sure
He'll apologize in a minute or two.

TYSON. The boy
Is a silly boy, he's a silly boy; and I'm going
To punish him.

MARGARET. Where are Humphrey and Nicholas?

TYSON. Now, Margaret——

RICHARD.   They were where the prisoners are,
Down in the cellars.

MARGARET.   Not talking to that witch?

RICHARD. There isn't a witch. They were sitting about on barrels.
It seemed that neither would speak while the other was there
And neither would go away. Half an hour ago.
They may be there still.

TYSON.   I must remind you, Margaret,
I was speaking to this very stupid boy.
He is going to scrub the floor. Yes, scrub it.
Scrub this floor this evening before our guests
Put in an appearance. Mulish tasks for a mulish
Fellow. I haven't forgotten his refusal
To fetch the constable.

RICHARD.   Has Alizon Eliot
Been left sitting alone?

MARGARET.   Alizon Eliot
Is not for you to be concerned with, Richard.

TYSON. Am I supposed to be merely exercising my tongue
Or am I being listened to? Do you hear me?

RICHARD. Yes; scrub the floor.—No, she is not;
I know that.

TYSON.   Furthermore, you'll relegate
Yourself to the kitchen to-night, fetching and carrying.
If you wish to be a mule you shall be a mule.
                              [*He hands* RICHARD *a note.*
And take this to whatever splendid fellow's
On duty. You will return with the prisoners
And tell them to remain in this room till I send for them.

—Tactics, Tappercoom: the idea that came to me.
You'll think it very good.—You may go, Richard.

[*Exit* RICHARD.

TAPPERCOOM. I am nothing but the Justice here, of course,
But, perhaps, even allowing for that, you could tell me
What the devil you're up to.

Enter NICHOLAS *with a gash on his forehead, followed more slowly
by* HUMPHREY.

NICHOLAS.   Look, Chaplain: blood.
Fee, fi, fo, fum. Can you smell it?

MARGARET. Now what have you been doing?

NICHOLAS.   Isn't it beautiful?
A splash from the cherry-red river that drives my mill!

CHAPLAIN. Well, yes, it has a cheerful appearance,
But isn't it painful?

MARGARET.   I am sure it's painful.
How did you——

HUMPHREY.   Mother, I make it known publicly:
I'm tired of my little brother. Will you please
Give him to some charity?

NICHOLAS.   Give me to faith
And hope and the revolution of our native town.
I've been hit on the head by two-thirds of a brick.

HUMPHREY. The young fool climbed on the wall and addressed
the crowd.

NICHOLAS. They were getting discouraged. I told them how
happy it made me
To see them interested in world affairs

And how the conquest of evil was being openly
Discussed in this house at that very moment
And then unfortunately I was hit by a brick.

MARGARET. What in the world have world affairs
To do with anything? But we won't argue.

TYSON. I believe that brick to have been divinely delivered,
And richly deserved. And am I to understand
You boys have also attempted conversation
With the prisoners?

HUMPHREY.   Now surely, uncle,
As one of the Town Council I should be allowed
To get a grasp of whatever concerns the welfare
Of the population? Nicholas, I agree,
Had no business on earth to be down there.

NICHOLAS.   I was on
Business of the soul, my sweetheart, business
Of the soul.

MARGARET.   You may use that word once too often,
Nicholas. Heaven or someone will take you seriously
And then you *would* look foolish. Come with me
And have your forehead seen to.

NICHOLAS.   But my big brother
Was on business of the flesh, by all the fires
Of Venus, weren't you, Humphrey?

HUMPHREY.   What the hell
Do you mean by that, you little death-watch beetle?

MARGARET. Nicholas, will you come?

NICHOLAS.   Certainly, mother.

[*Exit* MARGARET *and* NICHOLAS.

TYSON. How very remarkably insufferable
Young fellows can sometimes be. One would expect them
To care to model themselves on riper minds
Such as our own, Tappercoom. But really
We might as well have not existed, you know.

TAPPERCOOM. Am I to hear your plan, Tyson, or am I
Just to look quietly forward to old age?

TYSON. My plan, ah, yes. Conclusive and humane.
The two are brought together into this room.—
How does that strike you?

TAPPERCOOM.   It makes a complete sentence:
Subject: they. Predicate: are brought together——

TYSON. Ah, you will say 'with what object?' I'll tell you. We,
That is: ourselves, the Chaplain, and my elder nephew—
Will remain unobserved in the adjoining room
With the communicating door ajar.—And how
Does that strike you?

TAPPERCOOM.   With a dull thud, Tyson,
If I may say so.

TYSON.   I see the idea has eluded you.
A hypothetical Devil, Tappercoom,
Brought into conversation with a witch.
A dialogue of Hell, perhaps, and conclusive.
Or one or other by their exchange of words
Will prove to be innocent, or we shall have proof
Positive of guilt. Does that seem good?

TAPPERCOOM. Good is as good results.

HUMPHREY.   I should never have thought
You would have done anything so undignified
As to stoop to keyholes, uncle.

TYSON.   No, no, no.
  The door will be ajar, my boy.

HUMPHREY.   Ah yes,
  That will make us upright.—I can hear them coming.

TYSON [*going*]. Come along, come along.

CHAPLAIN.   'The ears of them that hear
  Shall hearken.' The prophet Isaiah.

TYSON.   Come along, Chaplain.

TAPPERCOOM [*following*]. A drink, Tyson. I wish to slake the
    dryness
  Of my disbelief.

                          [*They go in. The* CHAPLAIN *returns.*

CHAPLAIN.   I musn't leave my mistress.
  Where are you, angel? Just where chucklehead left her.

              Enter RICHARD *with* JENNET *and* THOMAS.

RICHARD. He wants you to wait here till he sends for you.
  If in some way—I wish—! I must fetch the scrubbers.

                                          [*Exit* RICHARD.

CHAPLAIN. Ah ... ah ... I'm not really here. I came
  For my angel, a foolish way to speak of it,
  This instrument. May I say, a happy issue
  Out of all your afflictions? I hope so.—Well,
  I'm away now.

THOMAS. God bless you, in case you sneeze.

CHAPLAIN. Yes; thank you. I may. And God bless you.

                                         [*Exit* CHAPLAIN.

THOMAS [*at the window*]. You would think by the holy scent of it
    our friend
  Had been baptizing the garden. But it's only
  The heathen rainfall.

JENNET.   Do you think he knows
What has been happening to us?

THOMAS.   Old angel-scraper?
He knows all right. But he's subdued
To the cloth he works in.

JENNET.   How tired I am.

THOMAS. And palingenesis has come again
With a hey and a ho. The indomitable
Perseverance of Persephone
Became ludicrous long ago.

JENNET.   What can you see
Out there?

THOMAS.   Out here? Out here is a sky so gentle
Five stars are ventured on it. I can see
The sky's pale belly glowing and growing big,
Soon to deliver the moon. And I can see
A glittering smear, the snail-trail of the sun
Where it crawled with its golden shell into the hills.
A darkening land sunken into prayer
Lucidly in dewdrops of one syllable,
Nunc dimittis. I see twilight, madam.

JENNET. But what can you hear?

THOMAS.   The howl of human jackals.

Enter RICHARD *with pail and scrubbing-brush.*

RICHARD. Do you mind? I have to scrub the floor.

THOMAS. A good old custom. Always fornicate
Between clean sheets and spit on a well-scrubbed floor.

JENNET. Twilight, double, treble, in and out!
If I try to find my way I bark my brain
On shadows sharp as rocks where half a day
Ago was a soft world, a world of warm

Straw, whispering every now and then
With rats, but possible, possible, not this,
This where I'm lost. The morning came, and left
The sunlight on my step like any normal
Tradesman. But now every spark
Of likelihood has gone. The light draws off
As easily as though no one could die
To-morrow.

THOMAS.   Are you going to be so serious
About such a mean allowance of breath as life is?
We'll suppose ourselves to be caddis-flies
Who live one day. Do we waste the evening
Commiserating with each other about
The unhygienic condition of our worm-cases?
For God's sake, shall we laugh?

JENNET.   For what reason?

THOMAS. For the reason of laughter, since laughter is surely
The surest touch of genius in creation.
Would *you* ever have thought of it, I ask you,
If you had been making man, stuffing him full
Of such hopping greeds and passions that he has
To blow himself to pieces as often as he
Conveniently can manage it—would it also
Have occurred to you to make him burst himself
With such a phenomenon as cachinnation?
That same laughter, madam, is an irrelevancy
Which almost amounts to revelation.

JENNET.   I laughed
Earlier this evening, and where am I now?

THOMAS.   Between
The past and the future which is where you were
Before.

JENNET. Was it for laughter's sake you told them
   You were the Devil? Or why did you?

THOMAS.   Honesty,
   Madam, common honesty.

JENNET.   Honesty common
   With the Devil?

THOMAS.   Gloriously common. It's Evil, for once
   Not travelling incognito. It is what it is,
   The Great Unspurious.

JENNET.   Thank you for that.
   You speak of the world I thought I was waking to
   This morning. But horror is walking round me here
   Because nothing is as it appears to be.
   That's the deep water my childhood had to swim in.
   My father was drowned in it.

THOMAS.   He was drowned in what?
   In hypocrisy?

JENNET.   In the pursuit of alchemy.
   In refusing to accept your dictum 'It is
   What it is'. Poor father. In the end he walked
   In Science like the densest night. And yet
   He was greatly gifted.
   When he was born he gave an algebraic
   Cry; at one glance measured the cubic content
   Of that ivory cone his mother's breast
   And multiplied his appetite by five.
   So he matured by a progression, gained
   Experience by correlation, expanded
   Into a marriage by contraction, and by
   Certain physical dynamics
   Formulated me. And on he went
   Still deeper into the calculating twilight

Under the twinkling of five-pointed figures
Till Truth became for him the sum of sums
And Death the long division. My poor father.
What years and powers he wasted.
He thought he could change the matter of the world
From the poles to the simultaneous equator
By strange experiment and by describing
Numerical parabolas.

THOMAS.   To change
The matter of the world! Magnificent
Intention. And so he died deluded.

JENNET. As a matter of fact, it wasn't a delusion.
As a matter of fact, after his death
When I was dusting the laboratory
I knocked over a crucible which knocked
Over another which rocked a third, and they poured
And spattered over some copper coins which two days later
By impregnation had turned into solid gold.

THOMAS. Tell that to some sailor on a horse!
If you had such a secret, I
And all my fiendish flock, my incubi,
Succubi, imps and cacodemons, would have leapt
Out of our bath of brimming brimstone, crying
Eureka, cherchez la femme!—Emperors
Would be colonizing you, their mistresses
Patronizing you, ministers of state
Governmentalizing you. And you
Would be eulogized, lionized, probably
Canonized for your divine mishap.

JENNET. But I never had such a secret. It's a secret
Still. What it was I spilt, or to what extent,
Or in what proportion; whether the atmosphere

Was hot, cold, moist or dry, I've never known.
And someone else can discolour their fingers, tease
Their brains and spoil their eyesight to discover it.
My father broke on the wheel of a dream; he was lost
In a search. And so, for me, the actual!
What I touch, what I see, what I know; the essential fact.

THOMAS. In other words, the bare untruth.

JENNET.   And, if I may say it
Without appearing rude, absolutely
No devils.

THOMAS.   How in the miserable world, in that case,
Do you come to be here, pursued by the local consignment
Of fear and guilt? What possible cause——

JENNET.   Your thumbs.
I'm sure they're giving you pain.

THOMAS.   Listen! by both
My cloven hooves! if you put us to the rack
Of an exchange of sympathy, I'll fell you to the ground.
Answer my question.

JENNET.   Why do they call me a witch?
Remember my father was an alchemist.
I live alone, preferring loneliness
To the companionable suffocation of an aunt.
I still amuse myself with simple experiments
In my father's laboratory. Also I speak
French to my poodle. Then you must know
I have a peacock which on Sundays
Dines with me indoors. Not long ago
A new little serving maid carrying the food
Heard its cry, dropped everything and ran,
Never to come back, and told all whom she met
That the Devil was dining with me.

THOMAS. It really is
Beyond the limit of respectable superstition
To confuse my voice with a peacock's. Don't they know
I sing solo bass in Hell's Madrigal Club?
—And as for you, you with no eyes, no ears,
No senses, you the most superstitious
Of all—(for what greater superstition
Is there than the mumbo-jumbo of believing
In reality?)—you should be swallowed whole by Time
In the way that you swallow appearances.
Horns, what a waste of effort it has been
To give you Creation's vast and exquisite
Dilemma! where altercation thrums
In every granule of the Milky Way,
Persisting still in the dead-sleep of the moon,
And heckling itself hoarse in that hot-head
The sun. And as for here, each acorn drops
Arguing to earth, and pollen's all polemic.—
We have given you a world as contradictory
As a female, as cabbalistic as the male,
A conscienceless hermaphrodite who plays
Heaven off against hell, hell off against heaven,
Revolving in the ballroom of the skies
Glittering with conflict as with diamonds:
We have wasted paradox and mystery on you
When all you ask us for, is cause and effect!—
A copy of your birth-certificate was all you needed
To make you at peace with Creation. How uneconomical
The whole thing's been.
JENNET. This is a fine time
To scold me for keeping myself to myself and out
Of the clutch of chaos. I was already
In a poor way of perplexity and now

You leave me no escape except
Out on a stream of tears.

THOMAS [*falling over* RICHARD *scrubbing*]. Now, none of that!—
Hell!

RICHARD. I beg your pardon.

THOMAS. Now that I'm down
On my knees I may as well stay here. In the name
Of all who ever were drowned at sea, don't weep!
I never learnt to swim. May God keep you
From being my Hellespont.

JENNET. What I do
With my own tears is for me to decide.

THOMAS. That's all very well. You get rid of them.
But on whose defenceless head are they going to fall?

JENNET. I had no idea you were so afraid of water.
I'll put them away.

THOMAS. O Pete, I don't know which
Is worse; to have you crying or to have you behaving
Like Catharine of Aix, who never wept
Until after she had been beheaded, and then
The accumulation of the tears of a long lifetime
Burst from her eyes with such force, they practic'ly winded
Three onlookers and floated the parish priest
Two hundred yards into the entrance-hall
Of a brothel.

JENNET. Poor Catharine!

THOMAS. Not at all.
It made her life in retrospect infinitely
More tolerable, and when she got to Purgatory
She was laughing so much they had to give her a sedative.

JENNET. Why should you want to be hanged?

THOMAS.   Madam,
I owe it to myself. But I can leave it
Until the last moment. It will keep
While the light still lasts.

JENNET.   What can we see in this light?
Nothing, I think, except flakes of drifting fear,
The promise of oblivion.

THOMAS.   Nothing can be seen
In the thistle-down, but the rough-head thistle comes.
Rest in that riddle. I can pass to you
Generations of roses in this wrinkled berry.
There: now you hold in your hand a race
Of summer gardens, it lies under centuries
Of petals. What is not, you have in your palm.
Rest in the riddle, rest; why not? This evening
Is a ridiculous wisp of down
Blowing in the air as disconsolately as dust.
And you have your own damnable mystery too,
Which at this moment I could well do without.

JENNET. I know of none. I'm an unhappy fact
Fearing death. This is a strange moment
To feel my life increasing, when this moment
And a little more may be for both of us
The end of time. You've cast your fishing-net
Of eccentricity,
Caught me when I was already lost
And landed me with despairing gills on your own
Strange beach. That's too inhuman of you.

THOMAS.   Inhuman?
If I dared to know what you meant it would sound disastrous!

JENNET. It means I care whether you live or die.

THOMAS. Will you stop frightening me to death?
Do you want our spirits to hobble out of their graves
Enduring twinges of hopeless human affection
As long as death shall last? Still to suffer
Pain in the amputated limb! To feel
Passion *in vacuo*! That is the sort of thing
That causes sun-spots, and the lord knows what
Infirmities in the firmament. I tell you
The heart is worthless,
Nothing more than a pomander's perfume
In the sewerage. And a nosegay of private emotion
Won't distract me from the stench of the plague-pit,
You needn't think it will.—Excuse me, Richard.—
Don't entertain the mildest interest in me
Or you'll have me die screaming.

JENNET.   Why should that be?
If you're afraid of your shadow falling across
Another life, shine less brightly upon yourself,
Step back into the rank and file of men,
Instead of preserving the magnetism of mystery
And your curious passion for death. You are making yourself
A breeding-ground for love and must take the consequences.
But what are you afraid of, since in a little
While neither of us may exist? Either or both
May be altogether transmuted into memory,
And then the heart's obscure indeed.—Richard,
There's a tear rolling out of your eye. What is it?

RICHARD. Oh, that? I don't really know. I have things on my mind.

JENNET. Not us?

RICHARD. Not only.

THOMAS.   If it's a woman, Richard,
   Apply yourself to the scrubbing-brush. It's all
   A trick of the light.

JENNET.   The light of a fire.

THOMAS.   And, Richard,
   Make this woman understand that I
   Am a figure of vice and crime——

JENNET.   Guilty of——

THOMAS.   Guilty
   Of mankind. I have perpetrated human nature.
   My father and mother were accessaries before the fact,
   But there'll be no accessaries after the fact,
   By my virility there won't! Just see me
   As I am, me like a perambulating
   Vegetable, patched with inconsequential
   Hair, looking out of two small jellies for the means
   Of life, balanced on folding bones, my sex
   No beauty but a blemish to be hidden
   Behind judicious rags, driven and scorched
   By boomerang rages and lunacies which never
   Touch the accommodating artichoke
   Or the seraphic strawberry beaming in its bed:
   I defend myself against pain and death by pain
   And death, and make the world go round, they tell me,
   By one of my less lethal appetites:
   Half this grotesque life I spend in a state
   Of slow decomposition, using
   The name of unconsidered God as a pedestal
   On which I stand and bray that I'm best
   Of beasts, until under some patient
   Moon or other I fall to pieces, like

A cake of dung. Is there a slut would hold
This in her arms and put her lips against it?

JENNET. Sluts are only human. By a quirk
Of unastonished nature, your obscene
Decaying figure of vegetable fun
Can drag upon a woman's heart, as though
Heaven were dragging up the roots of hell.
What is to be done? Something compels us into
The terrible fallacy that man is desirable
And there's no escaping into truth. The crimes
And cruelties leave us longing, and campaigning
Love still pitches his tent of light among
The suns and moons. You may be decay and a platitude
Of flesh, but I have no other such memory of life.
You may be corrupt as ancient apples, well then
Corruption is what I most willingly harvest.
You are Evil, Hell, the Father of Lies; if so
Hell is my home and my days of good were a holiday:
Hell is my hill and the world slopes away from it
Into insignificance. I have come suddenly
Upon my heart and where it is I see no help for.

THOMAS. We're lost, both irretrievably lost——

Enter TYSON, TAPPERCOOM, HUMPHREY, *and the* CHAPLAIN.

TAPPERCOOM.   Certainly.
The woman has confessed. *Spargere auras
Per vulgum ambiguas.* The town can go to bed.

TYSON. It was a happy idea, eh, Tappercoom? This will be
A great relief to my sister, and everybody
Concerned. A very nice confession, my dear.

THOMAS. What is this popping-noise? Now what's the matter?

JENNET. Do they think I've confessed to witchcraft?

TAPPERCOOM. Admirably.

CHAPLAIN [*to* JENNET]. Bother such sadness. You understand,
    I'm sure:
  Those in authority over us. I should like
  To have been a musician but others decreed otherwise.
  And sin, whatever we might prefer, cannot
  Go altogether unregarded.

TAPPERCOOM. Now,
  Now, Chaplain, don't get out of hand.
  Pieties come later.—Young Devize
  Had better go and calm the populace.
  Tell them faggots will be lit to-morrow at noon.

HUMPHREY. Have a heart, Mr. Tappercoom; they're hurling
    bricks.

JENNET. What do they mean? Am I at noon to go
  To the fire? Oh, for pity! Why must they brand
  Themselves with me?

THOMAS. She has bribed you to procure
  Her death! Graft! Graft! Oh, the corruption
  Of this town when only the rich can get to kingdom-
  Come and a poor man is left to groan
  In the full possession of his powers. And she's
  Not even guilty! I demand fair play
  For the criminal classes!

TYSON. Terrible state of mind.
  Humphrey, go at once to the gate——

HUMPHREY. Ah well, I can
  But try to dodge.

THOMAS [*knocking him down*]. You didn't try soon enough.
  Who else is going to cheat me out of my death?

Whee, ecclesiastic, let me brain you
With your wife!

> [*He snatches the* CHAPLAIN's *viol and offers to hit him on the head.*

CHAPLAIN. No, no! With something else—oh, please
Hit me with something else.

THOMAS. Exchange it
For a harp and hurry off to heaven.—Am I dangerous?
Will you give me the gallows?—Now, *now*, Mr. Mayor!
Richard, I'll drown him in your bucket.

> [JENNET *faints.*

RICHARD [*running to support her*]. Look, she has fallen!

CHAPLAIN. Air! Air!

TYSON. Water!

THOMAS. But no fire, do you hear? No fire!—How is she, Richard?
Oh, the delicate mistiming of women! She has carefully
Snapped in half my jawbone of an ass.

RICHARD. Life is coming back.

THOMAS. Importunate life.
It should have something better to do
Than to hang about at a chronic street-corner
In dirty weather and worse company.

TAPPERCOOM. It is my duty as Justice to deliver
Sentence on you as well.

THOMAS. Ah!

TAPPERCOOM. Found guilty
Of jaundice, misanthropy, suicidal tendencies
And spreading gloom and despondency. You will spend
The evening joyously, sociably, taking part
In the pleasures of your fellow men.

THOMAS.   Not
  Until you've hanged me. I'll be amenable then.

JENNET. Have I come back to consciousness to hear
  That still?—Richard, help me to stand.—You see,
  Preacher to the caddis-fly, I return
  To live my allotted span of insect hours.
  But if you batter my wings with talk of death
  I'll drop to the ground again.

THOMAS.   Ah! One
  Concession to your courage and then no more.
  Gentlemen, I'll accept your most inhuman
  Sentence. I'll not disturb the indolence
  Of your gallows yet. But on one condition:
  That this lady shall take her share to-night
  Of awful festivity. She shall suffer too.

TYSON. Out of the question, quite out of the question,
  Absolutely out of the question. What, what?

TAPPERCOOM. What?

THOMAS.   Then you shall spend your night in searching
  For the bodies of my victims, or else the Lord
  Chief Justice of England shall know you let a murderer
  Go free. I'll raise the country.

JENNET.   Do you think
  I can go in gaiety to-night
  Under the threat of to-morrow? If I could sleep——

THOMAS. That is the heaven to come.
  We should be like stars now that it's dark:
  Use ourselves up to the last bright dregs
  And vanish in the morning. Shall we not
  Suffer as wittily as we can? Now, come,
  Don't purse your lips like a little prude at the humour

Of annihilation. It is somewhat broad
I admit, but we're not children.

JENNET.   I am such
A girl of habit. I had got into the way
Of being alive. I will live as well as I can
This evening.

THOMAS.   And I'll live too, if it kills me.

HUMPHREY. Well, uncle? If you're going to let this clumsy-
Fisted cut-throat loose on the house to-night,
Why not the witch-girl, too?

CHAPLAIN.   Foolishly
I can't help saying it, I should like
To see them dancing.

TYSON. We have reached a decision.
The circumstances compel us to agree
To your most unorthodox request.

THOMAS.   Wisdom
At last. But listen, woman: after this evening
I have no further interest in the world.

JENNET. My interest also will not be great, I imagine,
After this evening.

CURTAIN ON ACT TWO

ACT THREE

Later the same night. The same room, by torchlight and moonlight. HUMPHREY *at the window. Enter* THOMAS, *who talks to himself until he notices* HUMPHREY.

THOMAS. O tedium, tedium, tedium. The frenzied
Ceremonial drumming of the humdrum!
Where in this small-talking world can I find
A longitude with no platitude?—I must
Apologize. That was no joke to be heard
Making to myself in the full face of the moon.
If only I had been born flame, a flame
Poised, say, on the flighty head of a candle,
I could have stood in this draught and gone out,
Whip, through the door of my exasperation.
But I remain, like the possibility
Of water in a desert.

HUMPHREY.   I'm sure nobody
Keeps you here. There's a road outside if you want it.

THOMAS. What on earth should I do with a road, that furrow
On the forehead of imbecility, a road?
I would as soon be up there, walking in the moon's
White unmolared gums. I'll sit on the world
And rotate with you till we roll into the morning.

HUMPHREY. You're a pestering parasite. If I had my way
You'd be got rid of. You're mad and you're violent,
And I strongly resent finding you slightly pleasant.

THOMAS. O God, yes, so do I.

Enter NICHOLAS.

NICHOLAS. As things turn out
I want to commit an offence.

THOMAS. Does something prevent you?

NICHOLAS. I don't know what offence to commit.

THOMAS. What abysmal
Poverty of mind!

NICHOLAS. This is a night
Of the most asphyxiating enjoyment that ever
Sapped my youth.

HUMPHREY. I think I remember
The stars gave you certain rights and interest
In a little blonde religious. How is she, Nicholas?

NICHOLAS. Your future wife, Humphrey, if that is who
You mean, is pale, tearful, and nibbling a walnut.
I loved her once—earlier to-day—
Loved her with a passionate misapprehension.
I thought you wanted her, and I'm always deeply
Devoted to your affairs. But now I'm bored,
As bored as the face of a fish,
In spite of the sunlit barley of her hair.

HUMPHREY. Aren't I ready to marry her? I thought that was why
We were mooning around celebrating. What more
Can I do to make you take her off my hands?
And I'm more than ready for the Last Trump as well.
It will stop old Mrs. Cartwright talking.

NICHOLAS. Never.
She's doom itself. She could talk a tombstone off anybody.

Enter MARGARET.

MARGARET. Oh, there you are. Whatever's wrong? You both
Go wandering off, as though our guests could be gay

Of their own accord (the few who could bring themselves
To bring themselves, practically in the teeth
Of the recording angel). They're very nervous
And need considerable jollying. Goose liver,
Cold larks, cranberry tarts and sucking pig,
And now everyone looks as though they only
Wanted to eat each other, which might in the circumstances
Be the best possible thing. Your uncle sent me
To find you. I can tell he's put out; he's as vexed
As a hen's hind feathers in a wind. And for that
Matter so am I. Go back inside
And be jolly like anyone else's children.

NICHOLAS.   Mother,
I'd as soon kiss the bottom of a Barbary ape.
The faces of our friends may be enchantment
To some, but they wrap my spirits in a shroud.—
For the sake of my unborn children, I have to avoid them.
Oh now, be brave, mother. They'll go in the course of nature.

MARGARET. It's unfortunate, considering the wide
Choice of living matter on this globe,
That I should have managed to be a mother. I can't
Imagine what I was thinking of. Your uncle
Has made me shake out the lavender
From one of my first gowns which has hung in the wardrobe
Four-and-twenty unencouraging years,
To lend to this Jennet girl, who in my opinion
Should not be here. And I said to her flatly
'The course of events is incredible. Make free
'With my jewel box.' Where is she now?

THOMAS.   No doubt
Still making free. Off she has gone,
Away to the melting moody horizons of opal,

Moonstone, bloodstone; now moving in lazy
Amber, now sheltering in the shade
Of jade from a brief rainfall of diamonds.
Able to think to-morrow has an even
Brighter air, a glitter less moderate,
A quite unparalleled freedom in the fire:
A death, no bounds to it. Where is she now?
She is dressing, I imagine.

MARGARET.   Yes, I suppose so.
I don't like to think of her. And as for you
I should like to think of you as someone I knew
Many years ago, and, alas, wouldn't see again.
That would be charming. I beg you to come,
Humphrey. Give your brother a good example.

HUMPHREY. Mother, I'm unwell.

MARGARET.   Oh, Humphrey!

NICHOLAS.   Mother,
He is officially sick and actually bored.
The two together are as bad as a dropsy.

MARGARET. I must keep my mind as concentrated as possible
On such pleasant things as the summer I spent at Stoke
D'Abernon. Your uncle must do what he will.
I've done what I can.

                                        [*Exit* MARGARET.

NICHOLAS.   Our mother isn't
Pleased.

HUMPHREY. She has never learnt to yawn
And so she hasn't the smallest comprehension
Of those who can.

THOMAS.   Benighted brothers in boredom,
Let us unite ourselves in a toast of ennui.

I give you a yawn: to this evening, especially remembering
Mrs. Cartwright. [*They all yawn.*] To mortal life, women,
All government, wars, art, science, ambitions,
And the entire fallacy of human emotions!

> [*As they painfully yawn again, enter* JENNET, *bright with
> jewels, and twenty years exquisitely out of fashion.*

JENNET. And wake us in the morning with an ambrosial
Breakfast, amen, amen.

NICHOLAS.   Humphrey, poppin,
Draw back the curtains. I have a sense of daylight.

HUMPHREY. It seems we're facing east.

THOMAS.   You've come too late.
Romulus, Remus and I have just buried the world
Under a heavy snowfall of disinterest.
There's nothing left of life but cranberry tarts,
Goose's liver, sucking pig, cold larks,
And Mrs. Cartwright.

JENNET.   That's riches running mad.
What about the have-not moon? Not a goose, not a pig,
And yet she manages to be the wit
Of heaven, and roused the envious Queen of Sheba
To wash in mercury so that the Sheban fountains
Should splash deliriously in the light of her breast.
But she died, poor Queen, shining less
Than the milk of her thousand shorthorn cows.

THOMAS.   What's this?
Where has the girl I spoke to this evening gone
With her Essential Fact? Surely she knows,
If she is true to herself, the moon is nothing
But a circumambulating aphrodisiac
Divinely subsidized to provoke the world

Into a rising birth-rate—a veneer
Of sheerest Venus on the planks of Time
Which may fool the ocean but which fools not me.

JENNET. So no moon.

THOMAS. No moon.

NICHOLAS. Let her have the last quarter.

JENNET. No;
If he says no moon then of course there can be no moon.
Otherwise we destroy his system of thought
And confuse the quest for truth.

THOMAS. You see, Nicholas?

JENNET. I've only one small silver night to spend
So show me no luxuries. It will be enough
If you spare me a spider, and when it spins I'll see
The six days of Creation in a web
And a fly caught on the seventh. And if the dew
Should rise in the web, I may well die a Christian.

THOMAS. I must shorten my sail. We're into a strange wind.
This evening you insisted on what you see,
What you touch, what you know. Where did this weather blow
    from?

JENNET. Off the moors of mortality: that might
Be so. Or there's that inland sea, the heart—
But you mustn't hinder me, not now. I come
Of a long-lived family, and I have
Some sixty years to use up almost immediately.
I shall join the sucking pig.

NICHOLAS. Please take my arm.
I'll guide you there.

HUMPHREY. He shall do no such thing.
Who's the host here?

THOMAS.   They have impeccable manners
   When they reach a certain temperature.

HUMPHREY.   A word
   More from you, and you go out of this house.

THOMAS. Like the heart going out of me, by which it avoids
   Having to break.

JENNET.   Be quiet for a moment. I hear
   A gay modulating anguish, rather like music.

NICHOLAS. It's the Chaplain, extorting lightness of heart
   From the guts of his viol, to the greater glory of God.

                    Enter HEBBLE TYSON.

TYSON. What I hear from your mother isn't agreeable to me
   In the smallest—a draught, quite noticeable.
   I'm a victim to air.—I expect members of my family——

THOMAS. Is this courtesy, Mr. Mayor, to turn your back
   On a guest?

JENNET.   Why should I be welcome? I am wearing
   His days gone by. I rustle with his memories!
   I, the little heretic as he thinks,
   The all unhallows Eve to his poor Adam;
   And nearly stubbing my toes against my grave
   In his sister's shoes, the grave he has ordered for me.
   Don't ask impossibilities of the gentleman.

TYSON. Humphrey, will you explain yourself?

HUMPHREY.   Uncle,
   I came to cool my brow. I was on my way back.

NICHOLAS. Don't keep us talking. I need to plunge again
   Into that ice-cap of pleasure in the next room.
   I repeat, my arm.

HUMPHREY.   I repeat that I'm the host.
I have the right——

JENNET.   He has the right, Nicholas.
Let me commit no solecism so near
To eternity. Please open the door for us.
We must go in as smoothly as old friends.

> [*Exeunt* JENNET, HUMPHREY, *and* NICHOLAS.

THOMAS. Well, does your blood run deep enough to run
Cold, or have you none?

TYSON.   That's enough. Get away.

THOMAS. Are you going to cry-off the burning?

TYSON.   Worthless creatures,
Both; I call you clutter. The standard soul
Must mercilessly be maintained. No
Two ways of life. One God, one point of view.
A general acquiescence to the mean.

THOMAS. And God knows when you say the mean, you mean
The mean. You'd be surprised to see the number
Of cloven hoof-marks in the yellow snow of your soul.
And so you'll kill her.
Time would have done it for her too, of course,
But more cautiously, and with a pretence of charm.
Am I allowed on bail into your garden?

TYSON. Tiresome catarrh. I haven't any wish to see you,
Not in the slightest degree: go where you like.

THOMAS. That's nowhere in this world. But still maybe
I can make myself useful and catch mice for an owl.

> [*Exit* THOMAS.

Enter TAPPERCOOM.

TAPPERCOOM. The young lunatic slipping off, is he?
Cheered up and gone? So much the less trouble for us.
Very jolly evening, Tyson. Are you sober?

TYSON. Yes, yes, yes.

TAPPERCOOM.   You shouldn't say that, you know.
You're in tears, Tyson. I know tears when I see them,
My wife has them. You've drunk too deep, my boy.
Now I'm sober as a judge, perhaps a judge
A little on circuit, but still sober. Tyson,
You're in tears, old fellow, two little wandering
Jews of tears getting 'emselves embrangled
In your beard.

TYSON.   I won't stand it, Tappercoom:
I won't have it, I won't have evil things
Looking so distinguished. I'm no longer
Young, and I should be given protection.

TAPPERCOOM.   What
Do you want protecting from now?

TYSON.   We must burn her,
Before she destroys our reason. Damnable glitter.
Tappercoom, we musn't become bewildered
At our time of life. Too unusual
Not to be corrupt. Must be burnt
Immediately, burnt, burnt, Tappercoom,
Immediately.

TAPPERCOOM. Are you trying to get rid of temptation,
Tyson? A belated visit of the wanton flesh
After all these years? You've got to be dispassionate.
Calm and civilized. I am civilized.
I know, frinstance, that Beauty is not an Absolute.
Beauty is a Condition. As you might say

Hey nonny no or Hey nonny yes.
But the Law's about as absolute an Absolute—
Hello, feeling dicky, Chaplain?

> [*The* CHAPLAIN *has entered, crying.*

CHAPLAIN.   It would be
So kind if you didn't notice me. I have
Upset myself. I have no right to exist,
Not in any form, I think.

TAPPERCOOM.   I hope you won't
Think me unsociable if I don't cry myself.
What's the matter? Here's the pair of you
Dripping like newly weighed anchors.
Let the butterflies come to you, Chaplain,
Or you'll never be pollinated into a Bishop.

CHAPLAIN. No, it's right and it's just I should be cast down.
I've treated her with an abomination
That maketh desolate:—the words, the words
Are from Daniel——

TAPPERCOOM.   Hey, what's this? The young woman again?

CHAPLAIN. My patient instrument. I made my viol
Commit such sins of sound—and I didn't mind:
No, I laughed. I was trying to play a dance.
I'm too unaccomplished to play with any jollity.
I shouldn't venture beyond religious pieces.

TYSON. There's no question of jollity. We've got
To burn her, for our peace of mind.

TAPPERCOOM.   You must wait
Until to-morrow, like a reasonable chap.
And to-morrow, remember, you'll have her property
Instead of your present longing for impropriety.
And her house, now I come to think of it,

Will suit me nicely.
A large mug of small beer for both of you.
Leave it to me.

CHAPLAIN.   No, no, no,
I should become delighted again. I wish
For repentance——

Enter RICHARD.

TAPPERCOOM.   You shall have it. I'll pour it out
Myself. You'll see: it shall bring you to your knees.

CHAPLAIN. I'm too unaccomplished. I haven't the talent,
But I hoped I should see them dancing. And after all
They didn't dance——

TAPPERCOOM.   They shall, dear saint, they shall.

[*Exit* TAPPERCOOM *and the* CHAPLAIN.

RICHARD. I was to tell you, Mr. Tyson——

TYSON.   I'm not
To be found. I'm fully occupied elsewhere.
If you wish to find me I shall be in my study.
You can knock, but I shall give you no reply.
I wish to be alone with my own convictions.
Good-night.

[*Exit* TYSON. THOMAS *looks through the window.*
Enter ALIZON.

THOMAS [*to* RICHARD]. The Great Bear is looking so geometrical
One would think that something or other could be proved.
Are you sad, Richard?

RICHARD.   Certainly.

THOMAS.   I also.
I've been cast adrift on a raft of melancholy.
The night-wind passed me, like a sail across
A blind man's eye. There it is,

The interminable tumbling of the great grey
Main of moonlight, washing over
The little oyster-shell of this month of April:
Among the raven-quills of the shadows
And on the white pillows of men asleep:
The night's a boundless pastureland of peace,
And something condones the world, incorrigibly.
But what, in fact, *is* this vaporous charm?
We're softened by a nice conglomeration
Of the earth's uneven surface, refraction of light,
Obstruction of light, condensation, distance,
And that sappy upshot of self-centred vegetablism
The trees of the garden. How is it we come
To see this as a heaven in the eye?
Why should we hawk and spit out ecstasy
As though we were nightingales, and call these quite
Casual degrees and differences
Beauty? What guile recommends the world
And gives our eyes the special sense to be
Deluded, above all animals?—Stone me, Richard!
I've begun to talk like that soulless girl, and she
May at this moment be talking like me! I shall go
Back into the garden, and choke myself with the seven
Sobs I managed to bring with me from the wreck.

RICHARD. To hear her you would think her feet had almost
Left the ground. The evening which began
So blackly, now, as though it were a kettle
Set over her flame, has started to sing. And all
The time I find myself praying under my breath
That something will save her.

THOMAS.   You might do worse.
Tides turn with a similar sort of whisper.

ALIZON. Richard.

RICHARD.   Alizon!

ALIZON.   I've come to be with you.

RICHARD. Not with me. I'm the to-and-fro fellow
To-night. You have to be with Humphrey.

ALIZON.   I think
I have never met Humphrey. I have met him less
And less the more I have seen him.

THOMAS.   You will forgive me.
I was mousing for a small Dutch owl.
If it has said towoo t-wice it has said it
A thousand times.

                    [*He disappears into the garden.*

RICHARD.   Hey! Thomas—! Ah well.—
The crickets are singing well with their legs to night.

ALIZON. It sounds as though the night-air is riding
On a creaking saddle.

RICHARD.   You must go back to the others.

ALIZON. Let me stay. I'm not able to love them.
Have you forgotten what they mean to do
To-morrow?

RICHARD.   How could I forget? But there are laws
And if someone fails them——

ALIZON.   I shall run
Away from laws if laws can't live in the heart.
I shall be gone to-morrow.

RICHARD.   You make the room
Suddenly cold. Where will you go?

ALIZON.   Where
Will you come to find me?

RICHARD.   Look, you've pulled the thread
In your sleeve. Is it honest for me to believe
You would be unhappy?

ALIZON.   When?

RICHARD.   If you marry Humphrey?

ALIZON. Humphrey's a winter in my head.
But whenever my thoughts are cold and I lay them
Against Richard's name, they seem to rest
On the warm ground where summer sits
As golden as a humblebee.
So I did very little but think of you
Until I ran out of the room.

RICHARD.   Do you come to me
Because you can never love the others?

ALIZON.   Our father
God moved many lives to show you to me.
I think that is the way it must have happened.
It was complicated, but very kind.

RICHARD.   If I asked you
If you could ever love me, I should know
For certain that I was no longer rational.

ALIZON. I love you quite as much as I love St. Anthony
And rather more than I love St. John Chrysostom.

RICHARD. But putting haloes on one side, as a man
Could you love me, Alizon?

ALIZON.   I have become
A woman, Richard, because I love you. I know
I was a child three hours ago. And yet
I love you as deeply as many years could make me,
But less deeply than many years will make me.

RICHARD. I think I may never speak steadily again.
What have I done or said to make it possible
That you should love me?

ALIZON.   Everything I loved
Before has come to one meeting place in you
And you have gone out into everything I love.

RICHARD. Happiness seems to be weeping in me, as
I suppose it should, being newly born.

ALIZON. We must never leave each other now, or else
We should perplex the kindness of God.

RICHARD.   The kindness
Of God in itself is not a little perplexing.
What do we do?

ALIZON.   We cleave to each other, Richard.
That is what is proper for us to do.

RICHARD. But you were promised to Humphrey, Alizon.
And I'm hardly more than a servant here
Tied to my own apron-strings. They'll never
Let us love each other.

ALIZON.   Then they will have
To outwit all that ever went to create us.

RICHARD. So they will. I believe it. Let them storm.
We're lovers in a deep and safe place
And never lonely any more.—Alizon,
Shall we make the future, however much it roars,
Lie down with our happiness? Are you ready
To forgo custom and escape with me?

ALIZON. Shall we go now, before anyone prevents us?

RICHARD. I'll take you to the old priest who first found me.
He is as near to being my father

As putting his hand into a poor-box could make him.
He'll help us. Oh, Alizon, I so
Love you. Let yourself quietly out and wait for me
Somewhere near the gate but in a shadow.
I must fetch my savings. Are you afraid?

ALIZON.   In some
Part of me, not all; and while I wait
I can have a word with the saints Theresa and Christopher:
They may have some suggestions.

RICHARD.   Yes, do that.
Now: like a mouse.

> [*When she has gone he goes to the window.*
                 Only let me spell
No disillusion for her, safety, peace,
And a good world, as good as she has made it!

> [RICHARD *starts to fetch his money.*

Enter MARGARET.

MARGARET. Now, Richard: have you found Mr. Tyson?

RICHARD.   Yes;
He's busy with his convictions.

MARGARET.   He has no business
To be busy now. How am I to prevent
This girl, condemned as a heretic, from charming us
With gentleness, consideration and gaiety?
It makes orthodoxy seem almost irrelevant.
But I expect they would tell us the soul can be as lost
In loving-kindness as in anything else.
Well, well; we must scramble for grace as best we can.
Where is Alizon?

RICHARD.   I must—I must——

MARGARET. The poor child has gone away to cry.
  See if you can find her, will you, Richard?

RICHARD. I have to— have to——

MARGARET.   Very well. I will go
  In search of the sad little soul myself.
  Oh dear, I could do with a splendid holiday
  In a complete vacuum.

                    [*Exit* MARGARET *one way,* RICHARD, *hastily, another.*
Enter JENNET. *She seems for a moment exhausted, but crosses to the*
                window. Enter NICHOLAS *and* HUMPHREY.

NICHOLAS.   Are you tired of us?

HUMPHREY.   Why on earth
  Can't you stop following her?

NICHOLAS.   Stop following me.

JENNET. I am troubled to find Thomas Mendip.

NICHOLAS.   He's far gone—
  As mad as the nature of man.

HUMPHREY.   As rude and crude
  As an act of God. He'll burn your house.

JENNET.   So he has.—
  Are you kind to mention burning?

HUMPHREY   I beg your pardon.

NICHOLAS. Couldn't you to-morrow by some elementary spell
  Reverse the direction of the flames and make them burn down-
      wards?
  It would save you unpleasantness and increase at the same
  Time the heat below, which would please
  Equally heaven and hell.
  I feel such a tenderness for you, not only because
  I think you've bewitched my brother, which would be

A most salutary thing, but because, even more
Than other women, you carry a sense of that cavernous
Night folded in night, where Creation sleeps
And dreams of men. If only we loved each other
Down the pitshaft of love I could go
To the motive mysteries under the soul's floor.
Well drenched in damnation I should be as pure
As a limewashed wall.

HUMPHREY.   Get out!

JENNET.   He does no harm.—
Is it possible he still might make for death
Even on this open-hearted night?

HUMPHREY.   Who might?

JENNET. Thomas Mendip. He's sick of the world, but the world
Has a right to him.

HUMPHREY.   Damn Thomas Mendip.

NICHOLAS.   Nothing
Easier.

        Enter RICHARD, *upset to see his escape cut off.*

        You're just the fellow, Richard:
We need some more Canary, say five bottles
More. And before we go in, we'll drink here, privately,
To beauty and the sombre sultry waters
Where beauty haunts.

RICHARD.   I have to find—to find——

NICHOLAS. Five bottles of Canary. I'll come to the cellars
And help you bring them. Quick, before our mother
Calls us back to evaporate into duty.

           [*Exit* NICHOLAS, *taking* RICHARD *with him.*

HUMPHREY. He's right. You have bewitched me. But not by
　　brews
　　And incantations. For all I know
　　You may have had some traffic with the Devil
　　And made some sinister agreement with him
　　To your soul's cost. If so, you will agree
　　The fire is fair, as fair goes:
　　You have to burn.

JENNET.　　　　　　　It's hard enough to live
　　These last few hours as the earth deserves.
　　Do you have to remind me how soon the night
　　Will leave me unprotected, at the daylight's mercy?
　　I'm tired, trying to fight those thoughts away.

HUMPHREY. But need you? These few hours of the night
　　Might be lived in a way which wouldn't end
　　In fire. It would be insufferable
　　If you were burned before I could know you.
　　I should never sit at ease in my body again.

JENNET. Must we talk of this? All there is
　　To be said has been said, and all in a heavy sentence.
　　There's nothing to add, except a grave silence.

HUMPHREY. Listen, will you listen? There is more to say.
　　I'm able to save you, since all official action
　　Can be given official hesitation. I happen
　　To be on the Council, and a dozen reasons
　　Can be found to postpone the moment of execution:
　　Legal reasons, monetary reasons—
　　They've confiscated your property, and I can question
　　Whether your affairs may not be too disordered.
　　And once postponed, a great congestion of quibbles
　　Can be let loose over the Council table——

JENNET. Hope can break the heart, Humphrey. Hope
Can be too strong.

HUMPHREY.   But this is true: actual
As my body is. And as for that—now, impartially,
Look what I risk. If in fact you have
Done anything to undermine our fairly
Workable righteousness, and they say you have,
Then my status in both this town and the after-life
Will be gone if either suspect me of having helped you.
I have to be given a considerable reason
For risking that.

JENNET.   I fondly hope I'm beginning
To misconstrue you.

HUMPHREY.   Later on to-night
When they're all bedded-down in their beauty-sleep
I'll procure the key and come to your cell. Is that
Agreeable?

JENNET.   Is it so to you?
Aren't you building your castles in foul air?

HUMPHREY. Foul? No; it's give and take, the basis
Of all understanding.

JENNET.   You mean you give me a choice:
To sleep with you, or to-morrow to sleep with my fathers.
And if I value the gift of life,
Which, dear heaven, I do, I can scarcely refuse.

HUMPHREY. Isn't that sense?

JENNET.   Admirable sense.
Oh, why, why am I not sensible?
Oddly enough, I hesitate. Can I
So dislike being cornered by a young lecher
That I should rather die? That would be

The maniac pitch of pride. Indeed, it might
Even be sin. Can I believe my ears?
I seem to be considering heaven. And heaven,
From this angle, seems considerable.

HUMPHREY. Now, please, we're not going to confuse the soul and
    the body.
This, speaking bodily, is merely an exchange
Of compliments.

JENNET.   And surely throwing away
My life for the sake of pride would seem to heaven
A bodily blasphemy, a suicide?

HUMPHREY. Even if heaven were interested. Or even
If you cared for heaven. Am I unattractive to you?

JENNET. Except that you have the manners of a sparrowhawk,
With less reason, no, you are not. But even so
I no more run to your arms than I wish to run
To death. I ask myself why. Surely I'm not
Mesmerized by some snake of chastity?

HUMPHREY. This isn't the time——

JENNET.   Don't speak, contemptible boy,
I'll tell you: I am not. We have
To look elsewhere—for instance, into my heart
Where recently I heard begin
A bell of longing which calls no one to church.
But need that, ringing anyway in vain,
Drown the milkmaid singing in my blood
And freeze into the tolling of my knell?
That would be pretty, indeed, but unproductive.
No, it's not that.

HUMPHREY.   Jennet, before they come
And interrupt us——

JENNET.   I am interested
  In my feelings. I seem to wish to have some importance
  In the play of time. If not,
  Then sad was my mother's pain, my breath, my bones,
  My web of nerves, my wondering brain,
  To be shaped and quickened with such anticipation
  Only to feed the swamp of space.
  What is deep, as love is deep, I'll have
  Deeply. What is good, as love is good,
  I'll have well. Then if time and space
  Have any purpose, I shall belong to it.
  If not, if all is a pretty fiction
  To distract the cherubim and seraphim
  Who so continually do cry, the least
  I can do is to fill the curled shell of the world
  With human deep-sea sound, and hold it to
  The ear of God, until he has appetite
  To taste our salt sorrow on his lips.
  And so you see it might be better to die.
  Though, on the other hand, I admit it might
  Be immensely foolish.—Listen! What
  Can all that thundering from the cellars be?

HUMPHREY. I don't know at all. You're simply playing for time.
  Why can't you answer me, before I'm thrown
  By the bucking of my pulse, before Nicholas
  Interrupts us? Will it be all right?

JENNET. Doesn't my plight seem pitiable to you?

HUMPHREY. Pitiable, yes. It makes me long for you
  Intolerably. Now, be a saint, and tell me
  I may come to your cell.

JENNET.   I wish I could believe

My freedom was not in the flames. O God, I wish
The ground would open.

[THOMAS *climbs in through the window.*

THOMAS.   Allow me to open it for you.
Admit I was right. Man's a mistake.
Lug-worms, the lot of us.

HUMPHREY.   Wipe your filthy boots
Before you start trespassing.

THOMAS.   And as for you
I'll make you the climax to my murders.
You can die a martyr to the cause
Of bureaucratic pollution.

JENNET.   Oh dear,
Is this lug-worms at war? And by what right, will you tell me,
Do you come moralizing in, dictating
What I should do?

THOMAS.   Woman, what are you saying?
Are you trying to tell me you'd even consider——

JENNET. I might prefer the dragon to St. George.

HUMPHREY. If he wants to fight me, let him. Come out into the
  garden.
If he kills me
Remember I thought you unfairly beautiful
And, to balance your sins, you should be encouraged
To spend your beauty in a proper way,
On someone who knows its worth.

THOMAS. Sound the trumpets!

JENNET.   Yes, why not? And a roll

Of drums. You, if you remember, failed
Even to give me a choice. You have only said
'Die, woman, and look as though you liked it.'
So you'll agree this can hardly be said to concern you.

THOMAS. All right! You've done your worst. You force me to
  tell you
The disastrous truth. I love you. A misadventure
So intolerable, hell could not do more.
Nothing in the world could touch me
And you have to come and be the damnable
Exception. I was nicely tucked up for the night
Of eternity, and, like a restless dream
Of a fool's paradise, you, with a rainbow where
Your face is and an *ignis fatuus*
Worn like a rose in your girdle, come pursued
By fire, and presto! the bedclothes are on the floor
And I, the tomfool, love you. Don't say again
That this doesn't concern me, or I shall say
That you needn't concern yourself with to-morrow's burning.

                          Enter NICHOLAS.

NICHOLAS. Do you know what that little bastard Richard did?
  He locked me in the cellars.

THOMAS.   Don't complicate
  The situation.—I love you, perfectly knowing
  You're nothing but a word out of the mouth
  Of that same planet of almighty blemish
  Which I long to leave. But the word so sings
  With an empty promise.—I shall lie in my grave
  With my hands clapped over my ears, to stop your music
  From riddling me as much as the meddling worms.
  Still, that's beside the point. We have to settle
  This other matter——

NICHOLAS.   Yes, I was telling you.
I went into the cellars to get the wine,
And the door swung after me, and that little son
Of a crossbow turned the key——

THOMAS [*to* JENNET].   Can we find somewhere
To talk where there isn't quite so much insect life?

NICHOLAS. And there I was, in cobwebs up to my armpits,
Hammering the door and yelling like a slaughter-house,
Until the cook came and let me out. Where is he?

JENNET. What should we talk of? You mean to be hanged.
Am I to understand that your tongue-tied dust
Will slip a ring on the finger of my ashes
And we'll both die happily ever after? Surely
The other suggestion, though more conventional,
Has fewer flaws?

THOMAS.   But you said, like a ray of truth
Itself, that you'd rather burn.

JENNET.   My heart, my mind
Would rather burn. But may not the casting vote
Be with my body? And is the body necessarily
Always ill-advised?

NICHOLAS.   Something has happened
Since I made the descent into those hellish cobwebs.
I'm adrift. What is it?

THOMAS.   Let me speak to her.
You've destroyed my defences, the laborious contrivance
Of hours, the precious pair of you. O Jennet,
Jennet, you should have let me go, before
I confessed a word of this damned word love. I'll not
Reconcile myself to a dark world
For the sake of five-feet six of wavering light,

For the sake of a woman who goes no higher
Than my bottom lip.

NICHOLAS.   I'll strip and fly my shirt
At the masthead unless someone picks me up.
What has been going on?

THOMAS.   Ask that neighing
Horse-box-kicker there, your matchless brother.

NICHOLAS. Ah, Humphrey darling, have there been
Some official natural instincts?

HUMPHREY.   I've had enough.
The whole thing's become unrecognizable.

JENNET [*to* THOMAS]. Have I a too uncertain virtue to keep you
On the earth?

THOMAS.   I ask nothing, nothing. Stop
Barracking my heart. Save yourself
His way if you must. There will always be
Your moment of hesitation, which I shall chalk
All over the walls of purgatory. Never mind
That, loving you, I've trodden the garden threadbare
Completing a way to save you.

JENNET.   If you saved me
Without wishing to save yourself, you might have saved
Your trouble.

NICHOLAS.   I imagine it's all over with us, Humphrey.
I shall go and lie with my own thoughts
And conceive reciprocity. Come on, you boy of gloom.
The high seas for us.

HUMPHREY.   Oh go and drown yourself
And me with you.

NICHOLAS.   There's no need to drown.
We'll take the tails off mermaids.

Enter MARGARET.

MARGARET.   Have any of you
  Seen that poor child Alizon? I think
  She must be lost.

NICHOLAS.   Who isn't? The best
  Thing we can do is to make wherever we're lost in
  Look as much like home as we can. Now don't
  Be worried. She can't be more lost than she was with us.

HUMPHREY. I can't marry her, mother. Could you think
  Of something else to do with her?
  I'm going to bed.

NICHOLAS.   I think Humphrey has been
  Improperly making a proper suggestion, mother.
  He wishes to be drowned.

MARGARET [*to* THOMAS].   They find it impossible
  To concentrate. Have you seen the little
  Fair-haired girl?

NICHOLAS.   He wishes to be hanged.

MARGARET [*to* JENNET]. Have you hidden the child?

NICHOLAS.   She wishes to be burned
  Rather than sleep with my brother.

MARGARET.   She should be thankful
  She can sleep at all. For years I have woken up
  Every quarter of an hour. I must sit down.
  I'm too tired to know what anyone's saying.

JENNET. I think none of us knows where to look for Alizon.
  Or for anything else. But shall we, while we wait
  For news of her, as two dispirited women
  Ask this man to admit he did no murders?

THOMAS. You think not?

JENNET.   I know. There was a soldier,
Discharged and centreless, with a towering pride
In his sensibility, and an endearing
Disposition to be a hero, who wanted
To make an example of himself to all
Erring mankind, and falling in with a witch-hunt
His good heart took the opportunity
Of providing a diversion. O Thomas,
It was very theatrical of you to choose the gallows.

THOMAS. Mother, we won't listen to this girl.
She is jealous, because of my intimate relations
With damnation. But damnation knows
I love her.

RICHARD [*appearing in the doorway*]. We have come back.

NICHOLAS. I want to talk to you. Who locked me in the cellars?

MARGARET [*as* ALIZON *enters*]. Alizon, where have you been?

ALIZON.   We had to come back.

MARGARET. Back? From where?

RICHARD.   We came across old Skipps.

ALIZON. We were running away. We wanted to be happy.

NICHOLAS. Skipps?

HUMPHREY.   The body of old Skipps? We'd better
Find Tappercoom.

                                    [*Exit* HUMPHREY.

MARGARET.   Alizon, what do you mean,
Running away?

RICHARD.   He is rather drunk. Shall I bring him
In? He had been to see his daughter.

JENNET [*to* THOMAS]. Who
Will trouble to hang you now? [*She goes up the stairs.*

THOMAS [*calling after her*]. He couldn't lie quiet
Among so many bones. He had to come back
To fetch his barrow.

TAPPERCOOM [*entering with* HUMPHREY]. What's all this I'm told?
I was hoping to hang on my bough for the rest of the evening
Ripe and undisturbed. What is it? Murder
Not such a fabrication after all?

ALIZON. We had to come back, you see, because nobody now
Will be able to burn her.

RICHARD. Nobody now will be able
To say she turned him into a dog. Come in,
Mr. Skipps.

Enter SKIPPS, *unsteady.*

TAPPERCOOM. It looks uncommonly to me
As though someone has been tampering with the evidence.
Where's Tyson? I'm too amiable to-night
To controvert any course of events whatsoever.

SKIPPS. Your young gentleman says Come in, so I comes in.
Youse only has to say muck off, and I goes, wivout argument.

TAPPERCOOM. Splendid, of course. Are you the rag-and-bone
merchant of this town, name of Matthew Skipps?

SKIPPS. Who give me that name? My granfathers and gran-
mothers and all in authrority undrim. Baptized I blaming was,
and I says to youse, baptized I am, and I says to youse, baptized
I will be, wiv holy weeping and washing of teeth. And immer-
sion upon us miserable offenders. Miserable offenders all—no
offence meant. And if any of youse is not a miserable offender, as
he's told to be by almighty and mercerable God, then I says to
him Hands off my daughter, you bloody-minded heathen.

TAPPERCOOM. All right, all right——

SKIPPS. And I'm not quarrelling, mind; I'm not quarrelling. Peace on earth and good tall women. And give us our trespassers as trespassers will be prosecuted for us. I'm not perfect, mind. But I'm as good a miserable offender as any man here present, ladies excepted.

THOMAS. Here now, Matt, aren't you forgetting yourself? You're dead: you've been dead for hours.

SKIPPS. Dead, am I? I has the respect to ask you to give me coabberation of that. I says mucking liar to nobody. But I seen my daughter three hours back, and she'd have said fair and to my face Dad, you're dead. She don't stand for no nonsense.

NICHOLAS. The whole town knows it, Skipps, old man. You've been dead since this morning.

SKIPPS. Dead. Well, you take my breaf away. Do I begin to stink, then?

HUMPHREY. You do.

SKIPPS. Fair enough. That's coabberation. I'm among the blessed saints.

TAPPERCOOM. He floats in the heaven of the grape. Someone take him home to his hovel.

SKIPPS [*roaring*]. Alleluia! Alleluia! Alleluia!

TAPPERCOOM. Now, stop that, Skipps. Keep your hosannas for the cold light of morning or we shall lock you up.

SKIPPS. Alleluia!

TAPPERCOOM. He'll wake your guests and spoil their pleasure. They're all sitting half sunk in a reef of collars. Even the dear good Chaplain has taken so many glassesful of repentance he's almost unconscious of the existence of sin.

SKIPPS. Glory, amen! Glory, glory, amen, amen!

MARGARET. Richard will take this old man home. Richard—
Where is Richard? Where is Alizon?
Have they gone again?

NICHOLAS.   Yes; Humphrey's future wife,
Blown clean away.

MARGARET.   Yes; that's all very well;
But she mustn't think she can let herself be blown
Away whenever she likes.

THOMAS.   What better time
Than when she likes?

SKIPPS.   As it was in the beginning,
Ever and ever, amen, al-leluia!

MARGARET. Take the old man to his home. Now that you've
made him
Think he's dead we shall never have any peace.

HUMPHREY. Nor shall we when he's gone.

NICHOLAS. Spread your wings, Matthew; we're going to teach
you to fly.

SKIPPS. I has the respect to ask to sit down. Youse blessed saints
Don't realize: it takes it out of you, this life everlasting. Alleluia!

NICHOLAS.   Come on.
Your second wind can blow where no one listens.

                    [*Exeunt* HUMPHREY, NICHOLAS, *and* SKIPPS.

TAPPERCOOM. That's more pleasant.
What was the thread, now, which the rascal broke?
Do I have to collect my thoughts any further?

MARGARET.   Yes:
Or I must. That poor child Alizon

Is too young to go throwing herself under the wheels
Of happiness. She should have wrapped up warmly first.
Hebble must know, in any case. I must tell him,
Though he's locked himself in, and only blows his nose
When I knock.

TAPPERCOOM.   Yes, get him on to a horse;
It will do him good.

MARGARET.   Hebble on a horse is a man
Delivered neck and crop to the will of God.
But he'll have to do it.

                                        [*Exit* MARGARET.

TAPPERCOOM.   Ah yes, he'll have to do it.
He's a dear little man.—What's to be the end of you?
I take it the male prisoner is sufficiently
Deflated not to plague us with his person
Any longer?

THOMAS.   Deflated? I'm overblown
With the knowledge of my villainy.

TAPPERCOOM.   Your guilt, my boy,
Is a confounded bore.

THOMAS.   Then let it bore me to extinction.

                        [JENNET *returns, wearing her own dress.*

TAPPERCOOM. The woman prisoner may notice, without
My mentioning it, that there's a certain mildness
In the night, a kind of somnolent inattention.
If she wishes to return to her cell, no one
Can object. On the other hand—How very empty
The streets must be just now.—You will forgive
A yawn in an overworked and elderly man.—

The moon is full, of course. To leave the town
Unobserved, one would have to use caution. As for me
I shall go and be a burden to my bed.
Good night.

JENNET.   Good night.

THOMAS.   Good night.

[*Exit* TAPPERCOOM.

THOMAS.   So much for me.

JENNET.   Thomas, only another
Fifty years or so and then I promise
To let you go.

THOMAS.   Do you see those roofs and spires?
There sleep hypocrisy, porcous pomposity, greed,
Lust, vulgarity, cruelty, trickery, sham
And all possible nitwittery—are you suggesting fifty
Years of that?

JENNET.   I was only suggesting fifty
Years of me.

THOMAS.   Girl, you haven't changed the world.
Glimmer as you will, the world's not changed.
I love you, but the world's not changed. Perhaps
I could draw you up over my eyes for a time
But the world sickens me still.

JENNET.   And do you think
Your gesture of death is going to change it? Except
For me.

THOMAS. Oh, the unholy mantrap of love!

JENNET. I have put on my own gown again,
But otherwise everything that is familiar,
My house, my poodle, peacock, and possessions,

I have to leave. The world is looking frozen
And forbidding under the moon; but I must be
Out of this town before daylight comes, and somewhere,
Who knows where, begin again.

THOMAS.   Brilliant!
So you fall back on the darkness to defeat me.
You gamble on the possibility
That I was well-brought-up. And, of course, you're right.
I have to see you home, though neither of us
Knows where on earth it is.

JENNET.   Thomas, can you mean to let
The world go on?

THOMAS.   I know my limitations.
When the landscape goes to seed, the wind is obsessed
By to-morrow.

JENNET.   I shall have to hurry.
That was the pickaxe voice of a cock, beginning
To break up the night. Am I an inconvenience
To you?

THOMAS.   As inevitably as original sin.
And I shall be loath to forgo one day of you,
Even for the sake of my ultimate friendly death.

JENNET. I am friendly too.

THOMAS.   Then let me wish us both
Good morning.—And God have mercy on our souls.

THE CURTAIN FALLS

A SLEEP OF PRISONERS

A Play

To

ROBERT GITTINGS

Dear Robert

    *It is nineteen years this summer since you persuaded me
to take a holiday from my full-time failure to make a
living, and sat me down, with a typewriter and a barrel of
beer, in the empty rectory at Thorn St. Margaret. I had
written almost nothing for five or six years, and I was to
write almost nothing again for five years following, but the
two months we spent at Thorn, two months (it seems to me
now) of continuous blazing sunshine, increased in me the
hope that one day the words would come. It was all very
well that I should look obstinately forward to plays which
I showed no sign of writing. It was an extraordinary faith
which made you also look obstinately forward to them.
The ten years in which you loyally thought of me as a
writer when clearly I wasn't, your lectures to me on my
self-defensive mockery of artists, and those two leisure
months under the Quantocks, were things of friendship
which kept me in a proper mind.*

    *We were talking even then, as we are talking, with
greater instancy, now, of the likelihood of war. And I
think we realized then, as we certainly now believe, that
progress is the growth of vision: the increased perception
of what makes for life and what makes for death. I have
tried, as you know, not altogether successfully, to find a
way for comedy to say something of this, since comedy is
an essential part of men's understanding. In A Sleep of
Prisoners I have tried to make a more simple statement,
though in a complicated design where each of four men is
seen through the sleeping thoughts of the others, and each,
in his own dream, speaks as at heart he is, not as he
believes himself to be. In the later part of Corporal Adams'
dream the dream changes to a state of thought entered into
by all the sleeping men, as though, sharing their prison life,
they shared, for a few moments of the night, their sleeping
life also.*

C.

A SLEEP OF PRISONERS

First performed in Oxford at the University Church on 23 April 1951 and in London at St. Thomas's Church, Regent Street, on 15 May 1951 with the following cast:

Private David King	LEONARD WHITE
Private Peter Able	DENHOLM ELLIOTT
Private Tim Meadows	HUGH PRYSE
Corporal Joe Adams	STANLEY BAKER

The play was produced by Michael MacOwan

CHARACTERS

PRIVATE DAVID KING

PRIVATE PETER ABLE

PRIVATE TIM MEADOWS

CORPORAL JOE ADAMS

The interior of a church, turned into a prison camp. One prisoner, PETER ABLE, *is in the organ loft, playing 'Now the day is over' with one finger. Another,* DAVID KING, *is looking at the memorial tablets on the wall. Four double bunks stand between the choir-stalls. A pile of straw and a pile of empty paillasses are on the chancel steps.*

DAVID [*shouting up to the organ loft*]. Hey, Pete, come down and tell me what this Latin
  Says. If it's Latin.

PETER [*still playing*]. Why, what for?

DAVID. For the sake of that organ. And because I want to know
  If 'Hic jacet' means what it looks like.

                [PETER *changes the tune to 'Three Blind Mice'.*
[*In a flash of temper.*]
  And because I said so, that's what for, because
  I said so! And because you're driving me potty.

PETER. Excuse me a minute: this is the difficult bit.

DAVID. If you want it difficult, go on playing. I swear
  I'll come up there and put my foot through you.

      [*As the playing goes on* DAVID *suddenly howls like a dog and starts tearing up a hymn-book.*

PETER [*the playing over*]. It's the universal language, Dave. It's
  music.

DAVID. Music my universal aunt. It's torture.
      [*He finds himself with a page or two of the hymn-book in his hand.*
  Here, I know this one.
  [*Sings.*] 'All things bright and beautiful——'

PETER [*coming down from the loft*]. That doesn't mean you, Davy.
  Put it down.

DAVID. 'All creatures great and small—'
  Well, one of those is me: I couldn't miss it.
  'All things wise and wonderful——'

> [CORPORAL JOE ADAMS *comes to the steps with more straw.*

ADAMS. Come and get it!

PETER   What is it? Soup?

ADAMS.   Straw.

PETER. Never could digest it.

> [TIM MEADOWS, *a middle-aged man—indeed he looks well
> on towards sixty—limps up to the pile of straw.*

ADAMS. How's the leg feel, Meadows?

MEADOWS.   Ah, all right.
  I wouldn't be heard saying anything about one leg
  I wouldn't say about the other.

PETER.   Where
  Did you get it, chum?

MEADOWS.   I had it for my birthday.
  Quite nice, isn't it? Five toes, it's got.

PETER. I mean where was the fighting, you wit?

MEADOWS [*jerking his head*].   Down the road.
  My Uncle George had a thumping wooden leg,
  Had it with him, on and off, for years.
  When he gave up the world, it got out in the wash house.

DAVID. Has anybody thought what it's going to be like
  Suppose we stay here for months or years?

ADAMS. Best they can do. You heard the towzer Commandant:
  'All more buildings blow up into sky.
  No place like home now. Roof here. Good and kind
  To prisoners. Keep off sun, keep off rain.'

PETER. Keep off the grass.

DAVID. It's a festering idea for a prison camp.
You have to think twice every time you think,
In case what you think's a bit on the dubious side.
It's all this smell of cooped-up angels
Worries me.

PETER.   What, us?

DAVID.   Not mother's angels,
Dumb-cluck, God's angels.

PETER.   Oh yes, them.
We're a worse fug to them, I shouldn't wonder.
We shall just have to make allowances.

DAVID.   Beg pardon:
I'm talking to no-complaints Pete: arrangements perfect.

ADAMS. Too many pricking thistles in this straw:
Pricked to hell.

                    [PETER *has wandered across to the lectern.*

PETER.   Note his early perpendicular
Language. Ecclesiastical influence.
See this? They've put us an English Bible.
There's careful nannies for you . . . 'These were the sons
Of Caleb the son of Hur, the firstborn of Ephratah:
Shobal the father of Kirjath-jearim, Salma
The father of Beth-lehem, Hareph the father
Of Beth-gader. And Shobal the father of Kirjath-
Jearim had sons: Haroeh, and half of the Manahethites——'
Interesting, isn't it?

DAVID.   Stuff it, Pete.

PETER. 'And these were the sons of David, which were born unto
Him in Hebron: the firstborn Amnon, of Ahinoam the

Jezreelitess: the second Daniel, of Abigail the
Carmelitess: the third Absalom the son of Maacah the
Daughter of Talmai king of Geshur: the fourth Adonijah
The son of Haggith: the fifth Shephatiah of Abital:
The sixth Ithream by Eglah his wife . . .'

Doing

All right, aren't you, Davey?

DAVID. So I did in Sunday school. You know what Absalom
Said to the tree? 'You're getting in my hair.'
And that's what I mean, so shut up.

PETER.   Shut up we are.
Don't mind me. I'm making myself at home.
Now all I've got to do is try the pulpit.

ADAMS. Watch yourself, Pete. We've got years of this.

DAVID [*his temper growing*]. Any damn where he makes himself at
home.
The world blows up, there's Pete there in the festering
Bomb-hole making cups of tea. I've had it
Week after week till I'm sick. Don't let's mind
What happens to anybody, don't let's object to anything,
Let's give the dirty towzers a cigarette,
There's nothing on earth worth getting warmed up about!
It doesn't matter who's on top, make yourself at home.

ADAMS. Character of Private Peter Able:
And not so far out at that. What we're in for
We've got to be in for and know just what it is.
Have some common sense, Pete. If you're looking for trouble
Go and have it in the vestry.

PETER [*up in the pulpit*]. How can I help it if I can't work myself up
About the way things go? It's a mystery to me.
We've had all this before. For God's sake

Be reasonable, Dave. Perhaps I was meant
To be a bishop.
[*He turns to the nave.*] Dearly beloved brothers
In a general muck-up, towzers included . . .

DAVID. What the hell do you think we're stuck here for
Locked in like lunatics? Just for a nice
New experience, with nice new friends
With nice new rifles to look after us?
We're at war with them, aren't we? And if we are
They're no blaming use!

PETER [*continuing to preach*]. We have here on my left
An example of the bestial passions that beset mankind.

> [DAVID, *beside himself, leaps up the steps and attacks* PETER
> *in the pulpit.*

Davey, Dave . . . don't be a lunatic!

ADAMS.   Come out of it,
King. Come down here, you great tomfool!

> [*He goes to drag* DAVID *away.* DAVID *has his hands on*
> PETER's *throat and has pushed him across the edge of the*
> *pulpit.*

DAVID [*raging*]. You laugh: I'll see you never laugh again.
Go on: laugh at this.

MEADOWS.   If you don't get your hands away
You'll wish you never had 'em. Give over! Give over!

> [DAVID *releases his hold. He pushes past* ADAMS *and comes*
> *down from the pulpit.*

I see the world in you very well. 'Tisn't
Your meaning, but you're a clumsy, wall-eyed bulldozer.
You don't know what you're hitting.

> [DAVID *goes past him without a word, and throws himself on*
> *to his bed.*

                                      Ah, well,
Neither do I, of course, come to that.

ADAMS. All right, Peter?

PETER.   Think so, Corporal,
I'm not properly reassembled yet.
There's a bit of a rattle, but I think I had that before.

ADAMS. Dave had better damp down that filthy volcano
Or let me know what.

PETER.   Oh, lord, I don't know,
It's who we happen to be. I suppose I'd better
Hit him back some time, or else he'll go mad
Trying to make me see daylight. I don't know.
I'll tell you my difficulty, Corp. I never remember
I ought to be fighting until I'm practically dead.
Sort of absent-fisted. Very worrying for Dave.

> [*They have come down from the pulpit.* PETER *sways on his
> feet.* ADAMS *supports him.*

ADAMS. You're all in, Pete.

PETER.   Say 'Fall out' and watch me
Fall.

ADAMS. All right, come on, we'll put you to bed.

> [MEADOWS *has limped across with two blankets for* PETER'S
> *bunk.* DAVID *is watching anxiously.*

DAVID. What's wrong, Pete?

ADAMS.   The best thing for you is keep
Out of this.

PETER.   Dog-tired, that's all. It comes
Of taking orders. Dog collar too tight.

DAVID. I'll see to him.

ADAMS. I've seen you see to him.
Get back on your bed.

DAVID. I've never killed him yet.
I'm a pal of his.

ADAMS. That's right. I couldn't have expressed it
Better myself. We'll talk about that tomorrow.

> [*He goes over to make up his own bunk.* DAVID *unlaces*
> PETER'*s boots.*

DAVID. How d'you feel now, Pete?

PETER. Beautiful.

DAVID. Why don't
You do some slaughtering sometimes? Why always
Leave it to me? Got no blood you can heat
Up or something? I didn't hurt you, did I,
Pete? How d'you feel?

PETER [*almost asleep*]. Um? Fine.

DAVID [*taking off* PETER'*s socks for him*]. The world's got to have
us. Things go wrong.
We've got to finish the dirty towzers. It's been
A festering day, and I'm stinking tired. See you
Tomorrow.

> [*He leaves* PETER *sleeping, goes over to his own bunk, and*
> *throws himself down.*

ADAMS [*to* MEADOWS]. I sometimes feel a bit like Dave
Myself, about Pete. You have to tell him there's a war on.

> [MEADOWS *has taken his boots and socks off and is lying on*
> *top of his blankets.*

MEADOWS. Sometimes I think if it wasn't for the words, Corporal,
I should be very given to talking. There's things
To be said which would surprise us if ever we said them.

ADAMS. Don't give us any more surprises, for God's sake.

MEADOWS. There's things would surprise us.

ADAMS [*studying the sole of his foot*]. Like the size of that blister.

MEADOWS. Or even bigger. Well, good night, Corporal.

ADAMS. G'night, boy.

MEADOWS.   I'm old enough to be
Your father.

ADAMS.   I thought you might be. How did you get
Pulled in on this?

MEADOWS.   I thought I would.
I got in under the fence. Not a soul
At the War Office had noticed me being born.
I'd only my mother's word for it myself,
And she never knew whether it was Monday washing-day
Or Thursday baking-day. She only knew
I made it hindering awkward.

ADAMS.   Are you glad
You came?

MEADOWS. Ah, now. Well,
Glad, yes, and sorry, yes, and so as that.
I remember how it came over me, as I
Was dunging a marrow bed. Tim, I said to me—
'Cos being a widower I do the old lady's
Talking for her, since she fell silent—Tim,
You're in the way to curse. Thinking of the enemy
And so as that. And I cursed up and about.
But cursing never made anything for a man yet.

So having had the pleasure of it, I came along
To take a hand. But there's strange divisions in us,
And in every man, one side or the other.
When I'm not too good I hear myself talking away
Like Tim Meadows M.P., at the other end of my head.
Sounds all right. I'd like to know what I say.
Might be interesting.

ADAMS.   I shouldn't worry.
I'm going to take a last look at Pete.
G'night, boy.

MEADOWS [*already almost asleep*]. Hope so.

                  [ADAMS *goes over to* PETER's *bunk.*

DAVID.   Corp.

ADAMS. Hullo.

DAVID.   How long are we here for?

ADAMS.   A million years.
So you'd better get to like it.

DAVID.   Give us
Cassock and surplice drill tomorrow, Joe.

ADAMS. O.K. Wash your feet.

DAVID.   How's Pete? Asleep?

ADAMS. Couldn't be more if he died.

DAVID [*starting up on his elbow*].   What do you mean?

ADAMS. I mean he's breathing like an easy conscience. Why don't
    you
Get down to it yourself? There's tomorrow to come,
According to orders. Good night, King of Israel.

DAVID.   Oh, go
And discard yourself. G'night, Corporal Joseph Adams.

    [ADAMS *goes to his bunk.* MEADOWS *turns in his sleep. The church clock strikes a single note.*

MEADOWS [*asleep*]. Who's that, fallen out? How many men?
How many? I said only one.
One was enough.
No, no, no. I didn't ask to be God.
No one else prepared to spell the words.
Spellbound. B-o-u-n-d. Ah-h-h-h . . .

    [*He turns in his sleep again.*

It's old Adam, old, old, old Adam.
Out of bounds. No one said fall out.
What time did you go to bad?
Sorrow, Adam, stremely sorrow.

    [CORPORAL ADAMS *comes towards him, a dream figure.*

Adam, Adam, stand easy there.

ADAMS. Reporting for duty, sir.

MEADOWS. As you were, Adam.

ADAMS. No chance of that, sir.

MEADOWS. As you were, as you were.

ADAMS. Lost all track of it now, sir.

MEADOWS. How far back was it, Adam?

ADAMS [*with a jerk of the head*]. Down the road. Too dark to see.

MEADOWS. Were you alone?

ADAMS.   A woman with me, sir.

MEADOWS. I said Let there be love,
And there wasn't enough light, you say?

ADAMS. We could see our own shapes, near enough,
But not the road. The road kept on dividing
Every yard or so. Makes it long.
We expected nothing like it, sir.
Ill-equipped, naked as the day,
It was all over and the world was on us
Before we had time to take cover.

MEADOWS. Stand at peace, Adam: do stand at peace.

ADAMS. There's nothing of that now, sir.

MEADOWS. Corporal Adam.

ADAMS.   Sir?

MEADOWS.   You have shown spirit.

ADAMS. Thank you, sir.
Excuse me, sir, but there's some talk of a future.
I've had no instructions.

MEADOWS [*turning in his sleep*]. Ah-h-h-h-h.

ADAMS. Is there any immediate anxiety of that?

          [DAVID, *as the dream figure of Cain, stands leaning on the
          lectern, chewing at a beet.*

How far can we fall back, sir?

DAVID [*smearing his arms with beet juice*]. Have you lost something?

ADAMS. Yes, Cain: yes, I have.

DAVID. Have you felt in all your pockets?

ADAMS. Yes, and by searchlight all along the grass
For God knows howling. Not a sign,
Not a sign, boy, not a ghost.

DAVID.   When do you last
Remember losing it?

ADAMS.   When I knew it was mine.
As soon as I knew it was mine I felt
I was the only one who didn't know
My host.

DAVID.   Poor overlooked
Old man. Allow me to make the introduction.
God: man. Man: God.

> [PETER, *the dream figure of Abel, is in the organ-loft finger-*
> *ing out 'Now the day is over'*.

ADAMS. I wish it could be so easy.

DAVID. Sigh, sigh, sigh!
The hot sun won't bring you out again
If you don't know how to behave.
Pretty much like mutiny. I'd like to remind you
We're first of all men, and complain afterwards.
[*Calling*.] Abel! Abel! Hey, flock-headed Peter,
Come down off those mountains.
Those bleating sheep can look after themselves.
Come on down.

PETER.   What for?

DAVID.   Because I said so!

PETER [*coming down*]. I overlooked the time. Is it day or night?

DAVID. You don't deserve to inherit the earth.
Am I supposed to carry the place alone?

PETER. Where will you carry it?
Where do you think you're going to take it to,
This prolific indifference?
Show me an ending great enough
To hold the passion of this beginning
And raise me to it.

Day and night, the sun and moon
Spirit us, we wonder where. Meanwhile
Here we are, we lean on our lives
Expecting purpose to keep her date,
Get cold waiting, watch the overworlds
Come and go, question the need to stay
But do, in an obstinate anticipation of love.
Ah, love me, it's a long misuse of breath
For boys like us. When do we start?

DAVID. When you suffering god'sbodies
Come to your senses. What you'll do
Is lose us life altogether.
Amply the animal is Cain, thank God,
As he was meant to be: a huskular strapling
With all his passions about him. Tomorrow
Will know him well. Momentous doings
Over the hill for the earth and us.
What hell else do you want?

PETER.   The justification.

DAVID. Oh, bulls and bears to that.
The word's too long to be lived.
Just if, just if, is as far as ever you'll see.

PETER. What's man to be?

DAVID.   Content and full.

PETER. That's modest enough.
What an occupation for eternity.
Sky's hollow filled as far as for ever
With rolling light: place without limit,
Time without pity:
And did you say all for the sake of our good condition,
All for our two-footed prosperity?

Well, we should prosper, considering
The torment squandered on our prospering.
From squid to eagle the ravening is on.
We are all pain-fellows, but nothing you dismay,
Man is to prosper. Other lives, forbear
To blame me, great and small forgive me
If to your various agonies
My light should seem hardly enough
To be the cause of the ponderable shadow.

DAVID. Who do you think you are, so Angel-sick?
Pain warns us to be master: pain prefers us.
Draws us up.

PETER.   Water into the sun:
All the brooding clouds of us!

DAVID.   All right.
We'll put it to the High and Mighty.
Play you dice to know who's favoured.

PETER. What's he to do with winning?

DAVID.   Play you dice.
Not so sure of yourself, I notice.

PETER. I'll play you. Throw for first throw.
Now creation be true to creatures.

ADAMS. Look, sir, my sons are playing.
How silent the spectators are,
World, air, and water.
Eyes bright, tension, halt.
Still as a bone from here to the sea.

DAVID [*playing*]. Ah-h-h-h!

ADAMS. Sir, my sons are playing. Cain's your man.
   He goes in the mould of passion as you made him.
   He can walk this broken world as easily
   As I and Eve the ivory light of Eden.
   I recommend him. The other boy
   Frets for what never came his way,
   Will never reconcile us to our exile.
   Look, sir, my sons are playing.
   Sir, let the future plume itself, not suffer.

PETER [*playing*]. How's that for a nest of singing birds?

ADAMS. Cain sweats: Cain gleams. Now do you see him?
   He gives his body to the game.
   Sir, he's your own making, and has no complaints.

DAVID. Ah! What are you doing to me, heaven and earth?

PETER. Friendly morning.

DAVID [*shaking the dice*]. Numbers, be true to nature.
                    Deal me high,
                    Six dark stars
                    Come into my sky.

                                        [*He throws.*

   Blight! What's blinding me
   By twos and threes? I'm strong, aren't I?
   Who's holding me down? Who's frozen my fist
   So it can't hatch the damn dice out?

PETER [*shaking and throwing*].
                    Deal me high, deal me low.
                    Make my deeds
                    My nameless needs.
                    I know I do not know.
   ... That brings me home!

                    [DAVID *roars with rage and disappointment.*

DAVID. Life is a hypocrite if I can't live
   The way it moves me! I was trusted
   Into breath. Why am I doubted now?
   Flesh is my birthplace. Why shouldn't I speak the tongue?
   What's the disguise, eh? Who's the lurcher
   First enjoys us, then disowns us?
   Keep me clean of God, creation's crooked.

ADAMS. Cain, steady, steady, you'll raise the world.

DAVID. You bet your roots I will.
   I'll know what game of hide and seek this is.
   Half and half, my petering brother says,
   Nothing of either, in and out the limbo.
   'I know I do not know' he says.
   So any lion can BE, and any ass,
   And any cockatoo: and all the unbiddable
   Roaming voices up and down
   Can live their lives and welcome
   While I go pestered and wondering down hill
   Like a half-wit angel strapped to the back of a mule.
   Thanks! I'll be as the body was first presumed.

PETER. It was a game between us, Cain.

DAVID [*in a fury*]. Your dice were weighted! You thought you
   could trick
   The life out of me. We'll see about that.
   You think you're better than you're created!
   I saw the smiles that went between
   You and the top air. I knew your game.
   Look helpless, let him see you're lost,
   Make him amiable to think
   He made more strangely than he thought he did!
   Get out of time, will you, get out of time!

       [*He takes* PETER *by the throat.* ADAMS *goes to part them.*

ADAMS. Cain, drop those hands!

> [*He is wheeled by an unknown force back against his bunk.*

O Sir,

Let me come to them. They're both
Out of my reach. I have to separate them.

DAVID [*strangling* PETER]. You leave us now, leave us, you half-
   and-half:
I want to be free of you!

PETER.   Cain! Cain!

ADAMS. Cain, Cain!

DAVID.   If life's not good enough for you
Go and justify yourself!

ADAMS. Pinioned here, when out of my body
I made them both, the fury and the suffering,
The fury, the suffering, the two ways
Which here spreadeagle me.

> [DAVID *has fought* PETER *back to the bed and kills him.*

O, O, O,
Eve, what love there was between us. Eve,
What gentle thing, a son, so harmless,
Can hang the world with blood.

DAVID [*to* PETER].   Oh,
You trouble me. You are dead.

ADAMS. How ceaseless the earth is. How it goes on.
Nothing has happened except silence where sound was,
Stillness where movement was. Nothing has happened,
But the future is like a great pit.
My heart breaks, quiet as petals falling
One by one, but this is the drift
Of agony for ever.

DAVID.   Now let's hope
  There will be no more argument,
  No more half-and-half, no more doubt,
  No more betrayal.—You trouble me,
  You trouble me.

MEADOWS [*in his sleep*]. Cain.

                         [DAVID *hides*

                              Cain. Where is
  Your brother?

DAVID.   How should I know? Am I
  His keeper?

ADAMS.   Where is keeping?
  Keep somewhere, world, the time we love.
  I have two sons, and where is one,
  And where will now the other be?
  I am a father unequipped to save.
  When I was young the trees of love forgave me:
  That was all. But now they say
  The days of such simple forgiveness are done,
  Old Joe Adam all sin and bone.

MEADOWS. Cain: I hear your brother's blood
  Crying to me from the ground.

DAVID. Sir, no: he is silent.
  All the crying is mine.

MEADOWS. Run, run, run. Cain
  Is after you.

DAVID.   What shall I do?

MEADOWS. What you have done. It does it to you.
  Nowhere rest. Cage of the world
  Holds your prowling. Howl, Cain, jackal afraid.

And nowhere, Cain, nowhere
Escape the fear of what men fear in you.
Every man's hand will be against you,
But never touch you into quietness.
Run! Run!

DAVID.   The punishment
Is more than I can bear. I loved life
With a good rage you gave me. And how much better
Did Abel do? He set up his heart
Against your government of flesh.
How was I expected to guess
That what I am you didn't want?
God the jailer, God the gun
Watches me exercise in the yard,
And all good neighbourhood has gone.
The two-faced beater makes me fly,
Fair game, poor game, damned game
For God and all man-hunters.

MEADOWS. They shall never kill you.

DAVID. Death was a big word, and now it has come
An act so small, my enemies will do it
Between two jobs. Cain's alive,
Cain's dead, we'll carry the bottom field:
Killing is light work, and Cain is easily dead.

MEADOWS. Run on, keep your head down, cross at the double
The bursts of open day between the nights.
My word is Bring him in alive.
Can you feel it carved on your body?

        [DAVID *twists as though he felt a branding iron touch him.*

DAVID. God in heaven! The drag!
You're tearing me out of my life still living!

This can't last on flesh for ever.
Let me sleep, let me, let me, let me sleep.
God, let me sleep. God, let me sleep.

> [*He goes into the shadows to his bed.*

MEADOWS [*turning in bed*]. This can't last on flesh for ever.
Let me sleep.

> [*There follows a pause of heavy breathing. The church clock
> in the tower strikes the three-quarters.* MEADOWS *wakes,
> props himself up on his elbow.*

Any of you boys awake?
Takes a bit of getting used to, sleeping
In a looming great church. How you doing?
I can't rest easy for the night of me.
. . . Sleeping like great roots, every Jack of them.
How many draughts are sifting under the doors.
Pwhee-ooo. And the breathing: and breathing: heavy and deep:
Breathing: heavy and deep.
Sighing the life out of you. All the night.

> [DAVID *stirs uneasily.*

DAVID. I don't have to stay here! I'm a King.

MEADOWS. David, that you? You awake, David?
A dream's dreaming him. This is no place
For lying awake. When other men are asleep
A waking man's a lost one. Tim, go byes.

> [*He covers his head with his blanket.*

DAVID [*in his sleep*]. I'm King of Israel. They told me so.
I'm doing all right. But who is there to trust?
There are so many fools. Fools and fools and fools,
All round my throne. Loved and alone
David keeps the earth. And nothing kills them.

[PETER, *as the dream figure of Absalom, stands with his back pressed against a wall as though afraid to be seen.*

PETER. Do you think I care?

DAVID. Who is that man down there
In the dark alley-way making mischief?

PETER. Do you think I care?

DAVID. Corporal Joab:
There's a man in the dark way. Do you see
That shadow shift? it has a belly and ribs.
It's a man, Joab, who shadows me. He lurks
Against my evening temper. Dangerous.

[ADAMS *appears as the dream figure of Joab.*

ADAMS. I think you know already.

DAVID. He has got to be named. Which of us does it?

ADAMS. He's your own son: Absalom.

DAVID. Now
The nightmare sits and eats with me.
He was boy enough.
Why does he look like a thief?

ADAMS. Because
He steals your good, he steals your strength,
He riddles your world until it sinks,
He plays away all your security,
All you labour and suffer to hold
Against the enemy.

DAVID. The world's back
Is bent and heavily burdened, and yet he thinks
He can leapfrog over. Absalom,
Absalom, why do you play the fool against me?

PETER. You and your enemies! Everlastingly
  Thinking of enemies. Open up.
  Your enemies are friends of mine.

DAVID. They gather against our safety. They make trash
  Of what is precious to us. Absalom,
  Come over here. I want to speak to you.

PETER [*running up into the pulpit*]. Do you think I care?

ADAMS.   If you let him run
  He'll make disaster certain.

DAVID.   Absalom,
  Come alive. Living is caring.
  Hell is making straight towards us.

PETER [*in the pulpit*]. Beloved, all who pipe your breath
  Under the salted almond moon,
  Hell is in my father's head
  Making straight towards him. Please forget it.
  He sees the scarlet shoots of spring
  And thinks of blood. He sees the air
  Streaming with imagined hordes
  And conjures them to come. But you and I
  Know that we can turn away
  And everything will turn
  Into itself again. What is
  A little evil here and there between friends?
  Shake hands on it: shake hands, shake hands:
  Have a cigarette, and make yourselves at home.
  Shall we say what we think of the King of Israel?
  Ha—ha—ha!

  [*Jeering laughter echoes round the roof of the church.*

DAVID. Don't do it to me, don't make the black rage
Shake me, Peter. I tremble like an earthquake
Because I can't find words which might
Put the fear of man into you.
Understand! The indecisions
Have to be decided. Who's against us
Reeks to God. Where's your hand?
Be ordinary human, Absalom.

ADAMS. Appeal's no use, King. He has
A foiling heart: the sharp world glances off
And so he's dangerous.

DAVID.   I think so too.
Who can put eyes in his head? Who'll do it,
Eh, Joab? We have to show him
This terse world means business, don't we, Corporal,
Don't we?

ADAMS.   He has to be instructed.

DAVID. Make a soldier of him. Make him fit
For conflict, as the stars and stags are.
He belongs to no element now. We have
To have him with us. Show him the way,
Joe Adams.

> [PETER *is lounging at the foot of the pulpit.* ADAMS *turns
> to him.*

ADAMS.   Get on parade.

PETER.   What's the music?

ADAMS. I'll sing you, Absalom, if you don't get moving.
And I'll see you singing where you never meant.
Square up.

PETER.   What's this?

ADAMS.   Square up, I said.

PETER. Where do we go from here?

ADAMS.   It's unarmed combat.
It's how your bare body makes them die.
It's old hey-presto death: you learn the trick
And death's the rabbit out of the hat:
Rolling oblivion for someone.
You've got to know how to get rid of the rats of the world.
They're up at your throat. Come on.

PETER. What nightmare's this you're dragging me into?

ADAMS. Humanity's. Come on.

PETER.   I know
Nothing about it. Life's all right to me.

ADAMS. Say that when it comes.

                        [*The unarmed combat*, ADAMS *instructing.*

DAVID. Where is he going now? He carries
No light with him. Does he know
The river's unbound: it's up above
Every known flood-mark, and still rising.

PETER [*who has got away from* ADAMS]. I'm on the other side of the
    river
Staying with friends, whoever they are.
Showery still, but I manage to get out,
I manage to get out.
The window marked with a cross is where I sleep.
Just off to a picnic with your enemies.
They're not bad fellows, once you get to know them.

DAVID [*to* ADAMS]. I have heard from my son.

ADAMS.   What's his news?

DAVID. He's with the enemy. He betrays us, Joab.
He has to be counted with them.
Are we ready?

ADAMS. Only waiting for the word.

DAVID. We attack at noon.

ADAMS. Only hoping for the time.
Good luck.

DAVID. Good luck.

> [ADAMS *walks down the chancel steps and crouches, keeping
> a steady eye on his wrist-watch.* ADAMS *gives a piercing
> whistle.* PETER *leaps up and hangs on to the edge of the
> pulpit.* ADAMS *cuts him down with a tommy-gun. He cries
> out.* DAVID *starts up in his bunk.* PETER *and* ADAMS *fall to
> the floor and lie prone.*

[*Awake.*] What's the matter, Peter? Pete! Anything wrong?

> [*He gets out of his bunk and goes across to Peter's.*

Pete, are you awake?

> [*He stands for a moment and then recrosses the floor.*

MEADOWS [*awake*]. Anything the matter?
Can't you sleep either?

DAVID [*getting back into his bunk*]. I thought I heard
Somebody shout. It woke me up.

MEADOWS. Nobody shouted.
I've been lying awake. It's just gone midnight.
There's a howling wind outside plays ducks and drakes
With a flat moon: just see it through this window:
It flips across the clouds and then goes under:
I wish I could run my head against some sleep.

This building's big for lying with your eyes open.
You could brush me off, and only think you're dusting.
Who's got the key of the crypt? [*He yawns.*]
Thanks for waking. It brings the population
Up to two. You're a silent chap. Dave?
Have you gone to sleep again already?
Back into the sea, like a slippery seal.
And here am I, high and dry.

DAVID [*asleep*]. Look, look, look.

MEADOWS.   Away he goes,
    Drifting far out. How much of him is left?
    Ah, lord, man, go to sleep: stop worrying.

                    [ADAMS *drags or carries* PETER *to Peter's bunk.*

DAVID. Joab, is that you? Joab, is that you?
    What are you bringing back?

ADAMS.   The victory.

DAVID. Are you sure it is the victory, Joab?
    Are we ever sure it's the victory?
    So many times you've come back, Joab,
    With something else. I want to be sure at last.
    I want to know what you mean by victory.
    Is it something else to me? Where are you looking?
    There's nothing that way. But look over here:
    There's something. Along the road, starting the dust,
    He wants to reach us. Why is that?
    So you're going to walk away.

ADAMS [*going to his bunk*]. I've done my best.
    I can't be held responsible for everything.

DAVID. Don't leave me, Joab. Stay and listen.

ADAMS [*covering himself over*].   I'm dead beat.
    The enemy's put to flight. Good night, you King of Israel.

DAVID. Bathed in sweat, white with dust. Call him here.
    Come up. I am the King.
    I shall wait patiently until your voice
    Gets back the breath to hit me. I'm here, waiting.

        [DAVID *sits on the edge of his bunk, a red army blanket*
        hanging from his shoulder.

MEADOWS [*awake*]. Where are you off to, Davey?
    Get you back to bed. A dream
    Has got you prisoner, Davey, like
    The world has got us all. Don't let it
    Take you in.

DAVID.   Come here to me, come over
    Here, the dusty fellow with the news,
    Come here. Is the fighting over? Unconditionally?

        [MEADOWS *has left his bunk and crossed to* DAVID.

MEADOWS. Lie down, boy. Forget it. It's all over.

DAVID. Is the young man Absalom safe?

MEADOWS   Lie down, Dave.
    Everybody's asleep.

ADAMS [*from his bunk*]. The boy's dead.
    You might as well be told: I say
    The boy's dead.

        [DAVID, *giving a groan, lies back on his bed.*

MEADOWS.   The night's over us.
    Nothing's doing. Except the next day's in us
    And makes a difficult sort of lying-in.
    Here, let's cover you up. Keep the day out of this.
    Find something better to sleep about.

Give your living heart a rest. Do you hear me,
Dave, down where you are? If you don't mind,
While I'm here, I'll borrow some of that sleep:
You've got enough for two.

> [*He limps back to his bunk, passing* ADAMS, *who wakes.*

ADAMS.   Hullo, Meadows:
What's worrying you?

MEADOWS.   Dave was. He couldn't
Let go of the day. He started getting up
And walking in his sleep.

ADAMS.   All right now?

MEADOWS. Seems running smoother.

ADAMS.   Is that him talking?

> [PETER *has begun to talk in his sleep.*

MEADOWS. Muttering monkeys love us, it's the other one now:
Peter's at it.

PETER.   Do I have to follow you?

ADAMS. You needn't hear him if you get your ears
Under the blankets. That's where I'm going.
Good-night, boy.

> [*He disappears under his blankets.* MEADOWS *climbs into his bunk.*

MEADOWS.   Hope so. It's a choppy crossing
We're having still. No coast of daylight yet for miles.

> [*He also disappears from view. A pause. The church clock strikes midnight.*

PETER [*asleep*]. Why did you call me? I'm contented here:
They say I'm in a prison. Morning comes
To a prison like a nurse.

A rustling presence, as though a small breeze came,
And presently a voice. I think
We're going to live. The dark pain has gone,
The relief of daylight
Flows over me, as though beginning is
Beginning. The hills roll in and make their homes,
And gradually unfold the plains. Breath
And light are cool together now.
The earth is all transparent, but too deep
To see down to its bed.

   [DAVID, *the dream figure of Abraham, stands beside* PETER.

DAVID.   Come with me.

PETER. Where are we going?

DAVID.   If necessary
To break our hearts. It's as well for the world.

PETER. There's enough breaking, God knows. We die,
And the great cities come down like avalanches.

DAVID. But men come down like living men.
Time gives the promise of time in every death,
Not of any ceasing. Come with me.
The cities are pitifully concerned.
We need to go to the hill.

PETER.   What shall we do?

DAVID. What falls to us.

PETER.   Falling from where?

DAVID. From the point of devotion, meaning God.
Carry this wood, Isaac, and this coil
Of rope.

PETER. I'm coming.

DAVID.   There has to be sacrifice.
I know that. There's nothing so sure.

PETER. You walk so fast. These things are heavy.

DAVID. I know. I carry them too.

PETER.   I only want
To look around a bit. There's so much to see.
Ah, peace on earth, I'm a boy for the sights.

DAVID. Don't break my heart. You so
Cling hold of the light. I have to take it
All away.

PETER.   Why are you so grave?
There's more light than we can hold. Everything
Grows over with fresh inclination
Every day. You and I are both
Immeasurably living.

> [DAVID *has been walking towards the pulpit.* PETER *still lies
> in bed. He starts to whistle a tune, though the whistling seems
> not to come from his lips but from above him.*

DAVID. What do you whistle for?

PETER.   I whistle for myself
And anyone who likes it.

DAVID.   Keep close to me.
It may not be for long. Time huddles round us,
A little place to be in. And we're already
Up the heavy hill. The singing birds
Drop down and down to the bed of the trees,
To the hay-silver evening, O
Lying gentleness, a thin veil over
The long scars from the nails of the warring hearts.

Come up, son, and see the world.
God dips his hand in death to wash the wound,
Takes evil to inoculate our lives
Against infectious evil. We'll go on.
I am history's wish and must come true,
And I shall hate so long as hate
Is history, though, God, it drives
My life away like a beaten dog. Here
Is the stone where we have to sacrifice.
Make my heart like it. It still is beating
Unhappily the human time.

PETER. Where is the creature that has to die?
There's nothing here of any life worth taking.
Shall we go down again?

DAVID.   There is life here.

PETER. A flinching snail, a few unhopeful harebells.
What good can they be?

DAVID.   What else?

PETER.   You, father,
And me.

DAVID.   I know you're with me. But very strangely
I stand alone with a knife. For the simple asking.
Noon imperial will no more let me keep you
Than if you were the morning dew. The day
Wears on. Shadows of our history
Steal across the sky. For our better freedom
Which makes us living men: for what will be
The heaven on earth, I have to bind you
With cords, and lay you here on the stone's table.

PETER. Are you going to kill me? No! Father!
   I've come only a short way into life
   And I can see great distance waiting.
   The free and evening air
   Swans from hill to hill.
   Surely there's no need for us to be
   The prisoners of the dark? Smile, father.
   Let me go.

DAVID.   Against my heart
   I let you go, for the world's own ends
   I let you go, for God's will
   I let you go, for children's children's joy
   I let you go, my grief obeying.
   The cords bind you against my will
   But you're bound for a better world.
   And I must lay you down to sleep
   For a better waking. Come now.

      [In mime he picks Isaac up in his arms and lays him across
      the front of the pulpit.

PETER *[in his bunk]*.   I'm afraid.
   And how is the earth going to answer, even so?

DAVID. As it will. How can we know?
   But we must do, and the future make amends.

PETER. Use the knife quickly. There are too many
   Thoughts of life coming to the cry.
   God put them down until I go.
   Now, now, suddenly!

DAVID *[the knife raised]*. This
   Cuts down my heart, but bitter events must be.

I can't learn to forgive necessity:
God help me to forgive it.

        [ADAMS *appears as the dream figure of the Angel.*

ADAMS.   Hold your arm.
There are new instructions. The knife can drop
Harmless and shining.

DAVID.   I never thought to know,
Strange voice of mercy, such happy descending.
Nor my son again. But he's here untouched,
And evening is at hand
As clear and still as no man.

PETER.   Father, I feel
The air go over me as though I should live.

DAVID. So you will, for the earth's while. Shall I
Undo the cords?

ADAMS.   These particular. But never all.
There's no loosening, since men with men
Are like the knotted sea. Lift him down
From the stone to the grass again, and, even so free,
Yet he will find the angry cities hold him.
But let him come back to the strange matter of living
As best he can: and take instead
The ram caught here by the white wool
In the barbed wire of the briar bush:
Make that the kill of the day.

DAVID.   Readily.

PETER. Between the day and the night
The stars tremble in balance.
The houses are beginning to come to light.
And so it would have been if the knife had killed me.

This would have been my death-time.
The ram goes in my place, in a curious changing.
Chance, as fine as a thread,
Cares to keep me, and I go my way.

MEADOWS [*a dream figure*]. Do you want a ride across the sands,
Master Isaac?

PETER.   Who are you?

MEADOWS.   Now, boy, boy,
Don't make a joke of me. Old Meadows,
The donkey man, who brought you up the hill.
Not remember me? That's a man's memory,
Short measure as that. Down a day.
And we've been waiting, Edwina and me,
As patient as two stale loaves, to take you down.

PETER. But I climbed the hill on foot.

MEADOWS [*patting the bunk*]. No credit, Edwina girl, no credit.
He thinks you're a mangy old moke. You tell him
There's none so mangy as thinks that others are.
You have it for the sake of the world.

PETER. All right, she can take me down. I'm rasping tired.
My whole body's like a three days' growth of beard.
But I don't know why she should have to carry me.
She's nothing herself but two swimming eyes
And a cask of ribs.

MEADOWS.   A back's a back.
She's as good as gold while she lives,
And after that she's as good as dead. Where else
Would you find such a satisfactory soul?
Gee-up, you old millennium. She's slow,
But it's kind of onwards. Jog, jog,
Jog, jog.

PETER.   There's a ram less in the world tonight.
My heart, I could see, was thudding in its eyes.
It was caught, and now it's dead.

MEADOWS.   Jog, jog,
Jog, jog, jog, jog, jog,
Jog, jog.

PETER. Across the sands and into the sea.
The sun flocks along the waves.
Blowing up for rain of sand.
Helter-shelter.

MEADOWS.   Jog. Jog. Jog.
Donkey ride is over. In under
The salty planks and corrugated iron.
Stable for mangy mokes. Home, old girl,
Home from the sea, old Millie-edwinium.
Tie up here.

> [*He has climbed into his bunk.*

PETER.   No eyes open. All
In sleep. The innocence has come.
Ram's wool hill pillow is hard.

> [*He sighs and turns in his bunk. The church clock strikes one.*
> *An aeroplane is heard flying over the church.* PETER *wakens*
> *and sits up in his bunk, listening.*

Is that one of ours?

MEADOWS [*his face emerging from the blankets*].
                         Just tell me: are you awake
Or asleep?

PETER.   Awake. Listen. Do you hear it?
Is it one of ours?

MEADOWS.   No question: one of ours.
  Or one of theirs.

PETER.   Gone over. Funny question:
  'Was I asleep?' when I was sitting up
  Asking you a question.

MEADOWS.   Dave's been sitting up
  Asking questions, as fast asleep as an old dog.
  And you've been chatting away like old knitting-needles,
  Half the night.

PETER.   What was I saying?

MEADOWS.   I know all
  Your secrets now, man.

PETER.   I wish I did.
  What did I say?

MEADOWS.   Like the perfect gentleman
  I obliterated my lug-holes:
  Under two blankets, army issue.
  A man must be let to have a soul to himself
  Or souls will go the way of tails.
  I wouldn't blame a man for sleeping.
  It comes to some. To others it doesn't come.
  Troubles differ. But I should be glad
  To stop lying out here in the open
  While you underearthly lads
  Are shut away talking night's language like natives.
  We only have to have Corporal Adams
  To make a start, and I might as well
  Give up the whole idea. Oh, lord, let me
  Race him to it. I'm going under now
  For the third time.

                              [*He covers his head with the blankets.*

PETER. Sorry if I disturbed you.
I'll go back where I came from, and if I can
I'll keep it to myself. Poor old Meadows:
Try thinking of love, or something.
Amor vincit insomnia.

MEADOWS. That's enough
Of night classes. What's it mean?

PETER. The writing on the wall. So turn
Your face to it: get snoring.

MEADOWS. Not hereabouts:
It wouldn't be reverent. Good night, then.

PETER. Same to you.

[*They cover their heads. A pause.* ADAMS, *asleep, lies flat
on his bunk, looking down over the foot of it.*

ADAMS. Fish, fish, fish in the sea, you flash
Through your clouds of water like the war in heaven:
Angel-fish and swordfish, the silver troops . . .
And I am salt and sick on a raft above you,
Wondering for land, but there's no homeward
I can see.

[*He turns on his back.*

God, have mercy
On our sick shoals, darting and dying.
We're strange fish to you. How long
Can you drift over our sea, and not give up
The ghost of hope? The air is bright between us.
The flying fish make occasional rainbows,
But land, your land and mine, is nowhere yet.

[DAVID, *a dream figure, comes to meet him.*

How can a man learn navigation
When there's no rudder? You can seem to walk,
You there: you can seem to walk:
But presently you drown.

DAVID.   Who wants us, Corporal?

ADAMS. I wish I knew. I'm soaked to the skin.
  The world shines wet. I think it's men's eyes everywhere
  Reflecting light. Presently you drown.

DAVID. Have you forgotten you're a prisoner?
  They marched us thirty miles in the pouring rain.
  Remember that? They, they, they, they.

> [PETER *comes down towards* DAVID, *marching but exhausted. As he reaches* DAVID *he reels and* DAVID *catches him.*]

PETER. What happens if I fall out, Dave?

DAVID. You don't fall out, that's all.

PETER. They can shoot me if they like.
  It'll be a bit of a rest.

DAVID. You're doing all right.

PETER. I wouldn't know. It. Feels.
  Damned. Odd. To me.

DAVID.   Corporal Adams,
  Man half-seas overboard!
  Can you lend a hand?

ADAMS [*jumping from his bunk*]. Here I come.
  Does he want to be the little ghost?
  Give us an arm. Dave and I will be
  Your anchor, boy: keep you from drifting
  Away where you're not wanted yet.

PETER. Don't think you've got me with you.
  I dropped out miles ago.

ADAMS. We'll keep the memory green.

> [*They do not move forward, but seem to be trudging.*

DAVID. They, they, they, they.

ADAMS. Be careful how you step. These logs we're on
  Are slimy and keep moving apart.

DAVID [*breaking away*]. Where do you think we are?
  We're prisoners, God! They've bricked us in.

ADAMS. Who said you were dismissed?

PETER.   Forget your stripes
  For a minute, Corporal: it's my birthday next month,
  My birthday, Corporal: into the world I came,
  The barest chance it happened to be me,
  The naked truth of all that led the way
  To make me. I'm going for a stroll.

> [*He wanders down towards the lectern.*

ADAMS. Where are you going? Orders are
  No man leaves unless in a state of death.

DAVID. There's nowhere to go, and he knows
  There's nowhere to go. He's trying to pretend
  We needn't be here.

PETER.   Don't throttle yourself
  With swallowing, Dave. Anyone
  Would think you never expected the world.
  Listen to the scriptures:
  [*As though reading the Bible.*]
      Nebuchadnezzar, hitting the news,
      Made every poor soul lick his shoes.

When the shoes began to wear
Nebuchadnezzar fell back on prayer.
Here endeth the first lesson. And here beginneth
The second lesson . . .

DAVID.   I'll read the second lesson:
God drown you for a rat, and let the world
Go down without you.

PETER.   Three blind mice of Gotham,
Shadrac, Meshac and Abednego:
They went to walk in a fire.
If the fire had been hotter
Their tales would have been shorter.
Here endeth——

ADAMS. Get into the ranks.

PETER. What's worrying you? We're not
On active service now. Maybe it's what
They call in our paybooks 'disembodied service':
So drill my spirit, Corporal, till it weeps
For mercy everywhere.

DAVID.   It had better weep,
It had better weep. By God, I'll say
We have to be more than men if we're to man
This rising day. They've been keeping from us
Who we are, till now, when it's too late
To recollect. [*Indicating* PETER.] Does he know?

ADAMS. Shadrac, Meshac, Abednego—
We didn't have those names before: I'll swear
We were at sea. This black morning
Christens us with names that were never ours
And makes us pay for them. Named,

Condemned. What they like to call us
Matters more than anything at heart.
Hearts are here to stop
And better if they do. God help us all.

PETER. Do I know what?

ADAMS.   We are your three blind mice:
Our names are Shadrac, Meshac, and Abednego.
This is our last morning. Who knows truly
What that means, except us?

PETER.   And which of us
Knows truly? O God in heaven, we're bound
To wake up out of this. Wake, wake, wake:
This is not my world! Where have you brought me?

DAVID. To feed what you've been riding pick-a-back.

PETER. I can believe anything, except
The monster.

DAVID.   And the monster's here.

ADAMS.   To make
Sure we know eternity's in earnest.

PETER. It's here to kill. What's that in earnest of?
But the world comes up even over the monster's back.
Corporal, can we make a dash for the hill there?

ADAMS. We're under close arrest.

DAVID.   O God, are we
To be shut up here in what other men do
And watch ourselves be ground and battered
Into their sins? Let me, dear God, be active
And seem to do right, whatever damned result.
Let me have some part in what goes on
Or I shall go mad!

PETER.   What's coming now
  Their eyes are on us. Do you see them?

ADAMS. Inspection. The powers have come to look us over
  To see if we're in fettle for the end.
  Get into line.

DAVID.   What, for those devils?
  Who are they?

ADAMS.   Nebuchadnezzar and his aides.
  Do what you're told.

PETER.   Is that him with one eye?

DAVID. Are they ours or theirs?

ADAMS.   Who are we, Dave, who
  Are we? If we could get the hang of that
  We might know what side they're on. I should say
  On all sides. Which is why the open air
  Feels like a barrack square.

PETER.   Is that him
  With one eye?

ADAMS.   If we could know who we are——

DAVID. I've got to know which side I'm on.
  I've got to be on a side.

ADAMS.   —They're coming up.
  Let's see you jump to it this time: we're coming
  Up for the jump. We can't help it if
  We hate his guts.—Look out.—Party, shun!

                              [*They all come to attention.*

  The three prisoners, sir.—Party, stand
  At ease!

PETER.   Purple and stars and red and gold.
  What are they celebrating?

DAVID.   We shall know soon.

ADAMS. Stop talking in the ranks.

> [*They stand silent for a moment.*

PETER.   What bastard language
  Is he talking? Are we supposed to guess?
  Police on earth. Aggression is the better
  Part of Allah. Liberating very high
  The dying and the dead. Freedoom, freedoom.
  Will he never clear his throat?

DAVID. He's moving on

ADAMS.   Party, at-ten-tion!
> [*They bring their heels together, but they cannot bring their
> hands from behind their backs.*

PETER. Corporal, our hands are tied!

DAVID.   They've played their game
  In the dark: we're theirs, whoever calls us.

ADAMS. Stand at ease.

DAVID.   Our feet are tied!

PETER.   Hobbled,
  Poor asses.

ADAMS.   That leaves me without a word of command
  Except fall on your knees.

PETER.   What's coming, Corporal?

ADAMS. You two, let's know it: we have to meet the fire.

DAVID. Tied hand and foot: not men at all!

PETER.   O how
  Shall we think these moments out
  Before thinking splits to fear. I begin

To feel the sweat of the pain: though the pain
Hasn't reached us yet.

ADAMS.   Have your hearts ready:
It's coming now.

DAVID.   Every damned forest in the world
Has fallen to make it. The glare's on us.

PETER.   Dead on.
And here's the reconnoitring heat:
It tells us what shall come.

ADAMS.   Now then! Chuck down
Your wishes for the world: there's nothing here
To charm us. Ready?

DAVID.   I've been strong.
The smoke's between us. Where are you, Adams?

ADAMS. Lost.

PETER.   Where are you, Adams?

                    [ADAMS *cries out and falls to his knees.*

DAVID. It's come to him, Peter!

PETER.   We shall know!

DAVID. Scalding God!

                    [*They, too, have fallen to their knees.*

ADAMS. What way have I come down, to find
I live still, in this round of blaze?
Here on my knees. And a fire hotter
Than any fire has ever been
Plays over me. And I live. I know
I kneel.

DAVID.   Adams.

ADAMS.   We're not destroyed.

DAVID. Adams.

PETER.   Voices. We're men who speak.

DAVID. We're men who sleep and wake.
   They haven't let us go.

PETER.   My breath
   Parts the fire a little.

ADAMS.   But the cords
   That were tying us are burnt: drop off
   Like snakes of soot.

PETER.   Can we stand?

DAVID. Even against this coursing fire we can.

PETER. Stand: move: as though we were living,
   In this narrow shaking street
   Under the eaves of seven-storeyed flames
   That lean and rear again, and still
   We stand. Can we be living, or only
   Seem to be?

ADAMS.   I can think of life.
   We'll make it yet.

DAVID.   That's my devotion.
   Which way now?

PETER.   Wait a minute. Who's that
   Watching us through the flame?

        [MEADOWS, *a dream figure, is sitting on the side of his bunk.*

DAVID.   Who's there?

ADAMS. Keep your heads down. Might be
   Some sniper of the fire.

                         [MEADOWS *crows like a cock.*

PETER.   A lunatic.

ADAMS [*calling to* MEADOWS]. Who are you?

MEADOWS.   Man.

ADAMS.   Under what command?

MEADOWS. God's.

ADAMS.   May we come through?

MEADOWS.   If you have
The patience and the love.

DAVID.   Under this fire?

MEADOWS. Well, then, the honesty.

ADAMS.   What honesty?

MEADOWS. Not to say we do
A thing for all men's sake when we do it only
For our own. And quick eyes to see
Where evil is. While any is our own
We sound fine words unsoundly.

ADAMS.   You cockeyed son
Of heaven, how did you get here?

MEADOWS. Under the fence. I think they forgot
To throw me in. But there's not a skipping soul
On the loneliest goat-path who is not
Hugged into this, the human shambles.
And whatever happens on the farthest pitch,
To the sand-man in the desert or the island-man in the sea,
Concerns us very soon. So you'll forgive me
If I seem to intrude.

PETER.   Do you mean to stay here?

MEADOWS. I can't get out alone. Neither can you.

But, on the other hand, single moments
Gather towards the striking clock.
Each man is the world.

PETER.   But great events
Go faster.

DAVID.   Who's to lead us out of this?

MEADOWS. It's hard to see. Who will trust
What the years have endlessly said?

ADAMS. There's been a mort of time. You'd think
Something might have come of it. These men
Are ready to go, and so am I.

PETER. But there's no God-known government anywhere.

MEADOWS. Behind us lie
The thousand and the thousand and the thousand years
Vexed and terrible. And still we use
The cures which never cure.

DAVID.   For mortal sake,
Shall we move? Do we just wait and die?

MEADOWS. Figures of wisdom back in the old sorrows
Hold and wait for ever. We see, admire
But never suffer them: suffer instead
A stubborn aberration.
O God, the fabulous wings unused,
Folded in the heart.

DAVID.   So help me, in
The stresses of this furnace I can see
To be strong beyond all action is the strength
To have. But how do men and forbearance meet?
A stone forbears when the wheel goes over, but that
Is death to the flesh.

ADAMS.   And every standing day
    The claims are deeper, inactivity harder.
    But where, in the maze of right and wrong,
    Are we to do what action?

PETER.   Look, how intense
    The place is now, with swaying and troubled figures.
    The flames are men: all human. There's no fire!
    Breath and blood chokes and burns us. This
    Surely is unquenchable? It can only transform.
    There's no way out. We can only stay and alter.

DAVID. Who says there's nothing here to hate?

MEADOWS. The deeds, not those who do.

ADAMS. Strange how we trust the powers that ruin
    And not the powers that bless.

DAVID.   But good's unguarded,
    As defenceless as a naked man.

MEADOWS. Imperishably. Good has no fear;
    Good is itself, what ever comes.
    It grows, and makes, and bravely
    Persuades, beyond all tilt of wrong:
    Stronger than anger, wiser than strategy,
    Enough to subdue cities and men
    If we believe it with a long courage of truth.

DAVID. Corporal, the crowing son of heaven
    Thinks we can make a morning.

MEADOWS.   Not
    By old measures. Expedience and self-preservation
    Can rot as they will. Lord, where we fail as men
    We fail as deeds of time.

PETER. The blaze of this fire
 Is wider than any man's imagination.
 It goes beyond any stretch of the heart.

MEADOWS. The human heart can go to the lengths of God.
 Dark and cold we may be, but this
 Is no winter now. The frozen misery
 Of centuries breaks, cracks, begins to move;
 The thunder is the thunder of the floes,
 The thaw, the flood, the upstart Spring.
 Thank God our time is now when wrong
 Comes up to face us everywhere,
 Never to leave us till we take
 The longest stride of soul men ever took.
 Affairs are now soul size.
 The enterprise
 Is exploration into God.
 Where are you making for? It takes
 So many thousand years to wake,
 But will you wake for pity's sake?
 Pete's sake, Dave or one of you,
 Wake up, will you? Go and lie down.
 Where do you think you're going?

ADAMS [*waking where he stands*]. What's wrong?

MEADOWS. You're walking in your sleep.
 So's Pete and Dave. That's too damn many.

ADAMS. Where's this place? How did I get here?

MEADOWS. You were born here, chum. It's the same for all of us.
 Get into bed.

PETER [*waking*]. What am I doing here?

MEADOWS. Walking your heart out, boy.

ADAMS.   Dave, Dave.

MEADOWS. Let him come to himself gentle but soon
   Before he goes and drowns himself in the font.

ADAMS. Wake up, Dave.

PETER.   I wish I knew where I was.

MEADOWS. I can only give you a rough idea myself.
   In a sort of a universe and a bit of a fix.
   It's what they call flesh we're in.
   And a fine old dance it is.

DAVID [*awake*].   Did they fetch us up?

MEADOWS. Out of a well. Where Truth was.
   They didn't like us fraternizing. Corp,
   Would you mind getting your men to bed
   And stop them trapsing round the precincts?

ADAMS. Dave, we're mad boys. Sleep gone to our heads.
   Come on.

DAVID.   What's the time?

ADAMS.   Zero hour.

DAVID. It feels like half an hour below. I've got cold feet.

PETER. [*already lying on his bunk*]   I've never done that before. I
      wonder now
   What gives us a sense of direction in a dream?
   Can we see in sleep? And what would have happened
   If we'd walked into the guard? Would he have shot us,
   Thinking we were trying to get out?

MEADOWS. So you were from what you said. I could stand
   One at a time, but not all three together.

It began to feel like the end of the world
With all your bunks giving up their dead.

ADAMS. Well, sleep, I suppose.

DAVID. Yeh. God bless.

PETER. Rest you merry.

MEADOWS. Hope so. Hope so.

[*They settle down. The church clock strikes. A bugle sounds
in the distance.*

THE PLAY ENDS

CURTMANTLE

A Play

SECOND EDITION

To

JOHN AND NANCY FRY

The play was first produced on 1 March 1961 at the state opening of the Stadsschouwburg, Tilburg, Holland, by the Ensemble Company, directed by Karl Guttmann

World première in English at the Edinburgh Festival, 4 September 1962

London première at the Aldwych Theatre, 6 October 1962, with the following cast:

William Marshal	ROY DOTRICE
Barber	JOHN HUSSEY
Wife	SUSAN ENGEL
Juggler	ROBERT JENNINGS
Huckster	KEN WYNNE
Blae	PATSY BYRNE
A man looking for justice	TREVOR MARTIN
Eleanor	MAXINE AUDLEY
Henry	DEREK GODFREY
Becket	ALAN DOBIE
Cleric	DONALD LAYNE–SMITH
Gilbert Foliot	JOHN NETTLETON
Earl of Leicester	PAUL DAWKINS
Christ Church monks	KEN WYNNE / JOHN HUSSEY
Young Henry / Richard / Geoffrey / John *the King's sons*	ROGER CROUCHER / DAVID BUCK / IAN McCULLOCH / MARTIN NORTON
Roger, *the King's son by Blae*	BRIAN SMITH
Messenger	SHAUN CURRY
Courtiers at Poitou	DARRYL KAVANN / EDWARD ARGENT
Constance, *Geoffrey's wife*	SUSAN ENGEL
Margaret, *Young Henry's wife*	MARIAN DIAMOND
Captain	TREVOR MARTIN
Philip of France	PETER McENERY
Old woman	MADOLINE THOMAS
Refugees	PAUL DAWKINS / ROY MARSDEN / CHERRY MORRIS / IAN RICKETTS

Bishops: EDWARD ARGENT, TERENCE GREENIDGE, ROBERT JENNINGS, HENRY KNOWLES

Courtiers and Soldiers: MARGARETA BOURDIN, IMOGEN HASSALL, CAROLINE HUNT, CAROLINE MAUD, MARK MOSS, KENNETH RATCLIFFE, STUART RICHMAN, LESLIE SOUTHWICK

Directed by STUART BURGE

FOREWORD

HENRY PLANTAGENET was born in 1133, the son of Matilda (daughter of Henry I) and Geoffrey Plantagenet, Count of Anjou. During his boyhood England was suffering an eight-year-long agony of civil war, fought between his mother and Stephen of Blois. At the age of twenty-one he was King, and the wealthiest ruler in Europe. At fifty-six he was dead, the sword of State pawned, his heart broken. But 'he had laid the foundations of the English Common Law, upon which succeeding generations would build. Changes in the design would arise, but its main outlines would not be altered.'[1]

Between these two dates there is a seething cauldron of events, conflicts, purposes, errors, brilliance, human endurance, and human suffering, which could provide, in those thirty-five years, all that we need for a lifetime's study and contemplation of mankind. No single play could contain more than a splash from the brew. What to use and what to lose out of this feverish concentration of life? How far should fidelity to historical events be sacrificed to suit the theatre?

If a playwright is rash enough to treat real events at all, he has to accept a double responsibility: to drag out of the sea of detail a story simple enough to be understood by people who knew nothing about it before; and to do so without distorting the material he has chosen to use. Otherwise let him invent his characters, let him go to Ruritania for his history.

To try to re-create what has taken place in this world (or, indeed, to write about life at all) is to be faced by the task of putting a shape on almost limitless complexity. The necessity for the shaping—for 'making a play of it'—is inherent in us, because pattern and balance

[1] Winston Churchill, *The History of the English-speaking Peoples*, Vol. I.

are pervading facts of the universe. It is tempting to make a misleading simplification. In the absence of any other household-god, simplification becomes a gross superstition. It gives us the security of 'knowing', of being at home in events. We even call it reality, or getting down to the truth. But everything that we ignored remains to confute us.

I can't pretend that the play which follows has solved the problems, but consideration of them has dictated the way it should go. Though it follows chronology, it is not a chronicle play. The form it takes is one of memory and contemplation. The stage is William Marshal's mind, as though he were remembering the life of Henry; and the deviations from historical accuracy are on the whole no greater than might occur in a man's memory. The episodes are telescoped, but nothing in the play is entirely invented. Even the incident of the old woman and her feather-bed is on record.

But because, as far as I could, I have tried to do away with time and place, and to convey thirty years in one almost uninterrupted action, a few manipulations of fact have crept in. For instance, when Henry gives his age as twenty-nine, it is not the age he was at that precise point in the story (he was twenty-five), but the age he was two pages later, when he offers Canterbury to Becket. Then, also, he didn't die at Le Mans; he went on to make the desperate ride which he only plans in the play, and the meeting with Philip and Richard took place at Colombières. Nor did he die on the old woman's feather mattress, but on a bed at Chinon. The final episode, which I give to the townspeople of Le Mans, rightly belongs to Henry's own servants.

The character of Roger is a combination of two illegitimate sons, one born of a prostitute, and another who became Geoffrey the Chancellor. I renamed him to avoid the confusion of having two characters called Geoffrey.

The play has two themes: one a progression towards a portrait of Henry, a search for his reality, moving through versions of

'Where is the King?' to the unresolved close of 'He was dead when they came to him'. The other theme is Law, or rather the interplay of different laws: civil, canon, moral, aesthetic, and the laws of God; and how they belong and do not belong to each other.

It adds up to no more than a sketch of Henry. Just as the thirty-five years of his reign contain a concentration of the human condition, so his character covers a vast field of human nature. He was simple and royal (his nickname of 'Curtmantle' derived from the plain short cloak he wore), direct and paradoxical, compassionate and hard, a man of intellect, a man of action, God-fearing, superstitious, blasphemous, far-seeing, short-sighted, affectionate, lustful, patient, volcanic, humble, overriding. It is difficult to think of any facet of man which at some time he didn't demonstrate, except chastity and sloth.

My starting place was Mrs. J. R. Green's *Henry the Second*. Among the other books I read on the period, I am particularly indebted to Amy Kelly's *Eleanor of Aquitaine*.

C. F.

May 1961

NOTE TO THE SECOND EDITION

DURING the rehearsals for the English production I made a certain number of minor textual alterations, and added two short scenes: the conversation between the two monks about Becket's escape from England, and the scene between Henry, Roger, and Richard, before we come to Le Mans. This was a considerably condensed version of a scene which was played in the Dutch production.

After the performances at the Edinburgh Festival I made some more small changes, and reshaped those pages which extend from the news of the birth of Philip of France, to Richard's song after the coronation. I also rehandled the scene of Eleanor's court at Poitou.

I have begun both the Prologue and Act III with some words from Marshal, to establish him as the memory in which the action of the play takes place.

For the English production I reduced the length of the Prologue by half, but I have left it in its full form in the printed text. An audience hasn't a reader's privilege of being able to skip at will.

C. F.

1965

CHARACTERS

(in order of their appearance)

BARBER
WIFE
JUGGLER
HUCKSTER
BLAE
ANESTY
ELEANOR
WILLIAM MARSHAL
HENRY
BECKET
CLERIC
GILBERT FOLIOT
EARL OF LEICESTER
YOUNG HENRY, *the King's Son*
RICHARD ⎫
GEOFFREY ⎬ *his brothers*
JOHN ⎭
ROGER
MESSENGER
BECKET'S CROSS-BEARER
CONSTANCE, *Geoffrey's wife*
MARGARET, *Young Henry's wife*
CAPTAIN
PHILIP OF FRANCE
OLD WOMAN
FOUR REFUGEES
BISHOPS, MONKS, COURTIERS, SOLDIERS

PROLOGUE

BARBER

WIFE

JUGGLER

HUCKSTER

BLAE

ANESTY

ACT ONE

ELEANOR

WILLIAM MARSHAL

HENRY

BECKET

CLERIC

GILBERT FOLIOT

PROLOGUE

MARSHAL. Memory is not so harsh as the experience. Who can recall now the full devastation of the time when young Henry Plantagenet first came into his Kingdom? Henry Curtmantle, we sometimes called him, with his cloak as short as his need for sleep. His energy was like creation itself; he was giving form to England's chaos, an England that, after eight years of civil war, had no trade, no law, no conscience. Up and down the land he went, sparing neither himself nor us who were hauled along after him. Order was being born out of the sweat of those days and nights: a time of pugnacious reality, that still plays in my mind— beginning and ending, as it did in his thoughts also, with the people he governed.

On the edge of an improvised encampment. Cart shafts hung with clothes to make sleeping quarters. A wind is blowing. A man, a HUCKSTER, *is beating a drum. The King's* BARBER *and his* WIFE *shouting to each other above the wind and the drumming. Enter through the shadows a third man, a* JUGGLER.

BARBER. We're on the edge of the marsh. It's the noise of the frogs you can hear!

WIFE. What is it?

BARBER. The croaking of frogs!

JUGGLER. Men are getting rough where I've just come from.

BARBER. Who's beating the drum?

JUGGLER. Shine the lantern over here, will you? I've got blood coming out of me.

BARBER [*moving towards the* HUCKSTER]. Give us a chance to sleep, what's the matter with you?

HUCKSTER. I'm discouraging away the evils of the night.

BARBER. Discourage that drum for one.

JUGGLER. Bring us the light. The clumsy, excitable sons of bitches have dug a hole in me.

BARBER. What's the matter?

JUGGLER. They've gone mad up in front there, arguing over who has the best right to accommodation. I was trying to get past 'em, and got stuck on a knife. Hold the light still.

BARBER. Anyway, you won't die of it.

JUGGLER. The clumsy, excitable sons of bitches!

HUCKSTER. I'd be better off in London, I'll tell you that. If it rains on us now—*mercy domine*! You have to be like iron to follow the King.

JUGGLER. Whose bucket of water?

BLAE [*emerging from the dark*]. It's mine, dearie. Come on here; I'll cure you.

JUGGLER. I can manage, love.

WIFE. So she's learnt to cure 'em as well; very useful, I should think.

BLAE. I learn not to listen, see, Jack, I say nothing.

WIFE. If my husband was anything of a man, he would see I was sleeping somewhere better than this.

BARBER. She tells me a man would have elbowed his way up to the front and made himself known. 'I'm the King's barber', she says a man would have said, 'and you can all go and hook yourselves up on a bush'.

JUGGLER. I wouldn't be a man on those terms, Barber. Look what I got, and I was only walking past them.

WIFE. It sounds like they're slaughtering rats.

JUGGLER. It's plain vicious brawling. It doesn't hurt the King to change his mind where he's going to. No harm to him to land us up ten miles from no place; and no daylight, either, to see where to spit. And a dirty night coming up on the wind. He's lying well out of the weather in the farmhouse, with ten or twelve of the best of the lords lying alongside him. But when you've had that, there's an old splay-footed barn, and then you're down to the cow-house and the pigsties; and that's where the trouble started. Who's to have the accommodation? Who's to have the honour and precedence to lie down in the muck in the pigsty? That's the beginning of the argument, rising up to blaspheming oratory, then shouldering and shoving, and simple Jack has to go and pass them just when they fetch out their damned cutlery.

[*A yell is heard above the brawling*.

BARBER. There's somebody accommodated.

WIFE. We're better off where we are.

BARBER. That's what I said.

HUCKSTER. What sort of a world is it, Jesus hear me? You'd think when a man goes travelling with the King's Court he'd make a fortune for himself. But what's the outcome of it? Grinding forward, day after day, through miles of mud, and find your night's lodging in a filthy swamp.

BARBER. You can tell yourself it's a great benefit to the kingdom. That's the outcome of it. Law and order is the outcome. Haven't you got a memory for the smoke and ruin this land was? Mad, and murderous, and lawless, bleeding away like raw meat.

HUCKSTER. I can have more of that at home in my own bed.

JUGGLER. What's here? There's a light coming.

WIFE. See it? Yes, look, there it is.

BARBER. Who else is out in the night, looking for somewhere to sleep?

HUCKSTER. That's the marshes down there. That's not an ordinary light. That leads you off to sink over your ears in a mucky death.   [*He nervously beats on the drum.*

BARBER. Give that a rest; give it up.

JUGGLER. Picking his way, the poor bloody man. We'll hollow at him.

BARBER. He's hollowing himself. [*To the* HUCKSTER.] Quiet, for God's sake!—Let's hear what he says.

        [RICHARD ANESTY, *the traveller, calls from a short distance.*

ANESTY. Who's there to hear me?

JUGGLER. Any number.

ANESTY. Have I caught up with the King?

JUGGLER. You're on the verge of him. Struggle on.

BARBER. Who would come to this place looking for the King, where we don't know where we are ourselves?

WIFE. Where we wouldn't be if we knew better.

HUCKSTER. A hell of a valley to come and lodge in.

        [*They wait for him. Enter* RICHARD ANESTY, *his sword drawn.*

JUGGLER. Draw into the circle, friend. We aren't quarrelsome.

ANESTY. God save you.

HUCKSTER. Let's hope so.

BARBER. You can save us your sword, as well.

JUGGLER. Put it by, man.

BARBER. If you think we're a lawless lot, no wonder, seeing us pitched out here in a black, spitting wind. But that's how the journey has gone, with the best of intentions. Otherwise we're decent men.

WIFE. He's the King's barber talking to you.

ANESTY. Then tell me where I can find the King.

JUGGLER. Show us your face.

ANESTY. Get me to the King.

BARBER. Steady, now, steady. What makes you think he'll see a gaunt, atrocious man rushing in on him out of the dark?

JUGGLER. Tell us your name.

ANESTY. Richard Anesty.

BARBER. What do you want with the King, Richard Anesty?

ANESTY. Simply a matter of birthright: of common justice. Where shall I find him?

BARBER. Wait, now, wait! Give us a proper explanation of yourself.

ANESTY. To satisfy the barber? So that's what I've come to. Well, the name is Anesty. My property was a fair property: was heft off me in the civil wars. It's taken five years, going through the courts, trying to get it back again. I'm sick of that particular labyrinth; it breaks the spirit. The King's the only answer. He'll see the matter set right: loves the law, hates the grabbing barony. He'll see the future gives me a world of my proper rights. Which way do I go to him?

BARBER. No way, at this hour of the night.

ANESTY. Who do you think will stop me now?

BARBER. You stay here, sir, as I say to you.

ANESTY. Not for a barber!

BARBER [*holding his arm*]. Then we'll have to keep you, for your own good!

JUGGLER [*taking the other;* ANESTY *struggles*]. Calm your soul, sir.

ANESTY. Right, when I've seen the King.

BARBER. And that's first thing in the morning. He's seeing all the

men then who have a reasonable cause for complaining, before
we move off.

BLAE. At six o'clock.

WIFE. You can believe her. She gets the accurate information
always, one way and another.

ANESTY. But I'm within yards of putting my hand to him. Do you
know what you're asking?

JUGGLER. Well, the time will pass easy enough if you're sleeping.

ANESTY. I've been searching for him seven weeks and two days.
I've had two horses die on the road, the last an hour or so ago,
three miles short of catching up with you. There was no way of
knowing, from one day to the next, where the King would be.

BARBER. Right, sir. That's his whole plan and purpose. Find out
the true state of the courts of law and the administration of his
kingdom, is what he is after; so come up on them unawares is
what he does. Thursday at Nottingham, says the itinerary. So the
judges at Nottingham keep sober Monday, Tuesday, Wednesday,
put off accepting any bribes till Friday, rub the dirt off their
hands, and sit down to business as punctual as the light. And
where is the King's majesty? The King's majesty is in Sheffield.

ANESTY. I know it very well.

JUGGLER. Well, here you are; get some sleep. The morning's not
so far off. You'll have no trouble from the King if you've got a
good claim.

HUCKSTER. Though you might wonder, looking at us here. He'll
march us all to death to get his law and order, though I'll say
this, he's sorry for you when you're dead. Concerning the foreign
sailors wrecked on our coast, per example, and the killing, robbing,
and stripping thereof, he wept like a sweating cistern, as we saw
at Whitstable. The veins in his head stood up the size of ropes,

condemning the practices to perjury-come. So we know to be butchered if we want to be well thought of.

BARBER [*indicating the* HUCKSTER *with his head*]. A highly nervous trading kind of man, with no wide thoughts at all for the world's good.—Haven't you got a memory for the smoke and ruin this land was? Mad, and murderous, and lawless, bleeding away like raw meat!

JUGGLER. Half a lifetime of it, if you can put that out of your memory.

BARBER. Foul injustice done to good men. As this good man here himself has suffered, so he tells us.

JUGGLER. This good man here is fast asleep.

BARBER. There it is, you see: good men can sleep now, under the wisdom of King Henry.

WIFE. Under a cart, if you wouldn't mind noticing.

BARBER. The wind is taking the clouds off. There it is: times are improving.

HUCKSTER. But I'm not, Jesus hear me.

JUGGLER. Six good hours insensible. I'll enjoy that. Goodnight, friends.

> [*The camp settles down to sleep. A horn begins to blow, coming nearer; shouts and a growing murmur.*]

JUGGLER [*groaning*]. What's the trouble now?

HUCKSTER. Isn't there to be any night between days in this King's world, for God's sake?

BARBER. We'd better find out.

VOICE [*coming nearer*]. Break up camp, get on the road!

HUCKSTER. They've gone out of their minds.

VOICE. Break up camp!

WIFE. What do they mean? Now? In the night?

VOICE. The King's in the saddle! Hurry yourselves! We're making for Kettering!

JUGGLER. What fool drunk has started this?

BARBER [*returning from inquiry*]. The camp's breaking up. We've got to move.

WIFE. Kettering!

JUGGLER. That means the best part of twenty miles before morning.

HUCKSTER. If a man can't have his lawful sleep, to hell with the law.

> [*The camp is busy and noisy, the lanterns moving, the carts being wheeled away.*

BARBER [*shaking* ANESTY *as he passes him*]. Better wake up, Richard Anesty. The King has left for Kettering.

ANESTY. The King—

BARBER. The King is riding off to Kettering.

ANESTY [*struggling to his feet*]. No, no, no! It isn't light yet. You swore to me you would bring me to him in the morning.

BARBER. So we thought we would, but we're moving on.

ANESTY. You don't know what you're saying! I have to see him! He has only got to lean a moment from his saddle! What can I do? How can I go on?—Where is the King?

> [*The stage empties and darkens.*

Where shall I find the King? A law that's just and merciful! Do I have to walk on for ever, looking for that?

> [*He trudges after the receding noise of the wagons.*

Where is the King?

> [*The wind blows in the dark, drops to a calm, and gradually the light increases on an empty hall in Westminster, no person there except the Queen,* ELEANOR, *standing alone.*

END OF PROLOGUE

Westminster. ELEANOR. *Enter* WILLIAM MARSHAL, *grinning.*

MARSHAL. The King's arrived in the yard, ma'am, with the
Chancellor.

ELEANOR. And every man in London appears to be smiling.
What is it, Marshal? Every man
Who has come in out of the street is either grinning,
Or sprawling a great hand across his mouth,
As though there were something of obscene pleasure in the world
    outside.

MARSHAL. Well, possibly it might be a general feeling of success.
As far as we can gather, the Chancellor has come back from
France with what he wanted. That's one cause for smiling.
When you think of the state of grievance the French have been
in, ever since you divorced their King and rode off with your own
property—that's a second cause for smiling. *Où se sont évanouis
le Poitou et l'Aquitaine?*

ELEANOR. Marshal, you've gone out of your mind.

MARSHAL. You must admit, ma'am, that was a pretty damned
effective joke. When you think of them seeing the Kingdom of
France reduced by a half, on one Palm Sunday afternoon.

ELEANOR. You expect me to believe that this grin on your face has
been there for eleven years? Now tell me the truth. What is the
joke? Are the filthy actors out in the yard?

MARSHAL. No, ma'am. It's the King and the Chancellor.

ELEANOR. Being witty enough to make all men smile. Or was it
horse-play?

MARSHAL. Both, ma'am.

ELEANOR. This island can never have been better entertained.

MARSHAL. There they were, the King and the Chancellor,
Riding together along Cheapside, the crown
And the croney, in great pleasure together.
There was a fairly disgusting beggar-man,
Best part naked, lifting up one of his crutches
Across the King's path. 'Poor lousy fellow',
The King said, reining in his horse.—'Dear lord of justice',
Said the beggar. He knew his onions; he understood
Just how to come at the King's generosity.
He said he was born at Le Mans, the same as the King.
Everybody knows what affection the King has
For his own birthplace. And then a hard-up story
That jerked a quick tear out of the King. 'Christ,'
He said, 'we'll have no naked men. Christ's
Charity, Thomas, let him have your cloak!'
'Give him yours, Henry,' Becket said:
'This is *your* deed of grace.' 'It's too old, and too short',
Said the King. 'It would be no charity to his arse.'
And he made a grab at the Chancellor's cloak—cinnamon
Velvet, a new one—and they wrestled on horseback, to take it
And keep it, until every man round was laughing himself
To water, and the Chancellor gave in.
So the King threw down the cloak, obliterating
The beggar, and we all rode forward happy.

ELEANOR. A deed of grace, gracefully done,
And very delicately reported. Here is the King.

> [WILLIAM MARSHAL *withdraws. Enter* HENRY, *chuckling,*
> *and* BECKET.

HENRY. His dignity shaken, but thanks to me
There's much joy in heaven over his charity.

BECKET. Ma'am, you will have to excuse a naked Chancellor.

ELEANOR. As God made you, Becket. I've no objection.

HENRY. Embrace him, Eleanor. He has worked his charms
  On Paris.

ELEANOR. I heard so. It's a happy thing
  That he lives in this modern world, to give us his company.

BECKET. There would be no Becket, without the King.
  Nor, I might add, much sign of the King's magnificence
  Without his Chancellor. I shall be ruined, Henry,
  Trying to keep up your personal splendour for you,
  To match the importance of your position!

HENRY.   You love it.

BECKET. It's just as well I love it. It impressed Louis.

ELEANOR. Poor Louis with his endless daughters.
  It would rather seem, if he is letting us marry
  Our young Henry to the baby Margaret,
  He despairs at last of having a son. The skies
  Are curiously empty for Louis, his long prayers
  Are ineffectual.

BECKET.   Completely so.
  And his disappointed Majesty of France
  Has come to an agreement with us over the question
  Of his daughter's dowry. He is willing—at least,
  I'll say he is prepared, when the children marry
  To make over to his daughter the country of the Vexin.

ELEANOR. With all its castles. Of course, Becket.
  It was what you went for.

HENRY.   So you can chew
  On that, Becket. No commendation from Eleanor.
  She learned her behaviour from an oracle;

What she expects, is what occurs. And what
You went for, we have got. And what we have got
Is natural, because it was necessary.
And that puts us clearly into the ascendent
For a term of good order, while we do our work.
From the Arctic circle to the Pyrenees
The King's peace is holding secure.

BECKET. And God's peace, too, no doubt.

HENRY.   No doubt.
It wouldn't surprise me.
Not a son is born to Louis, though he would give
God his place in his bed if he could get one.
But four good boys to me.
There's God articulate, if ever a god spoke.
Four strong Plantagenet males born
To a kingdom worthy of God's admiration.

ELEANOR. All being well.

HENRY.   What isn't well already
Is getting down on to its knees to be cured.
God's light, there's no anarchy to come worse
Than I've already transformed into good government,
Unless they drive me to a harrowing of hell.

ELEANOR. Or unless you drive them back to anarchy
To be free of your endless tramping up and down.
I never see a man in the Court who hasn't a limp,
The soles of his feet as raw with blisters
As yours are, Henry. For the Queen's peace,
Will you sit down?

HENRY. Why not? I should like to know if there's anything
Our dear friend here of the ten talents
Can fail at. Put him in command of the field,

You can see the horse under him grow two hands taller
While Becket stacks the countryside with Christian
Corpses. Eh, Tom? And has to be restrained.
Ship him to the continent as Chancellor
To work a delicate diplomacy,
He treats the road to Paris to such an immense
Procession of the mad world, and all singing in dialect:
Hawks, and dogs; and longtailed apes
Up on the backs of the horses: all his gold plate
And his private chapel, a holy menagerie
Of opulence and power—
Every mouth in France drops too wide open
To shut again in time to deny us
Anything we came to ask.
But then you see him here, dispensing charity,
There's the deacon in him. What are you, Becket?
Force, craft, or the holy apprentice?

BECKET. The King's representative. And full of faults.
    I do what I can.

HENRY. But you're not the whole of a man's capability,
    Thomas, for all your talents: I know you to be
    An incorruptible virgin: your virginity's
    As crass extravagant as the rest of your ways of living.
    If every man gave up women in God's name,
    Where in God's name would be the men
    To give up women in a generation's time?
    I tell you, Becket, for the sake of divine worship
    You'd better apply the flesh.

BECKET.   I am content,
    Henry, to be one man, and not the human race.

ELEANOR. It's as well that there should be someone in this country
    To undertake chastity for the King.

HENRY [*a pause*]. Well, there you have your permission.
  Fill the office of my virginity
  And scrape a living out of it if you can.

BECKET. Perfectly willing.

HENRY.   I shall expect a sainthood
  When my term of the world is over. Put it to the Pope.
                              [*He has shuffled over some documents.*
  Have you seen this, Becket? These crozier-clutching monkeys,
  Ramming home their shutters against the common
  Light of day: but the day comes, despite 'em!

BECKET. What is it?

HENRY [*throwing a parchment at him*]. There it is.

ELEANOR. Clearly the findings of an ecclesiastical court.

BECKET [*reading*]. The case of the Canon of Lincoln.

HENRY. The reverend Canon of rape and murder, who thinks
  Because they shaved his head in a holy circle
  He can grow the hair of an ape on his breast and his genitals.
  He thinks he has the divine right
  To cut throats and not hang for it.

BECKET.   The Bishop
  Could find no proof of his guilt. That was why he was acquitted.

HENRY. They can reverse the acquittal. The Sheriff
  Has sworn the man is guilty. They can pass him over
  To the secular arm, where a man is known by his crimes
  And not by his credentials. God's seat,
  I mean to make a fair and governable England;
  One justice, not two. The Church will soon
  Turn every criminal into a priest, to avoid the gallows;
  And the other honest, poor damned sons of Cain
  Who get slewed into crime in a five-minute passion
  Are hanged by the neck.

BECKET. All right, Henry.
Let's leave the poor damned sons of Cain to God, then.

ELEANOR. At least for this afternoon. We met here
To welcome Becket. As I am neither a Bishop
Nor a raping Canon
It's no argument which need detain me.

HENRY. I've heard no argument. Tom loves the law,
And he knows as well as I do the day is soon coming
When those who deviate will be compelled
Into the common pattern. There it is:
Patience restored. Sit down. I'll tell you
What my memory is celebrating today.
Not only Becket's triumphant return.
What else makes this a feast of the Angevin succession?

ELEANOR. What day is it?

HENRY. Unhorsed at the first shock.

ELEANOR. What day of the month?

BECKET. The sixteenth of September.
I can think of nothing: no battle, no marriage, no birth,
No death, no treaty, of which the anniversary
Falls on the sixteenth of September.

ELEANOR. I remember
Very well. It was the day, eleven years ago,
When I first met him; or, to be accurate,
The day I suffered his invasion:
For I can tell you, Becket,
He came forward to kiss my hand
Like a man who has just broken down the door.
I'm not at all certain he didn't ride in
Through the doorway on a horse.

HENRY.   Becket, I swear
  I sidled in like an egg-bound goose,
  I held her in such tremendous awe, this woman
  Who had been the inspiration of poets
  Ever since I could understand language,
  And the haunter of male imagination
  Ever since I could understand sex.

ELEANOR.   You hear him
  Working at his arithmetic, Becket,
  And grubbing up his advantage of years.

BECKET. Time walks by your side, ma'am, unwilling to pass.
  But Henry lives and does his work
  In a race of nights and days which are piling the years
  Up on him fast.

HENRY.   Twenty-nine, you methusalem!
  I can live to bury you twice over. God knows
  Time isn't a fellow workman to be trusted
  In any great patient endeavour. It's never
  Far from my mind. So much the more
  The men who impede me had better take care.

ELEANOR. We were beginning to tame him. Now he's off
  Trying to walk time to a standstill. Come back to the past,
  Henry—eleven years ago today—

HENRY. By God, I went to her cap in hand,
  Heart in mouth, and by God she was everything
  Reported of her.

BECKET.   And more, Henry.

ELEANOR.   No, no;
  I protest at that. Less, as God will judge me,
  I was less than reported. My reputation
  Wasn't spared in the French court then. And, to cap all,

As a variation of boredom, I gave to Louis
Another disastrous daughter. A waste of labour.
And the Abbot of Clairvaux—
After praying, I hope, for the accurate word—
Called me the evil genius of France.
That was at least something to be
In that miserable autumn, but not
My entire ambition. And, more or less then,
The door was torn off its hinges by the Duke of Normandy.
Henry was standing there eyeing me, ready
To start creating the world.

HENRY.   And not by accident,
This meeting with her. It was in the great
Pattern of events. Old Merlin predicted it.

BECKET. Stuff and nonsense.

HENRY.   That's your opinion.

BECKET. Well, I can think of better springs of action
Than a popular forgery.

HENRY.   Not the cause: I never said so:
But a welcome confirmation.

ELEANOR. You see how easily a woman is fooled, Becket.
In the tender fancy of my heart I thought
He was marrying me for my great possessions.
But you see I was only a superstition.
He took me, as he would take the salt he spilled,
And threw me over his shoulder to improve his luck.

HENRY. The Queen is angling for a quarrel, Becket,
Because she knows she is looking as ageless
As the Sea of Marmara, and no one has said so.

BECKET. I have said so.

HENRY.   Then say it again;
She likes to hear you.

ELEANOR.   Being the wife of Louis
Was like being married to a priest; with Henry
It is like being married to a jobbing Jupiter.
Tell me, how was Louis when you saw him, Becket?

BECKET. Courteous, ma'am, and over anxious.

ELEANOR. Unchanged. Frayed to ribbons whether to be
A king or an archbishop. It was always so.
He could never co-ordinate the two worlds.

BECKET. It was charming to see him
Pressing back against the wall at the sight
Of the least little monk, to let him take precedence,
Though the little monk drowned himself in blushes
And would have given his life
To have been allowed to bow himself out backwards.
But the King went on murmuring, 'No, no, dear and beloved
Brother in Christ Jesus, after you, if you please;
My kingdom is nothing to the kingdom of heaven;
You have the superiority; I must insist!'

HENRY. Excellent, I can hear him! You're any man
You want to be, Becket, I told you! Let's hear him again!

ELEANOR. As in Passion week eleven years ago.

HENRY. Louis, divorce your wife; excuse me,
I have a use for her.

ELEANOR.   Your evil spirit
Is prepared to leave you, Louis.

BECKET [*in the voice of Louis*].   Then may heaven
Help me with grace to suffer your going,
Amen; and France, taking the lower place,

Be first in God's mercy, and bear all things patiently
In the service of heaven.

HENRY.   Amen, amen.

ELEANOR.   Am I free, Louis?

BECKET [*in the voice of Louis*].
If to St. Peter's chair and in the will of God
We are not one, by my obedience we are two.

ELEANOR. Redemption by divine arithmetic!
                              [*They break into laughter.*

HENRY. Which reminds me, Tom: I'm giving you Canterbury.
By your own merit, Archbishop as well as Chancellor.
                    [*A silence.* BECKET *stands frozen.*

HENRY. Well, you immeasurable man. Your air
Of astonished innocence doesn't convince me. Don't
Pretend you never considered the chance of this
In one of your forward-looking silences
As soon as you knew that Theobald was dead?

BECKET. This is what Louis tried to do:
Insisting on his Chancellor for a bishopric
Against the nomination of the Chapter.
And you know what came of it. The Pope intervened
With anathema, and Louis had to give in.

HENRY. Louis can only get daughters, and I get sons,
Even on the same wife. What's the argument?

BECKET. There's one man in particular, Foliot of London,
And six or seven others besides, who by
Their learning, integrity, piety, loyalty
And cast of mind, are a better choice for Canterbury.

HENRY. And who is a better choice for England?

BECKET. Any mere minor canon or choirmaster
  Living as intently to his church
  As a workman who bows his head
  Over his chosen craft.

HENRY.   And who
  Is a better choice for me?

BECKET.   I am not.
  Ask any hundred random men,
  They'll tell you so. The Church itself
  Neither waits for me, nor wants me; rather
  Deplores me than otherwise. And I'm not a man
  Whose confidence thrives on its own. What I do well
  I do because men believe I will do it well
  Before ever the thing is begun. The fruit
  On the tree forms larger in a willing climate,
  Or anyway I found it so in my own
  Experience. I care for men's opinion.
  I doubt if I should ever be
  Sufficient in myself, to hold my course
  Without any approval. No one would say
  I was made of the stuff of martyrs. So if you ever
  Trusted to my perception—

HENRY.   Never,
  My friend. I trust your administration,
  Grasp of the law, charm of persuasion,
  And your like-thinking with my own thought—

BECKET. Natural in a Chancellor.

HENRY.   And natural
  In my long-tried friend, Tom Becket.

BECKET. But what is natural in an Archbishop?

HENRY. Precisely what is natural in Tom Becket.
    Your election is simple. To the majority
    Of men, inevitable.

BECKET.   One thing is simple.
    Whoever is made Archbishop will very soon
    Offend either you, Henry, or his God.
    I'll tell you why. There is a true and living
    Dialectic between the Church and the state
    Which has to be argued for ever in good part.
    It can't be broken off or turned
    Into a clear issue to be lost or won.
    It's the nature of man that argues;
    The deep roots of disputation
    Which dug in the dust, and formed Adam's body.
    So it's very unlikely, because your friend
    Becomes Primate of England, the argument will end.
    As Chancellor, my whole mind could speak for yours,
    Because I knew the Church had for her tongue
    A scholar and a saintly man who was not to be
    Brow-beaten. But now Theobald is dead.
    The English Church has lost its tongue. Do you mean
    That I should now become that tongue,
    To be used in argument between you and me?
    Because, if so, we shall not be as we have been.

HENRY. You will miss your falcons, of course, if you decide
    That blood sports are too secular.
    But which of us is going to change his nature
    Or his understanding? Together we have understood
    The claims men have on us
    And how to meet them. Whatever your office
    This truth is unalterable, the truth being one.

BECKET. The truth, like all of us, being of many dimensions,

And men so placed, they stake their lives on the shape of it
Until by a shift of their position, the shape
Of truth has changed.

ELEANOR.   Hardly a conclusion, I fancy,
  Which the good scholar and saintly man who trained you
  Would have applauded with both hands. Nevertheless
  Consider it, Henry. Conserve the blessings
  You have already.

HENRY.   The blessings I have already
  Are there to be blessed with.
  And the future is waiting to be blessed by us,
  In spite of the men who drag their feet. I can see
  He means to refuse.

BECKET.   I haven't said so.

HENRY. I can see he means to.

BECKET.   I haven't said so.
  But listen to the things I fear. However much
  We both imperatively want it otherwise,
  You're dividing us, and, what is more, forcing
  Yourself and me, indeed the whole kingdom,
  Into a kind of intrusion on the human mystery,
  Where we may not know what it is we're doing,
  What powers we are serving, or what is being made of us.
  Or even understand the conclusion when it comes.
  Delivering us up, in fact, to universal workings
  Which neither you nor I wish to comply with
  Or even to contemplate. If this should be so,
  Do you still propose that I should accept Canterbury?

ELEANOR. Well, which is it to be, Henry, to predict
  The future, Becket or Merlin?

HENRY.   Now he's master of excuses.
  Too complacent, is he, to enlarge himself
  To the size of the new world we have under our hand?
  But foresee this, then: if King and Archbishop
  Can work in affection, the Church will be content
  And calm. If not: waste of hours, energy,
  Opportunity; and much loss
  And peril to souls will come of it; and, worse,
  Loss of the time we need, to give England
  An incorruptible scaffolding of law
  To last her longer than her cliffs.

BECKET.   You remember
  When the Archbishop was dying, he sent for me
  And I didn't go. Now, on your own insistence,
  I see I do go after all, though now
  Too late to have any happiness in going.
  According to your will, then, Henry.

HENRY. All right, you confer the favour. I thought that I did.
  But what difference? We shall go ahead.
  Make away with your uncertainties, man.
  Anything unaccustomed has a doubtful look
  Till it grows to be a part of our thinking.
  Why shouldn't you keep your falcons?
  God will expect something of the kind
  From an Archbishop who was born in England.
  We'll make up to Him for it by establishing
  Order, protection, and justice
  For the man who has a shirt or the man who has not.
  A pity the whole of the earth is not to be
  Serene in our keeping. But there are still
  The four good Plantagenet males to come.
  We must leave them something to do.

Come and see that nest of young eagles, Tom.
You can describe to Harry the good points
Of Margaret of France, if you think you can make
An infant sound like a desirable wife.

ELEANOR. You've drawn blood from Becket, Henry.
The city sunshine, and the new English archbishop
Are equally cold and pale.
And besides, he has made a long journey for you.
You should give him time to rest.

BECKET.   The sea was rough.

HENRY. Do as you like, Tom. Be your own man
Until tomorrow.   [*Exit* HENRY.

ELEANOR.   And, ever after, be his
In every particular. The free and fallen
Spirits we may think we are,
You and I and the nest of young eagles,
Have our future state only in a world of Henry.
I should go and get your rest, Becket, before
You are led away into captivity by this new well-ordered world.
            [*She follows* HENRY. BECKET *stands unmoving.* WILLIAM
            MARSHAL *comes forward with a cloak.*

MARSHAL. They've brought over another cloak for you from the
Chancery, my lord Chancellor.—Will you wear it, my lord?—
They brought it to replace the one you parted with.—This is
your own, from the Chancery, sir.
                  [*He puts the cloak on to* BECKET's *shoulders.*

BECKET. Is the day much colder?

MARSHAL. I don't think so. But, if you remember, you gave away
your cloak—

BECKET. Tell me, Marshal, do you know yourself, who you are?

MARSHAL. I daresay I could pick myself out among two or three men, if I took thought.

BECKET. You have the best of it.—Take good care of the King.

MARSHAL. Why not? And the King can take good care of us. But what's your thought there, sir?

[BECKET *moves on out of sight.*

Why urge that on me?—[*He turns to the audience.*] I was soon to know. What was one had become two. The simple and reasonable action, at the very moment it came to life, was neither simple nor limited to reason. There it is. The logic of events has never been argued in the schools, as far as I know. There was the morning full of life, like an unbroken colt; but the moment the King, with a good will and strong knees, got astride it, God only knows what whistle it was answering; but it made history, whatever that is.— The day when Becket was consecrated Archbishop was a bright, fresh day; what clouds there were were easy-moving; and, except for a sharp indrawing of breath from the Chapter at Canterbury, we were all in the humour of progress, the rich men inside the cathedral, wary over their privileges, or the poor men outside, concerned with hope, all for the moment willing to presume a benefit from this move the King had made: firm, reasonable, new for those who looked for change, not too new for those who prospered in stability, and therefore promising, making for unity. The whole significance of unity was not debated, nor what fires can forge a diverse multitude into one mind. But for the present, at any rate. . . . Excuse me. [*He peers into the shadows.*] Come here.

[BLAE *comes forward.*

Who let you through?

BLAE. Nobody let me through. He was dead against it. I didn't need any youngster like that to tell me to stand and be recognized. I know who I am as well as he does. What I've come for is no business of his.

MARSHAL. This is no such free world, sweetheart. Come on, I'll see you safely outside again.

BLAE. I wouldn't put you to the trouble.—Keep your hands for your food.

MARSHAL. The boys all know where to find you, don't worry. If business is so bad, coming here isn't going to change it.

BLAE. Change isn't what I came for. I want something taken care of.

MARSHAL. I'll take care of you, for a good start. You can follow the Court when it's out on the road, but when we are back to London you stay home.

BLAE. So I do. But there's something I have to say to the King.

MARSHAL. You're not going to see the King.

BLAE. I don't have to; I can tell who he is in the dark.

MARSHAL. So that's what you're up to. Then let me say this to you, if you haven't got sense enough to know it; there's a private world, and a public world, there's a world of night, and a world of day, and if you dare to get one confused with the other I'll break my heart for the way you'll end up. The sooner I get you out of here, the better it will be for you.

BLAE. The King will see no harm comes to me, I can tell you that now.

MARSHAL. The King isn't going to have the chance.
                                        [*He throws her over his shoulder.*

BLAE. He won't have you do this, not to the mother of a son of his.
          [MARSHAL *stops and puts her down.* HENRY *stands upstage, unseen by them.*

MARSHAL. That's a pretty presentable story. Born with a label tied to his ear, *filius Henrici*, with a birth-mark of the Plantagenet leopard stamped sheer across him.

BLAE. You might have seen him. How did you know?

MARSHAL. Because otherwise you'd be out of your mind to risk laying charges against the King for the sake of what you can get out of it. I can tell you now what you'll get out of it—

HENRY. How do you know he's a boy of mine?

BLAE. It's him!

MARSHAL [*aside to her*]. Now will you run?

BLAE [*under her breath*]. I'm not doing wrong.

HENRY. How do you know he's a boy of mine?

BLAE. He says it himself, sir, in every pug look he gives me.

HENRY. What do you want?

BLAE. To know what's to be done with him. That's all, sir. What's to be done with you, I say to him, playing about with half the muck of your father's kingdom on your face and your knees?

HENRY. Go and take a look at him, Marshal. If he looks like mine, bring him to me. If he looks like mine to me, Becket can raise him and train him at the Chancery.

BLAE. Sir, you're a good King, a good man to all of us.

HENRY. Go and lick him clean, and give my face a chance to shine through him. And don't expect anything more from it.

BLAE. Nothing on earth, you can have my word. Myself is myself, sir, and that I can make do to look after. I give you my word—

HENRY. All right; exist unexplained. Get home.

BLAE. Yes, sir, my lord. [*Exit* BLAE.

HENRY. You see what comes, Marshal, of a wet summer.
That August at Hereford, the rain came down on us
Like a high sea slapping over a cockle boat

For six days, remember?
A week of good life wasted in a flood.

> [*A* CLERIC *has entered with a letter*.

What's this?

CLERIC. From his Grace of Canterbury, my lord.
He sends you his love and obedience.

HENRY. Two words, love and obedience. What
Does he expect me to do with them, when I never see him?
Haven't I given him time enough yet
To get used to being cock of the cloistral walk?
There's a child in him; he loves himself
In a new frock. That's it, Marshal, you fetch
That sprig of Plantagenet the whore has got,
And we'll make him as good a Chancellor in twenty years.
We'll see what life comes out of that churn-up
Of rain and Hereford mud and boredom and semen
And prostitution. Go and fetch him.

MARSHAL. I'll take a look, my lord, and try and judge what I find
there.

> [*Exit* MARSHAL. HENRY, *who has broken open the letter, reads it*.

HENRY. Did he tell you to say his love and obedience?

CLERIC. Yes, my lord.

HENRY. Then he told you a lie.

CLERIC. My lord?

HENRY. He made you bring me a damned lie! Watch out, you pious
little fellow, how much of your heart you give to faith. We've
hanged God once, to fulfil the scriptures. So now tell me what
reason God still has to keep the strain of treachery so active in us.
Eh? You tell me that.

CLERIC. Oh, my lord, watch your words.

HENRY. What kind of a farce is good faith and loyalty?

ELEANOR [*standing upstage*]. You tell me that.

HENRY [*looking at her*]. I am hurt by the child in this Tom Becket.
[*Enter* GILBERT FOLIOT, *Bishop of London, the King's confessor.*

ELEANOR. What has he done?

HENRY. Resigned from the Chancellorship, with his love and
obedience. Come here, Foliot. You'd better absolve me of a
blasphemy, or something of the sort. It upset our holy innocent,
here.

FOLIOT. Are you truly penitent?

HENRY. Yes, yes, yes, come on!
[FOLIOT *begins to speak in Latin, the words of absolution,
and then breaks off.*

FOLIOT. *Ego te absolvo*—My lord, will you give me your attention?

HENRY [*still reading Becket's letter*]. God in a suicide's grave! Will
you listen to this? . . . 'Not wishing now to be in the royal court
. . . diddle, diddle, diddle . . . to have leisure for prayers, and to
superintend the business of the Church . . .'—Who put him there
to pray? There are ten thousand monks, with nothing else to do
except say his prayers for him.
[FOLIOT *concludes the absolution, fairly hurriedly:*

FOLIOT. —*in nomine patris et filii et spiritu sancti.*

HENRY. Amen.—Christ in glory, what's been the truth of him over
these years? The whole motive and labour of his mind, as he
showed it to us, was the wise conduct of this poor, tormented
kingdom. And he made a fortune out of it, which I didn't grudge
him. But, by God, that was all he cared for, to be the unsurpass-
able Becket, and nothing at all for the shaping of a just world: his
mouth was making words at me, like a purse farting.

ELEANOR. Now he will see your justice demonstrated,
This angelic justice,
Hearing all voices, and weighing them in its heart,
Having no person or desires. Show us, Henry.

HENRY. Where is he, then? Ever since his consecration
He has turned his back on us, crouching down in Canterbury
As though he had conquered a rock, stuck his cross on it,
And meant to keep a sulking stretch of water
Between him and me.

CLERIC. Sir, speaking of what we see at Canterbury, you would
praise, as we do, how the finger of God has touched him; how
utterly he has put aside all ostentation; how he feasts the poor,
visits the sick, and every day washes the feet of thirteen beggars.

HENRY. A very sagacious and elaborate performance. I hope the
beggars are paid for it.

FOLIOT. We must remember, my lord, the difficulties for him are
very great. An immense talent, as we know; but, even so, even
you, my lord, must have expected an uncertain period of
readjustment. He is anxious to please. It will be interesting to see
how he achieves what you have set him to do.

HENRY. We know you will be interested. So does he. The devil of
an interest.

FOLIOT. False. I had no ambition to be in his place, though I
believe it was said.

HENRY. It was said so, I believe. But you deny it. Love and
obedience have been said. But here it's denied. When do we have
the truth?

Enter BECKET

ELEANOR. Ask him.   [HENRY *turns his head away.*
He has left his rock.

HENRY. What am I supposed to make of this?

BECKET. What is natural because it is necessary.
  I am one man, not two. My heart and reason
  Both give me the same answer.

HENRY.   I can see no heart.
  What reason?

BECKET.   You gave me spiritual charge of the kingdom.
  I take it, then, the kingdom's need
  Is that I should carry this charge in good earnest.

HENRY. The kingdom, not a country parish. You know
  Very well the need of the kingdom you serve.
  It's a living land, not a charge of kneeling peasants
  Obedient to a bell. And you know the Church
  That you're the head of, with its delight in substance
  Growing on itself like sin. Power and privilege,
  The swollen spiritual legs we have to stand on!
  I'll tell you, Becket, why it is you have drained
  All the warmth out of yourself down there in Canterbury.
  Because the King's truth is the truth you still believe.
  You kept clear of me to give yourself
  A spiritual authority you know you're weak in.
  What's your answer to that?

BECKET.   If it is true
  That I'm weak in spiritual authority—it isn't
  For me to deny it—should you not thank God
  That I mean to gain it? What is the worth of a kingdom
  If the head of its Church has no spiritual authority?

HENRY. What is the worth of spiritual authority
  If the lives under it are lived in anarchy?

BECKET. What have I done that proposes anarchy?

HENRY. Contradictory power is what you propose.
   There is hardly one thing I have reached out for
   In these last months, which hasn't been obstructed
   From Canterbury. But I see you, Becket:
   You mean the Church to be answerable for nothing
   Except itself, and yourself to be answerable
   Only to the old would-be infallible Italian
   Who rattles his keys of heaven and hell whichever
   Way expedience turns him.

FOLIOT.   *Te absolvo.* My lord,
   Whatever the provocation, there's no advantage
   In turning your scorn on the Holy Father.

HENRY. Is there not? Then I'm taking no advantage.

BECKET. Henry, one of us there has to be
   To whom the single care is not of this world.

HENRY. Very well; give up this world.
   Contend against me like an opposite.
   See that the spiritual power is powerful in the spirit.
   Indeed, go on, be smitten with a great light
   And relieve us all of a load of darkness.
   Show us, my friend—we are hungry to see it—
   The humility, the patience, and the poverty,
   The movement into grace, the entire surrender
   And sacrifice of the self.
   And not by a demonstration of foot-washing.

BECKET. Why suddenly talk like a woman,
   Contriving an argument when you know the answers?
   You, Henry, of all men, who cry out
   For a demonstration of order, for a house of men
   So lucid and strong it will never be confounded.
   See the Church likewise. If she should have

No definition in terms of the world, no shepherd
To guard her rule and substance, she would soon be thrust
Into any corner that man, trampling forward
Towards his places of possession,
Thought fit to leave open. What is not seen or heard
But yet endures has to be shown and spoken.
How, then, without rich form of ritual
And ceremony, shall we convey
The majesty of eternal government,
Or give a shape to the mystery revealed
Yet as a mystery?

HENRY. All right, perform the mystery, demonstrate
The mysterious order: baptize us, reprove us,
Absolve us, and bury us; but in so far
As your body sweats like the rest of us,
You owe me obedience.

BECKET.   And in so far
As you live, Henry, like the rest of us
In a universe of powers outside your government:
And in so far
As everything beyond the immediate moment
Ends in speculation: and in so far
As not even the predictions of Merlin
Can provide us with a living geometry
Of what we do, or what's done to us, in these
Things you owe your obedience to the Church.

HENRY. I owe no obedience to a man who cheats my trust in him.
None at all to an ostentatious humbug
Who dragged himself up by the shoulders of the kingdom
And once up, kicked it away. Your breeding
Wasn't prepared for the full extent of your talents,
Not to serve this world, or God either.

BECKET. You have borne with me pretty well. I must live in hope
That God's patience won't fall far short of yours, my lord.
—Your permission to withdraw.

HENRY.   In a fury, good;
You're still living, then; there's a warmth
Residing somewhere in this reverend cadaver.

BECKET. I will go apart for a time.

HENRY.   Do, for a time,
And scour yourself with an hour of good thinking.
Return Tom Becket, a man unwilling to deceive
Either himself or me.

> [BECKET *turns as though to speak again.* FOLIOT *touches his arm.*

FOLIOT. Apart, apart. You are not ready to speak. This need never
have happened. Come away.

> [BECKET *moves away,* FOLIOT *and the* CLERIC *with him.*
> HENRY *turns aside to* WILLIAM MARSHAL, *who has returned.*

HENRY. Well, what's the answer?

MARSHAL. I saw the boy. He struck at me with a fist the size of
an acorn and told me I was an old what I am not, my lord.

HENRY. Would you say he is mine?

MARSHAL. Dead sure he is.

HENRY. Did you fetch him away?

MARSHAL. Yes, I did; I brought him back in my arms, and had
my guts nearly kicked into my back. It's a painful commission,
bringing home the future. Do you want to see him, sir, before
I take him to the Chancery?

HENRY. When he's Chancellor he can go to the Chancery.

MARSHAL. But how's this, my lord? I thought you said—

HENRY. You can go to the Chancery; you can fetch young Henry out of Becket's care, and his little wife with him.

MARSHAL. He was shaping well. Why move him?

HENRY. There's a change in the spirit of the Chancery.

MARSHAL. The boy loves the Chancellor—the Archbishop; spiritual shepherd and uncle-schoolmaster. I doubt if he'll leave the Chancery without tears. And I'm already thoroughly drenched and salted from the first one.

HENRY. We have seen the remarkable steady mind of self-love. We've nothing further to learn of that, Marshal. Fetch the boy home, and keep him in your own charge. Teach him good faith.

MARSHAL. I? Teach him?

HENRY. Good faith.

MARSHAL. I'm no schoolmaster.

HENRY. Well, then, be the book. Leave him alone to study from you.

MARSHAL [*turning to go*]. As you say.

HENRY [*his voice rising in pain*].
Tell me how a man who has seen eye to eye with me
Can suddenly look at me as if he was blind?

MARSHAL [*turning back*]. Sir?

HENRY. Fetch the boy home.
[MARSHAL *pauses for a moment as though to speak, then goes gravely away.* HENRY *slowly turns and faces the place where* BECKET *stood, as though squaring up for a fight.*

HENRY. Now . . . Becket.

CURTAIN

END OF ACT ONE

ACT TWO

ELEANOR

BECKET

HENRY

GILBERT FOLIOT

WILLIAM MARSHAL

EARL OF LEICESTER

BLAE

YOUNG HENRY, *the King's son*

RICHARD

GEOFFREY } *his brothers*

JOHN

ROGER, *Blae's son*

MESSENGER

BECKET'S CROSS-BEARER

BISHOPS AND MEN OF THE COURT

BECKET, *with the* BISHOPS. *Enter* ELEANOR.

ELEANOR. I can hardly wish you Goodmorning, Archbishop,
When the morning is so unwilling to appear.
                    [*She bows to them, as they bow to her.*
My lords. Could you see your way across the yard?

BECKET. By groping, ma'am.

ELEANOR.   Have you come to find the King?
Today's a poor day for finding any man;
Only sounds and voices, and half creations of the fog
Which move like men but fade like spirits.

BECKET. It's a murk which penetrates the flesh
And wraps round the bones. No day for the mind.

ELEANOR. Or the light foot. It's a hard, subtle terrain
You have come to cross in Henry, Becket.
Please heaven some good comes out of it.
For me (a woman who dreads an abstract passion)
It presents a chilling prospect. These London streets,
Which I seem to have to walk as a penance
For loving life too warmly, tolerate me
Less every day. And you have lost
Your genius for life, that ready sense of the world
Which used to give your gravity a charm
And your laughter a solemnity,
As though you sang the complex heart of reality
And by singing mastered it. How could worship
Or prayer do better?

BECKET.　　　　　　　　Alas, madam.

ELEANOR.　　　　　　　　　　　　Alas,
  Becket!

BECKET. God must guide me.

ELEANOR.　　　　　　　　　　To guide the God
  A little is sometimes not without merit. But I see
  The only way I can have any part in life
  Is to stand and be the curious onlooker
  While two unproved worlds fly at each other.
  Be sure you draw blood, to lift my drooping spirits.
  The ground under your feet
  Has become the sand of the arena.
  And here's the bull you are matched with.
          [ELEANOR *moves away as* HENRY *enters, with* COURTIERS.

HENRY. You had better throw some light on this new man
  The Archbishop, Archbishop. We're losing precious weeks.
  Every day men are born into an island
  Not yet ready to receive them.
  I need reassurance.

BECKET.　　　　　　　Of what, reassurance of what?
  Whether indeed there can ever be a world
  Answering to the man created?

HENRY.　　　　　　　　　　To achieve
  That is our whole concern. Suppose you tell me
  How you see your own part in the process.

BECKET. To protect us from going aground on deceptive time,
  To keep our course in the deep reality.
  As time is contained in eternity
  So is temporal action contained in eternal truth.
  And that truth can't be put at the mercy of time.

HENRY. Nor time at the mercy of an ambitious Church.
I will remind you of what you know already.
There are certain customs,
Part of the growing nature of this island,
Which many generations in their need and experience
Have made their own in a common law. And these,
For what better will come of them, we mean to maintain.
You're well aware of them:
Clerics, for a crime against the common law,
To answer to the King's court.

BECKET.   No doubt
You have noticed, by my wish the bishops' courts
Have made their judgements more severe.

HENRY. Very tactful and unimpressive. There have been
Already in my time a hundred murders
Which were settled by nothing but a futile fine
Or the lick of a prison.

BECKET.   There would have been two hundred
If we had hanged the murderers. As it is,
There are now a hundred men who see we think
Lives of more account than they did: spirits
In trust, which we must never despair of.

HENRY. Men who make a profession of God should expect
The heavier punishment.

BECKET.   They are still men.

HENRY. Indeed they are! Therefore we need to know
Who is to govern them. Let me go on.
Laymen brought up for trial before a bishop
Must be given in every instance legal witnesses.
No archbishop, bishop, or beneficed clerk
To leave the kingdom without my authority.

No one holding land of me, nor any
Minister of mine to be excommunicated
Without my knowledge. For this is what you do,
You lords of the Church Arrogant,
Like an old god crazy with his thunderbolts.
As for the rest of the problems hindering our hope,
You know them closely, having shared them.
But that was then, when I knew you. As things are,
I need your word that you'll obey these Customs.

BECKET. God said 'I am Truth', not 'I am Custom'.

HENRY. Whose truth are you, you acrobat? These Customs
    Are the truth of the men whose lives shaped them.

BECKET. What a man knows he has by experience,
    But what a man is precedes experience.
    His experience merely reveals him, or destroys him;
    Either drives him to his own negation,
    Or persuades him to his affirmation, as he chooses.
    And this truth is not custom.
    This is not under the law, but under grace.
    What you see as the freedom of the State
    Within the law, I fear, as the enslavement
    Of that other state of man, in which, and in
    Which only, he can know his perfect freedom.
    So this is how I must answer you:
    We obey you in everything, unless it should threaten
    The will of God, and the laws and dignity of the Church.

HENRY. 'Unless' is nothing, no answer, and no vow!
    Who is to set the limit on your laws and dignity?
    Who, apart from your own reading of God,
    Is going to control your ambition? Very astute,
    Isn't it, to attach yourself to a power
    Which proceeds and communicates only through you.

BECKET. If by me you mean the Church, tell me
  Who controls the ambitions of the State?

HENRY. The well-being of the whole community.
  What man here will undertake
  To define the will of God? We have seen it
  Mauling humanity with visitations
  Of horror beyond belief.
  If you're so devoted to this will
  Why don't you go to its aid?
  Heave your house down when the hurricane shakes it,
  Piss in the flood water. Strip those robes off, Becket,
  And stand here shuddering
  In the icy air of God's will. Or talk better sense.

BECKET. And yet here, at the mercy of these elements,
  We exist more often unharmed.
  The vehement liberty of terror, which ignores our flesh,
  Is not the will,
  But it knows the will, returns to it in calm.
  Even when in rebellion it keeps
  The signature of light. In the avalanche of snow
  The star-figure of the flake is there unchanged.
  It was out of a whirlwind that God answered Job.
  And here, too, in the whirl of our senses,
  The way for this will has to be kept unthreatened.

HENRY. The will of the people is the will of God.

BECKET. They have many wills: many lusts and many thirsts:
  A will for death as well as a will for life.
  But, quick or dormant, in th'm they have a longing
  To be worked into the eternal fabric
  By God's love. And so we go with you faithfully,
  And swear we will, only saving our order.

HENRY. Which means whatever you like to make it.
   One order is going to be saved: mine in this kingdom!
   You know as well as I do, your saving clause
   Is more effective than what you swear. You, Foliot,
   Give me a straighter answer. You, you, you, you!
   You're not so brash in your calling.

FOLIOT.   Well, my lord,
   We are here as one body. It will have to be
   As the Church is led to reply: in everything
   Obedient saving our order.

A BISHOP.   Obedient
   Saving our order.

OTHERS.   Saving our order. Our order.
                     [HENRY's *anger is like an explosion of madness.*

HENRY [*with a roar*].
   Save your commonsense if you want to stay as you are!
   The Church never said this to a King before.
   By God, it's not going to begin with me!
   I had a demon for an ancestor.
   There are times I feel her wading in my blood and howling
   For a sacrifice of obscurantical fools.
   And by God, she shall have it!
   Your old immunity is over, you're trapped
   In a change of the world, my lords, which men deserve
   And are going to be given. The man who gets in the way
   Is of no more consequence than a skull
   Kicked about by oafs in a field,
   And that's what he will come to. Jesus whipped!
   You have reason to blench and hug your skirts round you,
   I'll tear the parts out of you—
   Hell doesn't have a monopoly in torment.

You will find as good here, if you pull your pious faces
When I ask for help. You'd better consider it.

> [*He leaves them in an uproar. An unnatural light begins to
> penetrate the fog. Faces are distorted by it. Shadows gesticu-
> late at a great height above the* MEN *of the Court, who rage
> against the* PRIESTS, *some advancing towards them waving
> axes. The* BISHOPS *harry* BECKET *in extreme anxiety.*

THE COURT [*the words that can be heard*].

Time it was said! They've got to learn where they live. They've
got a hold on the country beyond anything ever known. Grabbing
lands that haven't been theirs for a generation. Making us a property of Rome. [*They advance on the* BISHOPS, *some waving axes*:]
Consider, if you want to live. We'll split your heads open and
find your brains! If the road wants clearing, here's a cleaver to
do it. That's it, beat a retreat! Ah yes, now you know the times
you live in!

> [*At the same time the* BISHOPS *have moved crying out to*
> BECKET.]

BISHOPS. Have you thought where you lead us? How do we serve
the Church if we lose our Sees? Or our lives, perhaps: God
knows what he intends. You've lost us the friendship of the King.
The Holy Father said Be moderate; moderate, he said, moderate.
If you had shown a spark of your old will to please. . . . Is your
power to leave you, now you're powerful?

COURTIER. Take your time, Archbishop. The King's in dead
earnest.

BECKET. As I am.

COURT. What becomes of your influence if you rot out your life in
a dungeon, nobody even remembering where you are? And are
you so sure of your motives, with due respect, my lord? No self-
applause, no vainglory, no obstinacy? Anyway, your future, and
the Church's too, depends on the way you think.

A BISHOP. Have you thought of our distress?

BECKET [*suddenly, after silence*]. Where is the King?

ELEANOR. Ask yourself where it is you stand, saying
    Where is the King?
    Look round at the unreality of the light
    And the unreality of the faces in the light.
    You and he, you told him, would reach a place
    Where you might not know what was being made of you,
    Or understand the conclusion when it came.
    Certainly the familiar world has departed.
    A death-world here, where every move
    Is magnified on to the fog's blind face
    And becomes the gesture of a giant.

A BISHOP. You made your decision alone. Carry it alone.
        [*Enter* HENRY. *He stands in the strange light, looking at*
        BECKET. *All other eyes are also on* BECKET.

BECKET. Still with anxiety, but hoping, trusting
    That you mean to command nothing against my conscience,
    I will give you the Yes you ask for.
                [*An exhalation of relief from the* BISHOPS.

HENRY. Then we can go ahead. What do the rest say?

FOLIOT. Yes; in good faith.

BISHOPS.   In good faith. Good faith.

HENRY. You are men of admirable judgement.
    Here they are, the Customs of the kingdom,
    Codified, ready for your seal. And when it's done
    You can give us a burst of bell-ringing to clear the air.

BECKET. What's this?

HENRY. Your word made parchment. Fifteen paragraphs;
    You're familiar with all of them.

ELEANOR [*to herself*].　　　　　A false move.
　　Oh, never define!

BECKET.　　　　　　No! By all-prevailing
　　God: no! I'll never set my seal to this.

HENRY. Ah!

BECKET [*to the* BISHOPS]. You see where being accommodating
　　And afraid has brought us. Fear is the father of sin,
　　The devil's best weapon is a man's nerves!

HENRY.　　　　　　　　　　　He agrees
　　To cramming God into the words of dogma,
　　But evades the simple expression of law!

BECKET [*to the* BISHOPS]. You see
　　The pit that's dug for us under the spread branches.
　　Dreading that I should be cast out and alone
　　I was leading the Church to a broken back,
　　Betraying all heaven's charge that was trusted in me:
　　A poverty of spirit please God I never
　　Approach again. Harder the forgiveness
　　Which I now need to find. For now indeed
　　I'm alone. The knowledge of my fault
　　Is my only companion.　　　　　　[*He moves away.*

FOLIOT [*in despair*].　　Where are you leaving us?
　　Fairly lying between the hammer and the anvil!

HENRY. Now you begin to know him, the bewildering
　　Turns to maintain himself, first will, then won't:
　　Will in the abstract, won't in the definition.
　　He pretends to agree, to mask his real intentions,
　　Until his bluff is called. And now we're to have
　　A display of the anguished penitent
　　While he looks for a way out. But I shall help him
　　To bring order to this disarray of the spirit.

You reject your work as Chancellor. I'll relieve you
Of all shadow of that great and false expense.
You needn't be haunted by a sense of debt
Which might hamper your independence.
You shall pay me back every penny you received
From the estates and castles which were yours then.

BECKET [*turning*]. But you freed me from all secular obligations
The day I was consecrated.

HENRY.   Before you freed
Yourself from the purpose of the time you live in.
You will make good the sums you spent
On your war in Toulouse.

BECKET.   In the service of the State!

HENRY. It was in the service of recommending Becket
To himself and me.

BECKET.   It will somehow be paid.

HENRY [*now in full cry*].
And since the eternal account overlooks nothing,
To free your conscience by precise audit
You can pay the country back what you had from all
The vacant sees and abbeys while you were Chancellor.
Then devote yourself to God with a less hang-dog look.
> [*A moan of consternation from the* BISHOPS. BECKET *falls
> on one knee, and supports himself with a hand on the floor,
> like a pugilist waiting to rise before the end of the count.*

FOLIOT. Have you given yourself time, my lord,
To think what this means? Where will the Archbishop
Find the sureties for so much? Do you mean
To punish us all, to shake the whole spiritual power?

HENRY. Who will not be glad to share a burden
Which lightens a bowed conscience? The Archbishop

Prefers to abandon the things of this world. [*His anger returns.*]
Why should a man make God my enemy
And the enemy of a maturing nation,
As this man does? You shall see him as I found him:
A man depending on office, no nearer God
Than I am. Tell him to come back and face me.

CLERIC. Sir, he is ill, the Archbishop; he has to ask you
To excuse him; he is taken ill.

HENRY.   Contempt
Of the royal summons! He piles up his mistakes.
The more he squirms to free himself, the more
He tangles himself in guilt. Twice already
During the last month or two he has tried
To get to France without my authority,
And twice the ships have brought him back again.
It looks as if this island
Isn't large enough to contain both of us.

ELEANOR [*to herself*].
Who will grow large enough to contain the island?

HENRY. Either there are laws for every man,
And he is one; or there are no laws for any man.
The day is vital, and the world can't stand still
To be cheated, even under cover of God.

ELEANOR. Let me say this to the man who makes the world—
And also to the man who makes himself the Church.
Consider complexity, delight in difference.
Fear, for God's sake, your exact words.
Do you think you can draw lines on the living water?
Together we might make a world of progress.
Between us, by our three variants of human nature,
You and Becket and me, we could be

The complete reaching forward. Neither of you
Will dare to understand it. Have I spoken too late?

HENRY [*ignoring her*]. The issue is so great, the man so intractable,
It has come to this; he has to stand his trial,
And be judged by England, not by me,
By England's dawning knowledge of herself,
As though she tried herself in the trial of Becket.
We have done with privilege of person. None of us
Is anything more than the purpose of our time.

> [*He leaves, in the diminishing light.*

ELEANOR. Who has left the most blood on the sand, Marshal?

MARSHAL. Ma'am, the Archbishop is badly gored, that's certain.
But what wounds have been made on the King we still have to
discover. This business has grown too big for me.

ELEANOR. Grown very small, Marshal: the size of two men in a
   rage.
We are not going to see the great issues contending,
Nor the new spirit of England being forged in a fire.
We shall see the kicks and blows of angry men,
Both losing sight of the cause.
The high names
Of God and the State are now displaced
By hurt pride, self-distrust, foiled ambition,
And the rest of our common luggage.

MARSHAL. That may be. But, all the same, the Archbishop is on
trial.

ELEANOR. When the glorious battle turns into the vendetta
The great issues, no longer controlled by men,
Themselves take over command. Then at last he may listen
To some other voice than his own!

MARSHAL.   You mean the King?

ELEANOR. You saw, Marshal, how he turned away from me?
 Am I no more distinct than the men who walk in the fog?
 If I think I am a woman of flesh and blood,
 And unmistakeable spirit,
 He will soon undeceive me. He turned away
 As he would from his shadow on the wall.

MARSHAL. But, ma'am—

ELEANOR. Go to him, Marshal: love him as you can.
 He will have need of that.   [*Exit* ELEANOR.
        [*When the light returns,* FOLIOT *and another* BISHOP *are
        standing at one side. Enter* BECKET *with his cross-bearer*
        ALEXANDER LLEWELYN. *He takes the cross from*
        LLEWELYN.

FOLIOT. Look at this. Does he know what he's doing? [*To*
 BECKET.] You're ill advised, aren't you, Archbishop, to come
 here carrying your own cross? It's like drawing a sword out of
 the scabbard in the King's face. Suppose he should draw his own
 sword in reply? We should see a country at war with itself.

BECKET. We should know a man at war with himself. That's
 a risk we have to commit to God.
        [*He goes forward, using the cross as a staff in his left hand,
        as the* EARL OF LEICESTER *enters. He stops short as he sees*
        BECKET *advancing to take his seat.* BECKET *sits.*

FOLIOT [*to the* BISHOP].
 A fool he was, and a fool he always will be.

BECKET [*to* LEICESTER].
 What do you have to say to me? What is it?

LEICESTER. The verdict of the trial.

BECKET.   Such you call it.

LEICESTER. My lord, time has never seen before

Such a council as this, representing a whole nation
Sitting with the King in a conclave of law;
The evidence argued and weighed with deep anxiety.
And this new coherence of justice finds you
A perjurer and the King's traitor.

BECKET. Have you surrendered your mind so completely
That you can believe in this use of law?
Judgement is a sentence given after trial.
I was brought here on a pretext, not a charge.
So, for all your threshing of documents, the King
Thumbing his way through the always altering Customs,
Sweating for precedents and legal justification,
There has been no trial. And no trial can have no sentence.

LEICESTER. All you possess you hold from the King.

BECKET. Nothing. Nothing from the King. Whatever the Church
Holds is held in perpetual liberty.
I am your father, though you hold me in disdain:
Still and always your father, however vexed in thought,
Fallible in action, unpersuading in word,
Falling short in everything that makes
A man convince his times with truth. In spite
Of all, your father; and by a father's authority
I forbid you to give sentence.

LEICESTER.   Do I take
This answer to the King?

BECKET.   There is nothing
To be answered. I leave here as I came.
              [BECKET *moves away, bearing the cross, in a storm of threats*
              and mocks from those of the COURT *who are present. As*
              LEICESTER *turns to go, enter* HENRY.

HENRY. Where has he gone?

LEICESTER. He goes as he came, he said,
Refusing sentence, denying any trial.

HENRY. Fetch him back. We haven't done with him yet.

MARSHAL [*coming forward*].
This isn't the time to pursue him.
Three-quarters of the town followed him here,
And those who could, got down on their knees
And kissed the step he came in by. Take a look.
He can hardly get away or control his horse.

HENRY. There you have the measure of these people.
You can labour night and day to give them
A world that's comprehensible.
But their idolatry goes to any man—
Though he reeks of fault and cares less about their lives
Than he does for a point of heresy so fine
It wouldn't shake a hair in God's nostril—
So long as they think he bargains with a world beyond them.
Well, let them have his blessing,
Drawn with two fingers on the air.
I shall still bless them better in their daily lives;
And God can hear me and make the best of it.

Enter ELEANOR

ELEANOR. Other men have been busy with the ear of God.
There's news from Paris.

HENRY. Tonight he can lie
On his bed, and heave his breast with a sense
Of mastery which in fact is finished.

ELEANOR. Over how many years, I wonder,
Has Louis been pestering heaven for a male heir.
How many saints have been dragged from the calendar
To intervene? Almost a year ago

He lay flat on the chancel floor, refusing
To get up again until the Chapter had promised
To combine in one great assault of prayer.

HENRY. What is the news from Paris?

ELEANOR.   The power of prayer
Is the news from Paris. It has come in a letter
Written by Gerald of Wales three nights ago.
He was working late, he said, and had just put
His philosophy-fuddled head on to the pillow
When the frame of his bed began to shake
With a vibration of bells from every church in the city.
His dark room was all of a sudden
Staggering with torchlight. So he dived for his shirt
And made for the window. The whole of Paris was out
Streaming westwards. The prayers have reached their mark.

HENRY. It has taken them twenty years to get there.

ELEANOR. When he called from the window for news, an old woman
Waved a burning torch under his chin.
'Watch out for yourself,' she said,
'A king's been born in Paris tonight
'Who is going to be a hammer to your king of England!'—
So even the bricks and haycocks in France are dancing.
The child has got into their wine.

HENRY. They'd better make the most of it. He may die yet.

ELEANOR. They have called him Philip-Augustus, Dieu-Donné,
Given by God on an August night; hinting,
What's more, at empire, a name full of promise.
                              [HENRY *turns to the men of the* COURT.

HENRY. You can all go to your beds.
Except you, Marshal; bring Foliot here.
                              [HENRY *and* ELEANOR *alone.*

HENRY. You're pleased with the news from Paris.

ELEANOR. When heaven makes one of its rare rejoinders
I should have thought it the merest common civility
For all of us to attempt a smile.

HENRY. It's a smile against everything we've succeeded in.

ELEANOR. I smile however I am moved to smile.

HENRY. Even at the prospect of a troubled future.

ELEANOR. You haven't left my mind much else to do,
Except appreciate
Life's more acid comments on human endeavour.
And then I smile. Tell me, in fact,
What place do I have in your perfect order?
You served me, and your posterity is safe.
So much for you and me. And now I am nothing in this land,
Nothing but your occasional whore.
I have been a legend. What is left of that now?
You expect me to abandon
The inheritance of brain and heart
Which I received from my ancestors,
Who for generations have been a race of men
Born to act on events like sun on the vine.
But before the vows of marriage I accepted the vows
Of birth and blood. I shall be as faithful to mine
As you are to yours, though yours are lawless:
You who so struggle for order everywhere
Except in your own life.
If anarchy should prove to be a state which is indivisible,
Stretching from your own body across the face of the world,
You have stinging days ahead of you. Meanwhile
I smile, at this and that; and the boy born to France.

HENRY. The future of the young eagles means nothing to you.

ELEANOR. Does it not? I am their mother.

HENRY.   And I'm their father,
However at odds I may be with time and men;
However beset within and without, I am still
Their father; and your birth and blood
To which you say you intend to be true, mingle there
With mine. God above us, the house is a single thing!

ELEANOR. Though no man in the kingdom has enough fingers
To count your women: and all men know what tunes
You play on that Welsh harp, Rosamund de Clifford.
[*Sings to herself.*] 'By the flowing river a flower is growing.
'In a Thames bower gleams the king's own flower.
'Rosamunda, Rosamund, rose of the world . . .'
Curious I should forget how that song goes on. I hear it so
often, when the wind's my way; though usually whistled.
        Re-enter WILLIAM MARSHAL, *with* GILBERT FOLIOT.

HENRY. There's nothing to be said. The days are hot;
The thirst on the way demands a little shade
And fresh water. One thing I ask you to remember—

ELEANOR. You sent for London. Here he is.   [*Exit* ELEANOR.

HENRY. The labouring is most dark alone. Foliot,
There's a boy for France.

MARSHAL.   I told him.

FOLIOT.   I had heard.

HENRY. The scrap of flesh has given them a future.
France from now on has a new pair of eyes in its head.
We have to make sure those eyes look out on a future
Already decided, an established world.

FOLIOT. What man dictates the future?

HENRY. In this instance, I do. We'll put it in working order.
Young Harry can have the crown of England now.

MARSHAL. Two kings at once?

HENRY. We'll plant the saplings firmly in their place.
All the boys shall have their lands, and learn
To love and defend them while I am alive to see it.
Richard can have Poitou and Aquitaine.

FOLIOT.   The Queen's lands!

HENRY. Richard is the boy most hers; her lands
Fall naturally to him.

MARSHAL. Think a moment, sir; we know the young princes
Have a sight more vigour than experience.
What do you think they will make of a gift of power
Like this which you mean to give them?

HENRY.   Nothing but good,
Because the voice of Plantagenet is one voice,
Calling and answering along the same road.
The power I give them is trust and affection. How
Can this be ill spent?

FOLIOT.   Do you think the Archbishop
Will be prepared to crown the boy?

HENRY. What Archbishop?—It shall be done as I say.
Come on, we can discuss when and how. Do you see
The bated look the sky has? The way of the wind
Is altering. The trees are drawn with chalk on slate.
Spit in the air, Foliot. You will see how differently
The world looks in the morning when its plan
Is well drawn for a hundred years of peace.

                              [*Exeunt* HENRY *and* FOLIOT.

MARSHAL. But the morning was only another day. It emerged
sullen and bedraggled, after a night of bucketing rain, much as

we all did after a night of too little sleep. I heard the chanting of Compline, then of Mattins, and at last of Lauds. And the daylight was hard to face.

Enter TWO MONKS

1ST MONK. What is the news of him? How does he do, the Archbishop?

2ND MONK. He does very well. He has left us. So it goes.

1ST MONK. Is dead, do you mean?

2ND MONK. As far as the King's concerned, worse than dead. Last night one of the town gates was left unlocked, by the greased palm of a miracle. And heaven took the chance, and produced a storm of rain to cover up the sound of his riding away.

1ST MONK. He's out of the King's hands, then?

2ND MONK. Out of the King's hands, nearly out of the kingdom: disguised, heading for the coast; making for the French court. So it goes.

MARSHAL. Before noon the whispers had become a certainty. Before a month was over, Louis, to all Europe, was the man who protected the Kingdom of God, and Henry the man who was trying to destroy it.

1ST MONK. Thank God he is free.

2ND MONK. Thank God, if you like, for a father who deserts his children. That's the state we are in now.

1ST MONK. What are we to think of it, then?

2ND MONK. There is a toll to be paid to the devil on any road a man takes.

MARSHAL. As the day went on, the streets were choked with rumours. The man Becket was at large and the world rocked.—

But the King made his way as before, forcing new roads ahead of him. . . . There were other things to concern us. Today we've crowned the dark secret of the future. The young eagles are coming into their inheritance.

Enter BLAE

I was looking for you, sweetheart.

BLAE. Well, look who's here.

MARSHAL. I've brought you one of the new coins: struck to celebrate young Henry's coronation.

BLAE. How much more is it worth than the old ones?

MARSHAL. Not a ha'penny, but it's an interesting object. If you want to see them come back from the Abbey and take a look at your boy, I'll show you a place where you can squint through into the hall. [*He leads her to a point of vantage.*

BLAE [*as she goes*]. Thanks. I'd like to see him again. How is he growing?

MARSHAL. Not altogether up, but he thickens; and what he hasn't got in inches he piles on in intelligence. He sits at his books like a man who would rather eat paper than beef.

BLAE. Ah, God, that's the strange thing! To think that though I never had a brain in my head I once had those brains in my belly.

MARSHAL. The King means to have him for his Chancellor.

BLAE. Well, you never know what will come of your guts.

Trumpets. Enter, as from the Coronation, YOUNG HENRY, GEOFFREY, RICHARD, *and* JOHN, *his brothers*; BLAE'*s son* ROGER *and* HENRY *and* ELEANOR.

MARSHAL. Here they come now.

BLAE. That's not him, is it? No, that's not him, I know.

MARSHAL. That's the young prince Geoffrey, Count of Brittany
by the new mandate. . . . And there's Richard: sings like a min-
strel: his mother's boy.

BLAE. There's Roger now; I know him, I know my boy!

MARSHAL. There he is. He keeps a dogged, patient kind of manner,
considering the provocation he gets from the four legitimates.

BLAE. He's a man on the way all right, God bless him. I didn't
do half bad there. That's a thought worth keeping to end my
days with.

> [MARSHAL *leaves her and joins the Court. As the stage fills,*
> BLAE *is lost to view.*

HENRY. So I've seen beyond my death; what other man
Can say that? Blessed to rest, if only for a moment,
On the days which won't be my concern. And then
It was good, that passing salute of the sun
As we came out on the street.

ELEANOR.   And the sighing silence
Of the crowd who saw it.

> [*They go aside to disrobe.* MARSHAL *kneels to* YOUNG
> HENRY.

MARSHAL. My loyalty, for all the days I live.

YOUNG HENRY. There's not likely to come a time when I shall
doubt it.

HENRY. Help him off with his robes.

YOUNG HENRY.   No; I'll wear them.

RICHARD. He has the illusion of being a king, Marshal;
Don't disabuse him.

YOUNG HENRY.   Brother Richard is having
A morning of envy.

RICHARD.   Says the shadow of his dad.

HENRY [*raising a cup*].
   A long and prosperous life to Harry, to keep
   The flower of the broom golden when I'm gone.
   Pledge him, Richard,
   And you, Geoffrey. John, the health of your brother.

RICHARD. Prosperity, if you can get it.

GEOFFREY.   And good endeavour
   To our wives, to hurry on the generations:
   Especially to mine. Much pleasure to Constance.

JOHN. I shall reign before your children.

GEOFFREY.   Will you, sprat?
   You mean to live as long as that, do you?

ELEANOR. A long life to all my defiant eagles.
             [HENRY *sets refreshment before* YOUNG HENRY.

HENRY. May all men serve you well, and you them.

MARSHAL. Not many princes are given the dignity
   Of being served by a king.

YOUNG HENRY. If Becket had been there to crown me
   I should have known what my dignity was worth.

GEOFFREY. Good health to the troublesome Archbishop!
      [*A moment of silence. Except for a quick movement from*
      ROGER *towards the* KING, *no one moves, until the* KING,
      while MARSHAL *is speaking, swings round on the Court and*
      dismisses them.

MARSHAL. Each time he made a bold move to clear the way ahead,
   the ground became more dangerous than ever. When he thought
   he had finally disposed of Becket, the name of Becket was
   breathed out like fire all over Christendom. And now, when with
   love and trust, he stations the boys as sentinels to the Angevin
   world, the ground seems to crack where he stands.

YOUNG HENRY. Why shouldn't we speak of Becket. I am very fond
of him.

GEOFFREY. He does very well in France, I hear: hand-in-glove
with Louis.

YOUNG HENRY. They know how to value a man there, that's the
truth.

RICHARD. What do you put your value at, lord high brother? I'll
knock you down for a song.

HENRY. Good patience, do I have to plead with you
To think where your own interest lies?
Whoever makes harm for me harms you, and all
Those thousands of lives who look to us
For their safe conduct across time. We are bound
In one future, each depending on the others.

ELEANOR. And yet, you can no more make the future obey you
Than you can make yourself obey
Your own belief in the just mind.
Haven't you just driven out of your kingdom
Four hundred human lives, men, women, children,
In the middle of winter, out over a wild sea
With nowhere to go?—And their crime, what is their crime?
Simply their relationship to Becket.

YOUNG HENRY. Is this what he has done?

ELEANOR. They have gone to France, to spread the gospel
Of our just law-giving master of government,
To whose unknown fate my sons have been dedicated.

HENRY. To a strong peace in which they can thrive.

ELEANOR. You have set half Europe raging to see you brought
down.
I will tell you something certain about the future.
You will be alone. You have given my lands to Richard,

As though you considered me already dead.
It shall be so, then: to you I will be dead.
My life is in Poitou with Richard. There
At least, the warm sun will give me leave to smile.
And we shall make laws for sport and love
And put a little light in the eyes of Europe.

RICHARD. With three thousand men-at-arms at my disposal.

YOUNG HENRY. You caretaker of your mother's lands!

ELEANOR. You shall come to us there, Harry, all of you shall come,
Whenever you make yourselves your own masters,
Or when you need the sun to set your blood
Flowing more freely than ever it can here.

HENRY. That evil genius they called you once
Is alive again: turns now towards these boys.

ELEANOR. They shall show me how the world should be.
And I will believe there can be such a world.

HENRY. You were with me all through the time when I was shaping
The nightmare into an empire. Do you mean
To give the nightmare back to them? You can remember it.

ELEANOR. I know it still. But at last
I mean to wrench myself awake
And open my eyes to my own reality.

HENRY. Then please God you find that dawn less false
Than it is to me. Your true reality
Is in guarding what I have made.

ELEANOR. It's in myself, past, present, and to come.
Where will they find yours? They will break you open to find it.
                              [*Exit* ELEANOR. *The boys glance at one another.*

YOUNG HENRY. There are too many things wrong here
In the old world of your generation, father.

Hardly any content with the way things are going.
I have ears; I know what's going on.

> [RICHARD *gives a deflating twang on an instrument. There*
> *is silence for a moment.*

HENRY. Sons,
Look well into the human face.
You will see there the desert you must cross
If you mean to make the city. God knows
At first I could have believed all men
Were born of an act of love, though sometimes
To be contended with, or destroyed, or wept over,
Yet never altogether losing the trace
Of the good hunger which made them. Now there aren't
Many I can look at with much belief.
But, by Christ's blood, I'll give them the city of the law
Even if I have to make it by fearful means.
And then trust it complete into your hands,
Which are also of my making.
But first look well into the human face.   [*Exit* HENRY.

RICHARD [*strumming*]. 'So then they all to dinner went
                          Upon a carpet green . . .'
Do Harry; visit us in Poitou
When your crown starts to cut into your forehead.

YOUNG HENRY. I can see it's been cutting into yours all day.

RICHARD [*leaning towards him*]. Now look again: a flawless brow.
[*He tips* YOUNG HENRY's *crown.*] But what
Do we see here? It's the mark of the royal slavey.

GEOFFREY. Show him respect, Dick. You can still smell the holy
oil on him. Sing him the song you made for the coronation.

RICHARD. What is music to a man who has lost his liberty?
Well, we can try.

[*sings*]   To sing of a woman is no care.
        Only to mention breasts, belly, and thighs
          Is to have the music.
        Or sing of no more than her hair,
        The moist lips, the closing eyes,
          And there, there
          Are the words and the air.

        But praising a brother for a crown
        Which no more fits him than a basin,
          It's hard to do it.
        A shadow with a royal frown—
        What notes will fill the diapason?
          And where, where
          Are the—
            [YOUNG HENRY *leaps up and grabs the instrument.*

YOUNG HENRY. All right, I've stood enough!

RICHARD. Afraid of the truth?

YOUNG HENRY. Fed up with insolence and envy. I'll settle with
you.   [*He takes off his crown and robes.*

GEOFFREY. Oh, this is excellent! There's war among us!

RICHARD. Less arduous than making songs. Look, what ferocity!
      [*They draw their swords.* JOHN *puts on the robes and the
      crown, which are too large for him.*

JOHN. I'll be the king.

YOUNG HENRY. I'm ready for you; come on.

RICHARD. Pleasure, pleasure, pleasure.
      [GEOFFREY *has also taken a sword, and is ready to signal
      the start of the fight.* ROGER, *who has stood silently by until
      now, suddenly speaks.*

ROGER. Don't be such fools. Put the swords away.

RICHARD. Ding, dang.

GEOFFREY. Their blood's up. Now we really have come into our
inheritance. Mother Mary, this is very interesting.

> [*He starts the fight with a lift of his sword.* ROGER *gets
> between the fighting brothers. Unnoticed, he is wounded.*

ROGER. I tell you, you're not going to go on with this!

RICHARD. Look out, you bastard boy, we're busy.

YOUNG HENRY. Have you lost your senses? Get away from here.

GEOFFREY. Cut off his legs and continue.

YOUNG HENRY. Come over here, Dick.

ROGER. It's nothing to me if you want to slide about on your own
blood.

YOUNG HENRY. Then get out of the way.

ROGER. Except that it's my blood too, at least in part,
But, aside from that, it's the blood of the whole body
Of Plantagenet government; of the world's peace,
And the outcome of everything the king has lived for.
What thought have you given to that? What other man
Living could have gone so ahead of his time,
Holding so steadily to what he believes in,
While envy, prejudice, and self-interest
Are disputing every step he goes? And now
You can't keep the peace among yourselves! I tell you
If you don't know how to combine in one Plantagenet will
You might as well trundle the crown straight into the sea!

RICHARD. We'll show you how we combine to deal with a pompous,
impertinent ass!

GEOFFREY. Is the new King subdued by a cocky little bastard? . . .
Look out.

> [*He has seen* HENRY *and* MARSHAL *returning.*

ROGER. I seem to have taken . . . a cut from the swords . . . when
I . . . [*He falls. The three sons, with swords drawn, stand in a semi-
circle around* ROGER.

YOUNG HENRY. It wasn't any fault of ours. He got in the way.

GEOFFREY. A burst of oratory knocked him down. Well, we're very
sorry.

MARSHAL [*kneeling by* ROGER]. Quite a scratch here; he's been
losing blood. All right, he's coming round.

HENRY. So you mean to carry out the prophecy:
From the devil we came, and to the devil we'll go—
Brother against brother, the sons against the father.
I thought we might have got free from that curse.

GEOFFREY. Nobody was going to kill anybody, as far as I know.
[RICHARD *goes off, strumming the instrument;* GEOFFREY
with him. JOHN *leaves the crown and robes beside* YOUNG
HENRY, *who remains.* MARSHAL *has helped* ROGER *to his
feet, but he loses consciousness again and* MARSHAL *picks
him up in his arms.*

MARSHAL. It's not so long ago that I carried him here
Struggling like a bat in a veil. No serious
Damage is done that I see. [*Exit* MARSHAL.

HENRY. But how much
That none of you see.

YOUNG HENRY, What else could I have done?
Sit like a girl and let them mock at the crown?
They were trying to make a laughing-stock of me,
Said I was nothing but your shadow.
But I can make men follow me, and command them, too,
And strike fire out of my name as good as any
Or better.

HENRY.   You can find men to follow you:
   All the malcontents, hangers-on and family runts:
   They would follow you, if your brains were pig-swill.
   But if you want better than that, wait until time
   Has made something of you. As it is
   You're not fit to lead a crusade of children.

                              [YOUNG HENRY *puts his head in his hands.*
   Harry, have you never heard men mock at me,
   With a contempt for what I do, enlarging
   The errors, belittling the purpose, refusing
   To nourish the attempt; for all they're worth
   Increasing the chance of failure? When the world
   Laughs at its own opinion of you
   Don't let it destroy
   The man you are going to become.

YOUNG HENRY.   They shall see what I am.
       [*He takes his robes and crown and goes out, past* MARSHAL,
       who enters.

MARSHAL. He is in good hands. He will soon recover.

HENRY. I wish I could say the same of everything about us.
   But the days have been lamed, Marshal, somewhere in the mind.
   We may have to go on with that to the end now.
   Why do I see that arc of drawn swords
   And the falling body as though they would never leave me?
   Am I losing heart? Good man, that's not the trouble yet.
   I can go further and harder than we've come.
   But the health has gone out of the air.

MARSHAL. Sir, you remember at St. David's when you came
   To the great stone across the river, the woman
   Who screamed out at you Merlin's prophecy
   That the King would die as he walked across the stone.
   You hesitated; but you crossed.

HENRY [*chuckling*]. With my feet
   On Merlin's reputation. Right enough, Marshal,
   We shall reach the other side. You shall see
   How we change the look of things. The whole of Europe
   Is snarling at us, yes? Louis up in arms
   And off to invade Normandy, on the understanding
   That our day is over! Right! Now, Marshal,
   Observe the transformation. Henry Plantagenet
   Is in the mood for wooing. Our disturbing spirit
   Is prepared to humble itself,
   To cool the hot bellies, making such a gusty
   Rumble of indignation. Louis for a start:
   Catch him in Normandy, wake him up to see me
   There beside him, like his first shadow in the morning.

MARSHAL. Already he thinks you don't travel as other men do,
   But go on wings.

HENRY. Carrying persuasion, I hope.
   'Why, Louis, my liege, this won't do.
   'I've brought sad confusion to your mind,
   'Which my sorrow will mend. You who know so well
   'The extent of divine mercy, will want to see
   'A reconciliation between Becket and me.
   'I promise him a safe return to England
   'And full possession of his office; and he can crown
   'Young Harry all over again, with his and your
   'Young Margaret.'—And so we steady the days
   And begin to cross the stone, Marshal.

MARSHAL. And how
   Does the aggrieved heart of the Archbishop take it?

HENRY. Look, Marshal: I am going half way to meet him.
   And here we stand in Normandy, ready to float him
   Again towards England. And God knows I have shown him

Plenty of reverence—
Holding his stirrup for him while he dismounts,
Acknowledging that the less should serve the greater—
Louis could hardly do better.
And before God I would have things as they were.
I only ask him to treat me with tolerable respect
In front of these men who are watching us from their places.

> [MEN *are standing behind. Enter* BECKET.

Let us show each other all the good we can
And forget our quarrel.

BECKET.   I am very willing.

HENRY. The days behind us are thoroughly rebuked.
If we ever remember them
It will be with such fierce pain, the days ahead
Will double their virtue to overcome it.
There have been many kings of England before me,
Some greater, some less than I am. And many good
And holy Archbishops. Behave to me as the most
Holy of your predecessors behaved
To the least of mine, I'll be satisfied.

BECKET. I am touched by this. Yet we mustn't forget
That if our predecessors had settled everything well
We should never have had to undergo
These fearful years, of such harm to us both.

HENRY. Maybe so. Also remembering
That providence is a great maker of journeys,
And whoever refuses to go forward is dropped by the road.

BECKET. At least I take hopefully to the sea with you;
And surely England will take us up
Like a palm-branch in its hand, to see us riding
Together again on the road to London.

HENRY. Well, that must wait till I come there.

BECKET [*a pause*]. Does this mean
I'm returning alone?

HENRY. I can't come yet.
A little time will be yours to find your place again.

BECKET. This isn't the homecoming I expected.

HENRY. Your old weakness for riding in triumph, Becket.
I have to disappoint you. But if we go on soberly
The day for redeeming the past won't be far off.

BECKET. I pray it may come. But looking towards England now
Something tells me I am parting from you
As one you may see no more in this life.

HENRY. Heaven forgive us, do you think I intend
Any treachery to you?

BECKET. May it be a long way from your wish.
But sometimes in the mind's despair
When every thought and contrary thought, every
Act and opposing act, equally bear some taint
Of the man I am, I see I may be one of those
Whose life won't serve.

HENRY. Don't be too proud to live.
What's the matter with you? Can't you trust yourself
To accept the promise of things improving?—Becket,
The sea is running as smooth as a hound for you;
I'm sending you back with a pliant wind
All in your favour. And, if everything goes as it should,
You shall have the kiss of peace when I come to England.
Is this intention good enough to be blessed?

BECKET. In the name of Triune Majesty, the blessing
Of heaven on you.

HENRY.   And mine of the world on you.

                                              [*Exit* BECKET.

MARSHAL. It isn't the blessing of the world he's after now,
Nor yours; he is trying to find a success
Beyond human argument.

HENRY.   Looking
Into his eyes, Marshal, I could find nothing there
Which could help us to a new beginning. He makes me despair.

MARSHAL. Thinking back on it now, he seemed to me like a man
Who had gone through life saving up all passion
To spend at last on his own downfall.
What else are we to think, when we remember
How he behaved as soon as he reached England?
If that wasn't infatuation, that clumsy, aggressive
Unforbearance, before his shoes were dry
From the foam of the beach, there's no more charitable word.
I shall never forget the Bishop of London's face
When he brought us the first news of it.
He came pitching to Normandy, like a leap to safety.

Enter GILBERT FOLIOT

FOLIOT. It has been even worse than I feared it would be.
His rapturous welcome at Dover, and all the way
To Canterbury, so buoyed him up,
He might have been the lord of Spring
Making his progress on the winter roads.
Not a happy beginning to help him to moderation.
And as soon as a roof was over him, he struck
His note, in his most uncompromising key.
Excommunication for all who took part
In the crowning. And your men and his, my lord,
Had already clashed with some loss of life even before I left.

HENRY. I put him in the way of peace.

FOLIOT. You will never have it in his lifetime!

HENRY [*raging*].
What's the good of any of you, standing round
Like a lot of rotting pit-props, while you leave me
Wide open to the insolence of a fellow
Who came to me first on a limping mule, and now
Might as well spread his buttocks on the throne?
Do you all intend to sit about for ever
With your hands hanging slack between your knees,
Leaving him to foul the whole distance we've covered?
Who will get rid of this turbulent priest for me?
Are you all such feeble lovers of the kingdom?
      [FOUR MEN, *silently touching and beckoning each other,*
      leave the stage.

FOLIOT [*disturbed*].
I may have spoken with too much bitterness.
My world is too recently shaken to see these things
In a prudent light, but that is what we must do
With God's help; as we tried, my colleagues and I,
To nurse him through the dangers of his temperament,
Hoping for wisdom. And in return for this
He cuts us out of the Church's body like tumours.
But I know I spoke with too much feeling.

HENRY [*cool again*].
And great relish. We can take to the counsel-table,
Consider soberly the best way to move against him.
He has made his last mistake, and exempted me
From any promise I made to forget the past.
As he insists on being the sickness of the kingdom
It's up to us to be the physicians, to diagnose

The sickness, consult, and cure.

> [*He turns and sees the empty places.*
> What has become

Of the men who were with us?

FOLIOT. I was half aware of their going, that's true, and felt
A passing fear that your words might have been given
A more violent meaning than you meant to give them.

HENRY. What words of mine? You have some damnable thought.
What the devil do you mean?

MARSHAL. You may have more devoted men about you
Than you knew, or men with a devotion
To work off some score of their own, only waiting
For the first excuse to show their love for the kingdom.

HENRY. But they have no love for me! Neither have you
To have let them go. They had no permission to withdraw!
This was your doing, not mine, Foliot.
Get after them, Marshal; set men riding
On every road to the coast, search every port
And ship, and bring the lunatics back
If you kill your horses!   [MARSHAL *and others hurry away.*
I swear before God
This wasn't what I meant! It was not what I meant.
Go and pray; have the pain of prayer
Harsher than you have ever known it.

FOLIOT. I'm convinced we shall see them back, my lord.

HENRY. Convince your knees to pray until we know the answer.
[FOLIOT *bows and exits.* ROGER *stands pale and still at the
extreme right of the stage.*

HENRY. Dear Christ, the day that any man would dread
Is when life goes separate from the man,
When he speaks what he doesn't say, and does

What is not his doing, and an hour of the day
Which was unimportant as it went by
Comes back revealed as the satan of all hours,
Which will never let the man go. And then
He would see how the natural poisons in him
Creep from everything he sees and touches
As though saying, 'Here is the world you created
In your own image'. But this is not the world
He would have made. Sprung from the smallest fault,
A hair-fine crack in the dam, the unattended
Moment sweeps away the whole attempt,
The heart, thoughts, belief, longing
And intention of the man. It is infamous,
This life is infamous, if it uses us
Against our knowledge or will.

> [*The light is leaving the stage.* HENRY *moves restlessly.*]

I can hear the ice creaking on the river.
I could hear the horses on the frozen roads
In this taut air, half way from the coast.
How many days?

ROGER.   Two, my lord.

HENRY. They should have been back.
    Still have not come back.   [*He faces the audience in anguish.*
                    Did not come.
    [*He moves into the shadows. Enter a* MESSENGER. *He does
    not see* HENRY, *and stands for a moment undecided. Then he
    calls in the direction in which he came.*

MESSENGER. You said I should find the King here.

VOICE [*off stage*].   Is he not?

HENRY [*almost unseen*]. Speak from there.

MESSENGER [*moving*].   My lord—

HENRY   From where you are.

MESSENGER. I've been sent to bring you the news from England.

HENRY. Be afraid. Be afraid to say why they sent you.
You will never heal your mouth all your life long.
Leave it to a man who's already incurable.
I'll deliver your message.—It's the arc of swords.
Becket is dead.

> [*The* MESSENGER *is silent.* HENRY *gives a deep, low cry
> from the darkness. Suddenly he steps into the light like a
> madman.*

No men are fit to live, no-one in the world!
Foul and corrupt, foul and corrupt. All
Contagious. All due for death. Why should I spare
A man who can bear life and bring its messages?
They have made the King's name death.
It is treason now to breathe!

> [*He has the* MESSENGER *in his grip as though he would kill
> him.* ROGER *goes to part them;* MARSHAL *enters.*

ROGER. This is useless, my lord, useless, let him go!

HENRY. Take him out of my hands, take the thought of him
Out of my mind. There's been no news, nothing was said.
It's only here in my head, it's only here
Behind my eyes—only in my thoughts?

MARSHAL. No, my lord.

> [HENRY *turns and goes slowly away. At the farthest point he
> pauses, but does not turn.*

HENRY.   Let no one living come near me.

CURTAIN

END OF ACT TWO

ACT THREE

ACT THREE

HENRY

GILBERT FOLIOT

ELEANOR

YOUNG HENRY

RICHARD

GEOFFREY

CONSTANCE, *Geoffrey's wife*

MARGARET, *Young Henry's wife*

ROGER, *Blae's son, now Chancellor*

WILLIAM MARSHAL

A CAPTAIN

PHILIP OF FRANCE

OLD WOMAN

FOUR REFUGEES

SOME COURTIERS AND SOLDIERS

MARSHAL. For three years I watched him, living in his haunted mind. Three years, also, without a Queen: for the Queen was following her own fancies in Poitou, shaping her own dream of civilization. Alone, Henry tried to shake free of the shadow of Becket, going at last on a desperate pilgrimage of penance to Canterbury.

> [*The crypt at Canterbury, lit only by a few candles.* HENRY *is on his knees. The sound of monks singing the 119th Psalm.* HENRY *rises and sits on a stone seat against a pillar. He is barefooted, in a pilgrim's robe.*]

HENRY. It may be the day's first mass they are singing.
I can say the night has been crossed. Though you never know,
Crouching in prayers in this holy cellar,
Whether the light has broken
Or the night's as dark as ever.

Enter GILBERT FOLIOT

HENRY.   Is it day?

FOLIOT. The first hour, my lord, yes.

HENRY. The monks still awake to aim their lashing.

FOLIOT. They're waiting for you, at the high altar.

HENRY. Come on, then.

FOLIOT.   Should I let you make such a penance?
After three days of fasting, and twelve hours of vigil,
How can the body endure this discipline of rods,

Two hundred or more strokes from these seventy monks;
And some, my lord, who saw the Archbishop's death
Will give the rod their memory.

HENRY. Let it take away mine. I've stood enough
Of this perpetual shuddering of the nature
Which makes each day the moment before judgement.
Three years of it, the grinding of the thought,
Rat's teeth on the bones of the mind.
It was never my guilt, only in the rage of words.
But, if I think so, I diminish nothing.
I accept it all, if I can be rid of it all.
They're welcome to take their toll on my flesh
If I can be free of the world's loathing, and my
Self-sorrow. In Christ's name, let's go.

[*Exeunt* HENRY *and* FOLIOT.

[*Darkness. The chanting of the monks suddenly stops. A pause.*

[*Sunlight.* ELEANOR *with her Court at Poitou: the young queen* MARGARET; CONSTANCE (*Geoffrey's wife*). *Also* RICHARD, GEOFFREY, YOUNG HENRY *reading with his back to the others,* MEN *and* WOMEN *of the Court.*

ELEANOR. We are giving a new heart to the world
Here in Poitou, a new language for love,
Singers and poets with the tongue of Apollo,
Rivalling even France in the art of living.
We welcome Harry here, from the dark life
Of his father's kingdom. Here he will find the laws
Keep time in him like his own heart; for here
We govern as music governs itself within,
By the silent order whose speech is all visible things.
—But there is still business for this Court of Love.
How else can we define the world of woman
And man for you, before the Court adjourns?

COURTIER. Would the Love Court of Poitou consider
　　That true love can long survive in marriage?

GEOFFREY [*to* YOUNG HENRY].
　　You'd better give your attention to this, Harry!
　　Will our wives be judging themselves or us?

YOUNG HENRY. I had a cool enough welcome from mine.

GEOFFREY.　　　　　　　　　　　　　　　You've been
　　Away too long. The girl has forgotten the touch.

YOUNG HENRY. The whole enrapt colony of them
　　Has forgotten what the world is like. They're asleep in the sun.

GEOFFREY. You seem to have overlooked the mind of our mother.
　　She has a finger on every pulse in Christendom.

YOUNG HENRY. There's only one pulse in Christendom, the one
　　Self-will, overriding everything: our father!

GEOFFREY. Ssh, quiet! They've come to a decision.
　　This is interesting.

ELEANOR.　　　　　　We are not unanimous.

GEOFFREY. There's my Constance!

ELEANOR.　　　　　　　　　　　Nevertheless, consider
　　The nature of love. In love a man and woman
　　Are newly minted as in the beginning of the world,
　　Creating themselves out of each other's eyes.
　　But in marriage, whatever world is made,
　　Has the bones of the woman walled up in the foundations,
　　No air to breathe, nor any light to move in.

GEOFFREY.　　　　　　　　　　　I reject the statement!
　　No abatement of love in marriage, an increasing!
　　And there's my wife, carrying for you
　　The bulky demonstration under her heart.

CONSTANCE. You are called to order! This is contempt of court.

ELEANOR. It's a happy wife who finds love and marriage consonant.

YOUNG HENRY. Will you listen to what I have to say? Will you
    listen?
  In this drowsy hive you are all so in love with yourselves
  No facts can penetrate. Do we mean to let
  My father take all the world, and us with it?
  At Canterbury I saw him whipped like a boy,
  But, my God, now he has it all his own way.
  However fast the rebellions come
  Or the miracles flow from the dead Becket
  They disappear like snow from the heat of his flesh.
  At last I've got away from him: but if we mean
  To have any independent life, we should listen
  To what young Philip of France is saying. . . .

ELEANOR. There are murmurs of life still in this drowsy hive.
  I have young Philip's confidence, and he
  Has mine. Be with us here; you will come to know us better.—
  Well, there we have the session's end.
  Another day has gone ripening over the vineyards.
  As the dew settles on the dust, contentment
  Visit your evenings, and your sleep be untroubled.
                                    [HENRY *is standing among them.*

HENRY. There is one more thing before you go.

YOUNG HENRY [*hysterically*]. If he tries to drag me back
  To where I'm never given the powers that belong to me,
  I swear I'll throw myself down from the walls
  And finish what has never been a life anyway!

RICHARD. I've had no message that you meant to visit us.
  Forgive us if we haven't a welcome ready.

HENRY. Forgive yourselves if I come like a man among enemies.

ELEANOR. It's my world that you step into here, Henry.

HENRY. I know this place of yours, Eleanor,
  Where you nourish whatever can do me harm,
  Where you corrupt the hearts of my sons against me,
  And knit your fingers with any man who hates me.
  I know your world, where an acid wit
  Is valued higher than the mind hurt by it,
  Where rules dictate how a man should move, or love,
  Or cough, or betray, or do nothing:
  The unexceptionable dance of what
  Has withered within. Where every syllable's
  Up for valuation by the code
  Of the best poets, and nothing speaks from goodwill.
  I have understood at last the truth of the text:
  A man's enemies are the men of his own house.

ELEANOR. A man's own house is what he builds for himself.
  Here you're in mine, which faces its own way
  And looks towards other things.

HENRY.   Not any more.
  It has come to an end. You are under arrest.
      [*The sons cry out in protest.* ELEANOR *sees* HENRY's
      soldiers beside her.

ELEANOR. You take me back to yourself in the only way
  You know, by forcible possession,
  As you took your own vision of the world
  With a burly rape in the ditch. Your hopes, therefore,
  Are born bastards, outside the laws I recognize.
  The true law hides like the marrow of the bone,
  Feeding us in secret. And this hidden law may prove to be
  Not your single world, not unity but diversity,
  And then who will be the outlaw?

HENRY.   A fine secret law
  Which kills good faith among us! Yes, you can smile:

You think faith is a word I've no right to use.
But I can tell you, my love for women
Is more of a kind with God's laws
Than the aesthetic of adultery that you cultivate here:
And ever since Louis died
Political adultery with France
Is growing hot in all your dreams against me.
To which you add the violation of the minds
And hearts of these boys.
All this I'm bringing to an end.

ELEANOR.   You imagine so.
You can accuse me of nothing, except of following
The free course of events, the new order of things
Which is growing up round us. You bring nothing to an end.
You have kept young Harry breathing no air but yours,
Sleeping, riding, eating, always in your presence.
Is he any the more yours for that? He made
His escape from you. And so did Becket.
For what part of Becket, after all, has been done away with?
Only his human failings. Now he is rid of them.
His argument has become an incorruptible statement.
Purpose, however wise, is hardly blessed.
God thrives on chance and change.

HENRY. God use his eyes on me, this is sophistry!
If Becket had wanted peace he could have had it.
What's my crime? A secure Plantagenet empire
And a government of justice. Am I to be
The only man who goes begging for justice?
And begging it from sons who will benefit the most.
Affection they never lacked from me,
Patience they've drawn on as if from a bottomless well.
Let them try and deny it: and blame themselves

If I have to use harder means to make them know me.
[*To the* SOLDIERS:] Take the Queen to our care.

ELEANOR. You can drag me with you wherever you pace the earth,
Or leave me shut behind walls, you will know I am there.
Not I the prisoner. You, within yourself,
Are the one roped, waiting for punishment.
The shadows will only deepen for you. They will
Never lift again.

> [ELEANOR *withdraws, the* SOLDIERS *with her.*

GEOFFREY. Haven't you forgotten the prediction about our family?
What it is our blood inherits? Each of us against the other,
Brother against brother, the sons against the father.

YOUNG HENRY. That is one hereditary right you can't
Deprive us of.

RICHARD.   You can't rob us of your nature.

> [*Exeunt the* SONS. *The light changes. Enter* ROGER.

ROGER. Does a Chancellor, as fresh to office as I am,
Have a right to criticize his King?

HENRY. Any man has the right. But nobody
Can hit more painfully than my own thoughts.

ROGER. This is what I mean: this excess of grief
Against yourself is crippling your spirit.

HENRY. What did I do to lose them? First their love,
Then their lives? First Geoffrey, then Young Harry.
Geoffrey, a boy who spat with life
Suddenly by life spat away,
As though the fever said, like the voice of God:
'No more riding against your father.'
And then Harry, dying in a terrible anxiety
To have forgiveness. I doubt if a man
Can summon up enough grief to measure these things.

Enter RICHARD

RICHARD. Poor brother Harry. I have prayed that his soul
Shall be well received.
I imagine he is less perplexed now, taken
To the fountain-head. I shall miss the thought of him
Walking the world. I shall wonder about him.
We'll say no more. Death forgives most things.
I've come for your blessing, on my succession to England.

HENRY. You expect too much too soon.

RICHARD.   I only expect
What's mine by matter of course. Unless you want
To make it a matter of war. Do I have to show you
By force that I'm first in the hierarchy?

HENRY. A wiser ambition would be to be first in my heart,
A place you refuse to fill. But you have still
One brother left. There is still John.

RICHARD. Oh, yes, there is still the favoured one!
I can see a day coming when I shall find
John has been conveyed into my place
And England already disposed of.

HENRY. I dispose as I choose.
By God, you'd better submit to my peace:
And shall, till a world comes which I have no part in.

                                    [*Exeunt* HENRY *and* ROGER.

RICHARD. No, no, my father! Rather than that
I promise I'll drive you back across your life,
Town by town, over the road you have come,
Until I return you to your beginning
As lacking in power as when you were born.

                                    [*Exit* RICHARD.

MARSHAL. Ordeal by generation. This, then, was to be the end of
the universal argument: the ambition for the world transformed

into private grief. Is he the man left following behind, crying out for justice, or the man living out his faults? I have no answer. I only know that Richard and young Philip together, drove us back town by town as he said he would. We fell back through the king's memories one by one. 'Here it was . . .' he would say; 'and in this place . . .'. But each time it was a grimace he looked at; he said so. The memory had been different. The streets were like furrows; or scars, rather; and we were driven out, leaving dead men slumped on the walls. Until at last we withdrew here, into Le Mans, the King's birthplace. A thick mist was over the valley of the river. We smashed the bridge, and as we started driving spiles into the fords the mist lifted. We saw the pavilions where Richard and the French army had spent the night spread along the edge of the wood only a few yards away from the river. When the King saw them, he turned to me as though to someone who should wake him from a nightmare.

A CAPTAIN [*entering downstage*]. Where is the King?

MARSHAL. Not far away. We shall soon have him with us. Stand ready. [*Exit* CAPTAIN.

. . . He told us to fire the houses beside the river, destroy cover and hold the enemy back. But the wind veered, and the flames leapt roaring through the ramparts, and took hold of the city. The citizens have poured out through the gates, and here we are now, seven hundred men, fallen back to the fields outside the walls.

[*Three* MEN *and a* WOMAN *come out of the burning city, pushing a handcart piled with their possessions.*

1ST. Will you come on? Your mother's dead, isn't she, and the fire's gone over her.

4TH. O God, God, blessed Mary!

1ST. Well, come on, then.

4TH. Where can we go?

1ST. All the rest of them's a mile on the road, aren't they? Tie the stubborn bitch to the cart.

4TH. Leave me alone.

1ST. Then will you move yourself? You'll see what comes to you when the French army's across the river and wants a woman. Walk, will you?

> [*They move on. As they go, an* OLD WOMAN *enters, struggling along slowly, dragging a feather mattress and talking to it.*

OLD WOMAN. Ah, come on. What's the matter with you, you old feathers? You're not going to stay and be burnt. You'll come along with me. I haven't dragged you as far's this to lie down on you. It's to save you from the roasting.

MARSHAL. Here, you can't manage to take that along, old mother.

OLD WOMAN. I ought to manage. They was my own gooses. It took me seven Michaelmasses plucking them. And the feathers flew up light enough then, when they was wanted in the bloody bolster.

MARSHAL. Is this all that you've saved out of the city?

OLD WOMAN. I've brought away a spoon in my pocket; but the rest this old dreadful fire he can have it. Because he's sure to have it, after. As long as I keep the gooses' bed. In the end, I've had my days pretty comfortable. But there's my dying day I haven't had yet, and except for these gooses under me there won't be no other company then. So they can stop dragging and come of their selves.

MARSHAL. I'll take it a bit on the road. There's a cart ahead of you. [*He lifts the bed on to his shoulder.*] Ah Christ, your damn gooses! There's some burning smudge got into me!

> [*He lets the bed slide to the ground, takes off his helmet and flicks away the smudge.*

OLD WOMAN. Won't you lift it up again? Ah, ah! How am I going
　　to do, if the old devil has got into my bed?
　　　　　　　　　　　[MARSHAL *kicks the bed flat, and stamps on it.*
　　Is the old devil dead?

MARSHAL. May God do the same for the cares that scorch the King.
　　　　　　　　[HENRY, *dazed and half-blinded, enters from the city.*

HENRY. There's no more to come from God! I've seen what God's
　　mind is.
　　He knew I loved this city,
　　He knew if he ever looked into my heart,
　　He knew I loved the city I was born in.
　　And here my father lies in his grave. And I
　　Have thrust him in the fire.
　　I have burned my city, I have burned away
　　My own beginning, the one place in the world
　　Where memory could return untroubled, before
　　The earth began to bleed wherever I walked.
　　　　　　　　　　[*He looks up to the smoke-obscured sky.*
　　I meant the fire to save us! Do you think I kneel
　　To a God who can turn a brutal wind
　　To eat us up in fire? No,
　　I renounce all part in you: no such hands
　　As yours will have my soul. I'll burn it
　　Away like the city, I'll hurt you
　　In the centre of your love, as you do me.
　　Your eyes can sting like mine, and weep
　　With the same helpless water.
　　There's nothing left for either of us to save.—
　　We move out, Marshal.

MARSHAL.　　　　　　　　The men are waiting
　　Over in the meadow there, ready to stand or ride away.
　　All except Prince John. I thought he was with you.

HENRY. John not here? Damn him, it's a cool woman
Who can hold him down in this heat. But he'll be with us.
He's been close beside me all through these weeks;
He knows what has been endured, for the sake
Of his inheritance. How near have they come?

CAPTAIN. They're already wading the water, my lord.
Half Count Richard's men are across.

HENRY.   This time
He's not going to find a forgiving father, but days
Of riding after us till we make a stand
With the fresh troops of Anjou.
All right, sound retreat. And tell your men
No carrying away loot. This ride will find
The weak seams in all of them, men and horses.

                    Enter ROGER

ROGER. The people who have left the city have turned back on the
road.

MARSHAL. There's an old fording-place there if the French have
found it.

ROGER. The way out is getting narrower.

HENRY [*to the* CAPTAIN]. We'll go through the woods. Halt at the
first clearing.
I'll join you there.
          [*A trumpet call.* HENRY *is suddenly as gay as though he
          were a boy again.*
                    That trumpet will bring John.
I know every crawling root and low bough of these woods,
Hunted and roamed it all over in my boyhood:
Path, and turn, and brook, I'll show you the ways.
And we'll shake off Richard, leave him confounded.

Come on; the years are only beginning.
We head for Anjou; with Angevin men we can start again.
I turn my back, yes, I turn my back,
But when I turn my face—Marshal, Marshal—
Where are the horses? Get me into the saddle.

> [*He gasps with pain and grips the shoulders of* ROGER.

MARSHAL. Sir, we're ready; it's time to go.

HENRY. My own body now—my own body—

MARSHAL. What is it?

HENRY. —fights me. From the heels to the throat, Marshal!

MARSHAL. Lean on me. You'll crack the boy's bones.

ROGER. He can have my breath if it helps him.

MARSHAL. This is no place to stand. Walk these few paces. Come on, sir. The miles of the world have been nothing to you.

HENRY. Ah! Almighty God!

MARSHAL. Once through this you'll be back to everything you were.

HENRY. You think so, good.—But you don't know this pain! It hasn't—[*He pitches on to the gooses' bed.*] It hasn't a sense of mercy.

MARSHAL. You can defeat it, we must ride away.

HENRY. Cannot ride.

MARSHAL. Cannot? That has never been a word of yours, my lord.

HENRY. Cannot. It's mine now.

ROGER. Both armies are coming up: one out of the smoke, the other out of clouds of dust.

HENRY. Well, I'm here. And they come.

> [*He turns in agony on to his face.*

ROGER. Look how his breathing tugs him, Marshal.

MARSHAL. He must lie there, though we love him.

> [*A roll of drums from the left, answered from the right. The
> standard of Aquitaine is borne out from the city, the standard
> of France from the road. The clothes of the men are heavy
> with water.* RICHARD *comes forward, smiling, to* PHILIP *of
> France.*

RICHARD. We've come through that action, Philip France,
  Like sheep through a dip, sweating and red as fire,
  Damp as the water, but unscratched. Not a man
  To receive us. What sheep-faced fools do we look?

> [*He laughs, but* PHILIP *does not; his head turns, and his eyes
> rest on* HENRY.

PHILIP. Henry of England. Henry of England.

RICHARD. My father, God be with me! We have brought him
  down after all!

PHILIP. I was born to meet him at this moment. Wake him.

MARSHAL. He hears you, and knows whose voice it is.

RICHARD. It's the old dog's custom to take his sleep waking.

PHILIP. Does he mean to feed himself into the ground
  Now that his greatness has been so humbled?
  Tell him the time for that hasn't come yet.
  There are things to be said between us.

MARSHAL. He's in too much pain.

RICHARD.   He picks his time well.

MARSHAL. I'll come with you as a hostage; you can be sure
  He will meet you tomorrow.

RICHARD.   I love him for this!
  He can use the quick swerve, the double back,
  The dive for home, better than any ball player.
  But only Lucifer knew how to fall and then

Come back into a kingdom. My father is only
Demon by descent. But he made the most of it.

HENRY. If a son can make his tongue goad at a father
My body can be made to stand. You shall have your conference.
> [*He tries to struggle to his feet, but drops on to all fours, and
> moves towards them in this way.*

MARSHAL. Does this give you a pleasure you can bear?

PHILIP. Help him to his feet.

RICHARD.   He's playing for pity
Trying to shame us into leniency.
> [HENRY *gets to his knees, and then stands, putting* MARSHAL
> *aside.*

HENRY. Mind your own business, Marshal. Get it over,
You God-given boy. Get on with it.

PHILIP.   You have come
To the end of the proud years, when all events were Henry.
An old man now, with your self-appointed sorrows
To keep you company; no longer fit
For the care of the many people. The time has come
To make good the years of insult you gave my father,
As well as other men of worth,
Not least your son here. God with his gradual purpose
Has brought us face to face.

HENRY.   Spare us the piety.
What do you want?

PHILIP.   First of all the homage you owe me,
Placing yourself in my hands without question.
You will give to Richard: Poitou, Maine, Touraine,
Anjou, and Normandy.
Release his mother, your Queen, and call on your barons
To acknowledge him as your successor.

You'll pay an indemnity of twenty thousand marks,
For all the destruction of this campaign. Meanwhile
The castles which have fallen to us in this war,
As well as the castles of the Vexin, stay in our hands
Until everything demanded has been done.

> [HENRY *moves his head slowly towards* RICHARD.

RICHARD. This is all I ever asked. Except
For the indemnity, we make no other claims.

HENRY. All you asked. How much less is this than all?

PHILIP. The passing of years make their own justice.
> [*Still* HENRY *broods. The air is heavy and silent. Then a
> long mutter of thunder.* HENRY *raises his head.*

HENRY. Whose is this offence?
> [*A peal of thunder.* HENRY, *almost falling, is held by*
> MARSHAL.

Anything, anything. Stand back from me, Marshal.
And cover your ears. Further away. I am one
More who betrays the city.

> [*He turns to* PHILIP, *his voice very low.*
> You have my homage.
I can't get to my knees and up again, but you have it.
Everything you demand you know you can take.
That's done; the world has been altered; I can go.

PHILIP. We end the day with the kiss of peace, then.
> [PHILIP *gives* HENRY *the kiss of peace.* RICHARD *comes
> forward to do the same. As he kisses his father,* HENRY *speaks
> softly.*

HENRY. You have a lesson to learn. Death can wait
Until your brother John and I have made you
A fair return for this.

RICHARD.   My brother John?
And where do you suppose my brother John is?

HENRY. God forgive you. You've taken him prisoner.

RICHARD. Prisoner? John? My own dear brother? No.
He came over to us in the best of spirits this morning
To be on the side where the sun was rising.

HENRY.   Liar!

RICHARD. Brother John is allied with his brother Richard.

HENRY. He knows we undertook all this for him.

RICHARD. Who's for a rest, Philip? My throat's as rusty
As the earth here.

PHILIP.   There's a tent pitched in the field.
Water to wash in, and wine to swill down the dust.
Though in my spirits I could walk the world now.
                              [*Exeunt* PHILIP *and* RICHARD.

MARSHAL. Sir, sir, sir.

HENRY.   That's all, that's all that was left
To come. The rest can go on, on and on
As it will.

MARSHAL. Give way, sir; lie down here.

HENRY. Give way, go down . . . they all say it: go down,
Give way, go down.   [*He goes blindly on to the bed.*
                    Shame, shame, shame,
On a conquered king.
         [MARSHAL *crouches beside* HENRY, *and makes a pillow of
         his cloak while he speaks.*

MARSHAL.   You're only obeying
Your own body's knowledge of endurance
Which says Hold still for awhile, raging man.
Hour after hour, for thirty years,

You have shouldered up a world towards your mind,
Seen it thrown down more than once
As though for ever, and righted it, lifted it,
Borne it even higher. It would have broken
Twelve men's hearts, each of your own strength,
To have hewn their way through these years as you have.
The severe day begs for a little night to rest in.
Only a bruised, not a conquered King.

ROGER. Sir, believe what you've accomplished.
Your laws are fixed on England: grumbled at
Like the weather, but, like the weather, accepted
As a source of strength. The people have become
Their own law, in the twelve men representing them.
Unparalleled in Christendom, this new nature of the island.

HENRY [*in delirium*].
Hot on the road, eleven furlongs from Paris.
And now we're carrying half of France, the horse
Has good reason to stumble.

MARSHAL [*to* ROGER].   There's the fever talking.
I'll find somewhere where he can lodge before
The sun goes down. And out of the sound
Of that triumphant mob of France,
Singing there in the field, like a village wedding.
                                        [*Exit* MARSHAL.

HENRY. The bells are ringing—do you hear them, father?—to
celebrate my marriage. We've got the lustrous Queen. We can
start creating the world. My sweat could lie with hers and breed
rivers. It's too hot to ride any further. I'll get down into the water.
There's my father, washing the filthy summer sweat off him.
                              [*He struggles to get out of his clothes.*

ROGER. Wait a bit, sir: your father's not there now.

HENRY. Yes, he is there. Father, stay where you are. I'm coming. The grime of the journey is fearful. We have to wash it off.

ROGER. It's all right, sir: there it is: you have had your bathe.

HENRY. No. By no means. I'm not washed clean. [*He shudders.*] The water's been lying in the dark too long. It's icy cold. The caked sweat and dirt goes in so deep you have to wash to the bone.

ROGER. You're well washed now. Feel the water on you.
  [ROGER *guides the King's hand across the sweat on his body.*
  HENRY *turns his eyes to him.*

HENRY. On our way from Paris we bathed in a deep pool away from the sun. At night my father lay like this; in two days he was dead. Do you know who I am?

ROGER. The King, my lord.

HENRY. And who is this man the King?

ROGER. My father.

HENRY. That wasn't thought of when I got you. A bull night and an unfastidious whore, while the rain soaked through the tent. And by God's mercy you were made. I've done better things and been worse punished.

ROGER. I owe you a life, sir.
  [ROGER *dries the sweat from* HENRY's *body with a cloth.*
  Enter two or three MONKS. *They stand beside* HENRY.

ROGER. Why are you standing here? What do you want?

MONK. We have come a long way to reach the King. We come from Canterbury.

ROGER. Christ Church monks: this is no time or place for you.

MONK. We have found the King. And what better time for him to feel the troubles of other men than now, when he knows affliction ? We have come for a grant of our rights. No one but the King can give us the justice we need.

HENRY. You must wait until I come to England. Don't think because you see me stretched here on the rack, you can extort unfair promises. I'll hear you when I return.

MONK. What sort of answer is this to men who have struggled five hundred miles to see you ?

ROGER. You have heard the King. And you know he keeps his word. Go back to England, practise patience, he'll come to you.

[*The* MONKS *move away. One turns back, his face contorted with anger.*

MONK. By the merits of the blessed Thomas Becket, whose life and passion so pleased heaven, God will shortly do us justice on your body !

[HENRY's *head swings away, and he gasps.* ROGER *rises in rage, but* HENRY *pulls him down to his knees. Exeunt* MONKS.

HENRY. We have to hear it. I know this will never lift off me. . . . When you can, write for me to the Prior, tell him I think with concern of the difficulties which are his. Say that meanwhile they should consider deeply of the two sides, and think well of peace. Say they did harshly, to bring Becket out of the grave.

ROGER. Yes, my lord.

HENRY. You shall have this ring: the Plantagenet leopard.

ROGER. No, my lord, no. The leopard has to stay on your hand.

HENRY. It has bitten deep into my finger. There it is.

ROGER. I'll not take it until you are back to power, both in body and kingdom.

HENRY. Only you of the brood haven't confirmed that all my affections were a fool's errand. . . . What are you saying ?

ROGER. Sir, I was praying that God would soon return you to prosperity.

HENRY. The decision's already been made. There's no argument any more, and no more heavy blows between us. Go and call back that monk who cursed me with such pleasure that it made him tremble. Now he can absolve and bless me for his trouble. The formalities of allegiance. I believe in the law.

ROGER. Time for that when we've taken you to shelter.

HENRY. Call him now; while he still remembers me.

ROGER. I'll go when William Marshal comes back, my lord.

HENRY. Are you failing in obedience?

ROGER. I mean I can't leave you alone, my lord.

HENRY. What's the harm? I'm familiar with this place. Fetch him.
        [ROGER *rises and looks into the growing shadows where the*
        REFUGEES *are crouching.*

ROGER. Good people, while I'm away watch over him.
    You know he comes of your city, and you of his.
    Take care of him as a neighbour, and if he calls for me,
    Shout as you run to fetch me; I shall hear you.
                [*Exit* ROGER. *The* REFUGEES *move a little forward.*

3RD. You know, this was the king of the world, so men say.

4TH. He is looking.
                [*The* KING *and the* REFUGEES *gaze at one another.*

HENRY [*in great anxiety*]. I don't know . . .

1ST. What, then?

HENRY. . . . if the laws will hold.
        [*The* REFUGEES *gaze.* HENRY *turns his head away from
        them. A violence attacks his body. He tries to pull himself up.*
    It is all still to do!
                            [*He falls back, and is silent.*

1ST. Mary Virgin, but I think he's dead.

2ND. Shall I put my ear to his heart?

4TH. No, come away. You can't come close to a great king.
                    [*The* OLD WOMAN *is whimpering and praying.*

1ST. I wouldn't come close to a great king, but what we have here
    is a dead man. You've seen fifty like it or more. I'm thinking,
    we've had nothing from him yet, and he's lost us everything we
    had in this burning city. This dead fellow owes us a bit of justice.

2ND. But he's a dead man, so he doesn't pay.

1ST. Nor say No either. He doesn't refuse us. These things he has
    will only go to them who want nothing. For anyway he'll be
    stripped before they bury him, and washed and that.

4TH. I won't stay and see you lay hands on him.   [*Exit.*
                    [*The* 2ND *has nervously joined the* 1ST *in stripping the body.*

1ST. This is gold, do you see that?

OLD WOMAN. It's wicked work, it's wicked work.

1ST. We'll give you something, but shut your mouth.

OLD WOMAN. I won't have nothing of it. I'm only waiting here to
    have my gooses' bed.

3RD [*on watch*]. They're coming. Run, man!
                    [*As he runs past the cart he grabs some belongings.* 1ST *and*
                    2ND *take to their heels. The* OLD WOMAN *sits with the*
                    body of the KING, *gabbling her prayers.*
        Enter WILLIAM MARSHAL, *carrying a hurdle; and* ROGER *with*
                            the MONK.

MARSHAL. Mercy of God, look!

ROGER. O God in heaven! O my father! I should never have left
    him. I thought they were simple men, but they were devils. [*He*
    turns on the OLD WOMAN.] You sat watching this, without calling

for help which would have brought me to him. Did they kill him before they robbed him? Which way are they gone?

OLD WOMAN. I told them it was wicked work they did, wicked work they did. But he died in his own time, before they came up close. He was dead when they came to him.

ROGER. They'll be brought back and made to suffer for it.

MARSHAL. It serves no turn. It was in his heart to give them a world. Help me to lift him.

[*They lift* HENRY *from the bed to the hurdle.* ROGER *takes off his velvet cloak and spreads it over the body.*

MARSHAL. 'Christ,' he said, 'we'll have no naked men.'

[MARSHAL *and* ROGER *carry* HENRY *away on the hurdle, the* MONK *following.*

[*The* OLD WOMAN *sits for a moment. She gets up and goes to the feather mattress, tugs at it, and begins to drag it towards the cart.*

THE END

OXFORD

MORE OXFORD PAPERBACKS

This book is just one of nearly 1000 Oxford Paperbacks currently in print. If you would like details of other Oxford Paperbacks, including titles in the World's Classics, Oxford Reference, Oxford Books, OPUS, Past Masters, Oxford Authors, and Oxford Shakespeare series, please write to:

UK and Europe: Oxford Paperbacks Publicity Manager, Arts and Reference Publicity Department, Oxford University Press, Walton Street, Oxford OX2 6DP.

Customers in UK and Europe will find Oxford Paperbacks available in all good bookshops. But in case of difficulty please send orders to the Cash-with-Order Department, Oxford University Press Distribution Services, Saxon Way West, Corby, Northants NN18 9ES. Tel: 0536 741519; Fax: 0536 746337. Please send a cheque for the total cost of the books, plus £1.75 postage and packing for orders under £20; £2.75 for orders over £20. Customers outside the UK should add 10% of the cost of the books for postage and packing.

USA: Oxford Paperbacks Marketing Manager, Oxford University Press, Inc., 200 Madison Avenue, New York, N.Y. 10016.

Canada: Trade Department, Oxford University Press, 70 Wynford Drive, Don Mills, Ontario M3C 1J9.

Australia: Trade Marketing Manager, Oxford University Press, G.P.O. Box 2784Y, Melbourne 3001, Victoria.

South Africa: Oxford University Press, P.O. Box 1141, Cape Town 8000.

PAST MASTERS

General Editor: Keith Thomas

SHAKESPEARE

Germaine Greer

'At the core of a coherent social structure as he viewed it lay marriage, which for Shakespeare is no mere comic convention but a crucial and complex ideal. He rejected the stereotype of the passive, sex-less, unresponsive female and its inevitable concom-mitant, the misogynist conviction that all women were whores at heart. Instead he created a series of female characters who were both passionate and pure, who gave their hearts spontaneously into the keeping of the men they loved and remained true to the bargain in the face of tremendous odds.'

Germaine Greer's short book on Shakespeare brings a completely new eye to a subject about whom more has been written than on any other English figure. She is especially concerned with discovering why Shakespeare 'was and is a popular artist', who remains a central figure in English cultural life four centuries after his death.

'eminently trenchant and sensible . . . a genuine exploration in its own right' John Bayley, *Listener*

'the clearest and simplest explanation of Shake-speare's thought I have yet read' Auberon Waugh, *Daily Mail*

OXFORD POETS

A PORTER SELECTED

Peter Porter

This selection of about one hundred of Porter's best poems is chosen from all his works to date, including his latest book, *Possible Worlds*, and *The Automatic Oracle*, which won the 1988 Whitbread Prize for Poetry.

What the critics have said about Peter Porter:

'I can't think of any contemporary poet who is so consistently entertaining over such a variety of material.' John Lucas, *New Statesman*

'an immensely fertile, lively, informed, honest and penetrating mind.' Stephen Spender, *Observer*

'He writes vigorously, with savage erudition and wonderful expansiveness . . . No one now writing matches Porter's profoundly moral and cultured overview.' Douglas Dunn, *Punch*

OXFORD POETS

FLEUR ADCOCK

Time Zones

In this lively new collection, Fleur Adcock's subjects range from domestic matters—recalling the birth of her son some years back; remembering her father, the news of whose death in New Zealand reaches her, the expatriate, in England; working in her own London garden—to matters of contemporary concern, such as the Romanian bid for freedom in 1989, and support for Green causes, including the anti-nuclear stand.

'She is an eminently readable poet, whose quiet accuracy sometimes makes me laugh out loud.' Wendy Cope, *Guardian*

OXFORD POETRY LIBRARY

ALEXANDER POPE

Edited by Pat Rogers

Pope has been acknowledged as the most important poet of the first half of the eighteenth century. This selection includes his brilliant poems *An Essay on Criticism*, *Windsor Forest*, and his masterpiece of social satire, *The Rape of the Lock*. Together with a representative sample of Pope's other verse, Pat Rogers gives an eloquent defence of Pope's poetic practice.

OXFORD POETRY LIBRARY

LORD BYRON

Edited by Jerome J. McGann

Byron was one of the most acclaimed writers of his time, and he continues to be a highly popular Romantic poet with readers today. His mastery of a sweeping range of topics and forms is clearly reflected in this selection, which includes extracts from all his major poems such as *Childe Harold*, *Beppo*, and *Don Juan*, together with many shorter lyrics.

THE OXFORD AUTHORS

General Editor: Frank Kermode

THE OXFORD AUTHORS is a series of authoritative editions of major English writers. Aimed at both students and general readers, each volume contains a generous selection of the best writings—poetry, prose, and letters—to give the essence of a writer's work and thinking. All the texts are complemented by essential notes, an introduction, chronology, and suggestions for further reading.

OXFORD BOOKS

THE NEW OXFORD BOOK OF
IRISH VERSE

Edited, with Translations, by Thomas Kinsella

Verse in Irish, especially from the early and med-
ieval periods, has long been felt to be the preserve of
linguists and specialists, while Anglo-Irish poetry is
usually seen as an adjunct to the English tradition.
This original anthology approaches the Irish poetic
tradition as a unity and presents a relationship
between two major bodies of poetry that reflects a
shared and painful history.

'the first coherent attempt to present the entire
range of Irish poetry in both languages to an English-speaking readership' *Irish Times*

'a very satisfying and moving introduction to Irish
poetry' *Listener*

OXFORD BOOKS

THE OXFORD BOOK OF ENGLISH GHOST STORIES

Chosen by Michael Cox and R. A. Gilbert

This anthology includes some of the best and most frightening ghost stories ever written, including M. R. James's 'Oh Whistle, and I'll Come to You, My Lad', 'The Monkey's Paw' by W. W. Jacobs, and H. G. Wells's 'The Red Room'. The important contribution of women writers to the genre is represented by stories such as Amelia Edwards's 'The Phantom Coach', Edith Wharton's 'Mr Jones', and Elizabeth Bowen's 'Hand in Glove'.

As the editors stress in their informative introduction, a good ghost story, though it may raise many profound questions about life and death, entertains as much as it unsettles us, and the best writers are careful to satisfy what Virginia Woolf called 'the strange human craving for the pleasure of feeling afraid'. This anthology, the first to present the full range of classic English ghost fiction, similarly combines a serious literary purpose with the plain intention of arousing pleasing fear at the doings of the dead.

'an excellent cross-section of familiar and unfamiliar stories and guaranteed to delight' *New Statesman*

OXFORD REFERENCE

THE CONCISE OXFORD COMPANION TO ENGLISH LITERATURE

Edited by Margaret Drabble and Jenny Stringer

Based on the immensely popular fifth edition of the *Oxford Companion to English Literature* this is an indispensable, compact guide to the central matter of English literature.

There are more than 5,000 entries on the lives and works of authors, poets, playwrights, essayists, philosophers, and historians; plot summaries of novels and plays; literary movements; fictional characters; legends; theatres; periodicals; and much more.

The book's sharpened focus on the English literature of the British Isles makes it especially convenient to use, but there is still generous coverage of the literature of other countries and of other disciplines which have influenced or been influenced by English literature.

From reviews of *The Oxford Companion to English Literature*:

'a book which one turns to with constant pleasure . . . a book with much style and little prejudice' Iain Gilchrist, *TLS*

'it is quite difficult to imagine, in this genre, a more useful publication' Frank Kermode, *London Review of Books*

'incarnates a living sense of tradition . . . sensitive not to fashion merely but to the spirit of the age' Christopher Ricks, *Sunday Times*

ILLUSTRATED HISTORIES IN
OXFORD PAPERBACKS

THE OXFORD ILLUSTRATED HISTORY
OF ENGLISH LITERATURE

Edited by Pat Rogers

Britain possesses a literary heritage which is almost unrivalled in the Western world. In this volume, the richness, diversity, and continuity of that tradition are explored by a group of Britain's foremost literary scholars.

Chapter by chapter the authors trace the history of English literature, from its first stirrings in Anglo-Saxon poetry to the present day. At its heart towers the figure of Shakespeare, who is accorded a special chapter to himself. Other major figures such as Chaucer, Milton, Donne, Wordsworth, Dickens, Eliot, and Auden are treated in depth, and the story is brought up to date with discussion of living authors such as Seamus Heaney and Edward Bond.

'[a] lovely volume . . . put in your thumb and pull out plums' Michael Foot

'scholarly and enthusiastic people have written inspiring essays that induce an eagerness in their readers to return to the writers they admire' *Economist*